ENGLAND'S PRIDE

General Lord Wolseley by A. Besnard

ENGLAND'S PRIDE

*The story of the
Gordon Relief Expedition*

by JULIAN SYMONS

THE HISTORY BOOK CLUB · LONDON

This edition published 1966 by
The History Book Club Ltd
for sale only to its members
Originally published 1965 by
Hamish Hamilton Ltd

Printed in Great Britain by
Latimer Trend & Co Ltd, Plymouth

'Too late! Too late to save him.
In vain, in vain, they tried.
His life was England's glory,
His death was England's pride.'

Popular Song after
Gordon's death.

ACKNOWLEDGMENTS

MANY of the factual details relating to the Gordon Relief Expedition are contained in the volumes of memoranda, letters and official papers that Wolseley had specially bound up for his personal reference at the War Office. I am grateful to Mr. D. W. King, O.B.E., the War Office Librarian, and to his assistants for their help in guiding my steps in these lightly-trodden fields. More of Wolseley's personal papers are housed in Hove Public Library, and I must thank the Librarian, Mr. Jack Dove, for letting me examine them. Other important Wolseley material is to be found in the Royal United Services Institution, including Wolseley's correspondence with his wife, and various writings, among them some sketchy passages for the unpublished later volumes of his autobiography. My thanks are due to Brigadier J. Stephenson, O.B.E., Director of the Institution, for permission to consult these papers, and to Mr. David Erskine for searching among old trunks to find fresh material. I must acknowledge also the kindness of the Institution in letting me reproduce some of the rare photographs of the Expedition from an album in their possession. Messrs. Thomas Cook and Son kindly allowed me to consult their archives. Officials of the Public Record Office, the Manuscript Room of the British Museum and the Historical Manuscripts Commission have all been helpful.

CONTENTS

LIST OF ILLUSTRATIONS

PART ONE

THE MISSION

CHAPTER ONE

DEPARTURE OF A HERO

1. The Gladstone Government

THE great Midlothian campaign of 1879 which unseated Disraeli's Government was not only a triumph for Gladstone's eloquence, but evidence also of his extraordinary ability to sense the strength of the prevailing political wind. He had been offered, and had rejected, a safe seat in Edinburgh. Midlothian by contrast was firmly Unionist, a seat thought to be in the gift of the Duke of Buccleuch and contested by his son, Lord Dalkeith. In a fortnight Gladstone delivered twenty-two speeches, many of them outdoors, a few in the halls of market towns. He told his audiences of farmers and shopkeepers that he was in favour of Home Rule for various parts of the United Kingdom, in favour of free trade, against Government waste, and against illusory dreams of Imperial glory. His listeners liked the strong sense of moral virtue he imparted even more than they liked what he said. He made it clear that the war with Afghanistan was not only a waste of money but also a crime against God, the annexation of Cyprus not only a breach of 'the public law of Europe' but also law-breaking to no purpose, since the island was a valueless encumbrance. To feel that one's personal interests chime with public morality is always pleasant. Gladstone's audiences were in perfect sympathy with the general idea that commitments abroad and expenditure at home should be reduced, and they were not disturbed by the vaguely outlined prospect of some kind of Home Rule for Ireland, Scotland and Wales.

Midlothian was won, and the election was won, with 353

Liberals obtaining an absolute majority over 238 Unionists and
61 Irish Nationalists, yet the Government was formed with difficulty. Five years earlier Gladstone had retired from the leadership
of the Liberal party. 'At the age of sixty-five, and after forty-two
years of a laborious public life, I think myself entitled to retire
on the present opportunity', he had said, and since then his in-
cursions into politics had been often deeply embarrassing to the
party leadership, which was divided between Lord Hartington
in the House of Commons and his cousin Lord Granville in the
House of Lords. Who wanted to see Gladstone back in power?
Certainly not the Queen, who said positively that he was utterly
unacceptable to her, and that she would sooner abdicate than
send for the 'half-mad fire-brand who would soon ruin everything,
and be a Dictator'. Yet it was impossible to ignore the old man's
overwhelming ascendancy over the electorate. When the Queen
asked Hartington to form a Government he visited Gladstone,
and the visit destroyed any thought he may have nursed that he
or Granville might form an administration. It is true that the
first election results had stunned Gladstone into writing to Lord
Acton that he hoped and prayed for 'a decisive accession of the
Liberal party to power without me'. Now that this decisive
accession to power had come about, however, he told Hartington that he could accept no post in the Government except that
of Prime Minister, and although he added that he would support
it from outside, this must have sounded like a threat rather than
a promise. Hartington felt bound to advise the Queen that she
must send for Gladstone, and she did so, consoling herself with
the thought that it could be only a matter of a year or two before
age and ill health enforced his retirement.

Gladstone's conduct may appear hypocritical today, but to
Liberals at the time, even to Hartington and Granville, what happened seemed inevitable. He was the architect of victory, and
also the only man who could hold together a Liberal Government in which the component elements, Whigs and Radicals,
differed in many matters more than the Whigs differed from the
Unionist opposition. The divisions in the Government showed
from its inception. The Whig gentry, many of whom were

Liberal only in name, predominated in the Cabinet. Granville became Foreign Secretary and Hartington Secretary for India, and Whigs got most of the other important posts. The only positive Radicals were John Bright, whose politically active days were almost over, W. E. Forster, who was placed in charge of Irish affairs, and Joseph Chamberlain, who became President of the Board of Trade. Chamberlain and Sir Charles Dilke reached an agreement by which neither of them would accept any office at all unless one of the two was given a Cabinet post. Gladstone reluctantly chose Chamberlain, and Dilke accepted the post of Under-Secretary at the Foreign Office. Sir William Harcourt, the leader of the more Radically-minded Whigs rather than a Radical himself, went to the Home Office.

The Queen was disturbed by the presence of any Radicals at all in the Cabinet, but Granville soothingly assured her Private Secretary that 'the Government is like bread sauce—made of two substantial elements. The few peppercorns are very obvious, and perhaps give a little flavour, but do not affect the character of the food'. But two years later Dilke also was in the Cabinet, and although Gladstone pointed out that Bright and Forster had gone, so that the Cabinet might now be called a little less Radical than it had been, the Queen was not reassured. She sensed the power and purposefulness of Dilke and Chamberlain. As Dilke acutely pointed out, Gladstone acted as a kind of buffer between the Parliamentary power of the Whigs, who regarded the Liberal party as their own possession, and the Radical feeling of the country. 'Gladstone will say "You have got me; that is what you asked for", and will give us a Whig Cabinet.' This, certainly, was what he attempted to do, spreading his great healing shade over the frequently-quarrelling factions. His success was limited by the weakness of his two principal Whig lieutenants, Granville and Hartington.

The association between the two Whig peers was long and close. It went back to the eighteen fifties when Spencer Compton Cavendish had visited Russia as a young man in his early twenties, attached to the staff of his much older cousin, who had already become Lord Granville, and was representing the Queen

B

at the Tsar's coronation. Granville was already a prominent politician who had held positions in the Government, and had indeed been for a few months Foreign Secretary, in succession to Palmerston. Cavendish's political career began after his return from Russia, when he was returned as Member for North Lancashire. In the following year the sixth Duke of Devonshire died, and Cavendish became Marquis of Hartington when his father succeeded to the Dukedom. Since that time he had been Under Secretary for War under Palmerston, and Secretary for War later in the eighteen sixties during the short government of Lord Russell. Later he had been a reluctant Chief Secretary for Ireland, and after Gladstone's retirement had accepted with even greater reluctance the leadership of the Liberal Party. Hartington hesitated for nearly three weeks about accepting, and at one time said positively that nothing would induce him to allow his name to be put forward in any contest. His hesitation sprang from a real modesty about his own abilities, and from his sense that 'the Opposition consists of Whigs, Radicals and Home Rulers', and that his own lack of sympathy with anything but strict Whiggism unfitted him for the leadership. But in the end, after prolonged negotiations, there was no contest and Granville wrote to him: 'My dear Harty Tarty, you are in.' What Hartington's biographer calls the sentence of doom had been pronounced.

Hartington's leadership during the next five years was not conspicuously successful or energetic. He was hampered partly by the sympathy he felt for such Disraelian schemes as the purchase of Suez Canal shares, but partly also by the lack of some vital spark noticed by Gladstone when he wrote in 1874 that Hartington had given the public 'an inadequate idea of (his) force'. The legend of Hartington's indolence is contradicted by the abundance of his correspondence, but the force which comes from an ability to express passionate conviction in public was not in his make-up. He had instead an ox-like simplicity and straightforwardness which often made him the mouthpiece of subtler men, together with a brooding obstinacy that was sometimes impervious even to Gladstonian rhetoric.

Of his cousin Granville, who was Foreign Secretary during

the whole five years of this Government, there is less to be said. He had become by age and experience a kind of father confessor for the party and an adjudicator of disputes within it. He was certainly more indolent than Hartington, and this indolence was combined with a gift for evading immediate difficulties which in relation to foreign affairs was often disastrous. Sir Evelyn Baring remarked that 'his power of eluding the main point at issue was quite extraordinary', and Queen Victoria put the same thing in a different way when she said that he was as weak as water. It would not be right to say that Granville viewed the art of diplomacy as the avoidance of action, but it is certainly true that he had a horror of extreme steps and quick decisions, perhaps believing that all problems are lessened by subjection to the wearing process of time. The blessings of *laissez-faire*, Baring observed, had been largely negated by the extreme directness of Bismarck. 'Lord Granville always seemed to me to make the mistake of confounding the cases in which the dawdling *laissez-faire* policy was wise, with those in which it was necessary to take time by the forelock and have a clearly defined policy at an early date. This, in a Foreign Minister, is a great fault.' Both Granville and Hartington, who in 1882 became Secretary of State for War, found it difficult to arrive at firm decisions leading to action, and they were equally antipathetic to many of Gladstone's policies. At every turn of events Hartington consulted his conscience as other men look at their watches, but he hesitated to act on what the watch told him, for he was never sure that it gave the right time.

The hesitancy of the two leading Whigs was in contrast to what was for Gladstone the unwelcome Bismarckian directness of Dilke and Chamberlain. Their intransigence, their insistence on great personal freedom of action, and Chamberlain's deliberate use of meetings in the country to advocate such policies as the payment of Members of Parliament and the breaking-up of great estates as a step towards land reform, all distressed Gladstone. They did not irritate him, for he remained under the most extreme pressure of events wonderfully free from personal irritation.

2. Egypt

It was generally understood throughout the Liberal Party, and
not merely hoped by the Queen, that Gladstone was only coming back to office for a short time, but it soon became apparent
that the policies he had most at heart could not be carried out
unless he were Prime Minister. In general terms his policy was
characteristic of what would now be called Left-wing Liberalism,
involving domestic social reform and disentanglement from all
commitments abroad. His home policy was bedevilled by all
sorts of problems like Bradlaugh's refusal to take the oath of
allegiance, but such irrelevancies did not cause Gladstone to
swerve from his two main objectives, of giving some measure
of land reform and Home Rule to Ireland, and of extending the
franchise to artisans and labourers. His foreign policy was an
attempted reversal of almost all that had been done by Disraeli,
the abandonment of a pro-Turkish attitude in relation to Russia,
rejection of the 'forward policy' in Afghanistan, the granting
of self-government to the Transvaal. But the biggest foreign
thorn in his side was the question of Egypt.

'We do not want to have Egypt', Palmerston had said in 1857.
'We want to trade with Egypt, and to travel through Egypt,
but we do not want the burthen of governing Egypt.' To trade
with a country implies an interest in its financial viability, and
Britain and France became involved in propping up Egypt's
shaky financial structure by loans. In 1879 the two countries
presented what was in effect an ultimatum to the Khedive
Ismail, demanding his resignation. The Khedive held his position
through a firman from the fading Ottoman Empire, and the
Sultan was induced to agree to Ismail's replacement by his son
Tewfik. Two controllers, one French and one British, were put
in charge of Egypt's finances. The English controller, who had
previously served on the Commission considering the country's
debt, was Major Evelyn Baring.

This system of Dual Control was deeply humiliating to all
Egyptians. Baring and the French Controller, M. de Blignières,

held no public office, but they had seats in the Council of Ministers, their control over the country's finances included full rights of supervision and investigation, and they could not be dismissed without the consent of their Governments. Tewfik appeared to his people as a Franco-British puppet, and a revolt against him was inevitable. When it came, in 1882, it was headed by an Army Colonel named Arabi, and was strongly anti-European and even more strongly anti-Turk. The Egyptians, Arabi said, 'were imprisoned, exiled, strangled, thrown into the Nile, starved, and robbed according to the will of their masters. A liberated slave was a freer man than a freeborn Arab. The most ignorant Turk was preferred and honoured before the best of the Egyptians.' This infant nationalism was given short shrift. The bombardment of Alexandria by the British fleet (the French flinched from co-operating with them) was succeeded by the despatch of an army under Sir Garnet Wolseley. Arabi's army was destroyed in a matter of hours at the battle of Tel-el-Kebir, and Arabi himself was captured and sent to Cyprus.

The Egyptian situation posed unending moral problems for a Government like that headed by Gladstone. At the time of the bombardment of Alexandria and the battle of Tel-el-Kebir it was thought by some Whigs that Gladstone and the Radical ministers would resign rather than use force in Egypt, but Bright's was the only resignation. Gladstone was able to persuade himself that the war was not what it seemed. 'We have carried out this war from a love of peace, and, I may say, on the principle of peace', he said in one of those fine word-spinning flights that infuriated his opponents. But what was to happen now that the war was over? Gladstone longed to have done with Egypt in every sense except a financial one. 'I am afraid that there is no chance of getting Mr. Gladstone to pay any attention to Egypt while the Arrears Bill is going on', Hartington wrote to Granville, but in fact Egypt could not be ignored. More than 2,000 Europeans living at Alexandria presented a petition asking for a permanent British occupation, and a force remained in the city 'for the preservation of public tranquillity', as Granville put it. The system of Dual Control was ended against the wishes of the French, and a mission headed by Lord Dufferin was sent out to decide what should be done.

Basically there were only two possible courses. One was to assume complete control of the country in the way that Britain controlled India, but although Dufferin looked wistfully at this possibility he recognized that it would be entirely unacceptable to any Liberal Government. The other was to give Egypt back to the Egyptians, but this idea horrified Dufferin. 'It is frightful to contemplate the misery and misfortune which would be entailed on the population', he said, if the European advisers left the Egyptian Government 'a prey to dishonest speculators, ruinous contracts, and delusive engineering operations.' What the Government actually did was to put in hand several measures which implied a lengthy occupation of Egypt, control of its economy and support of its army, while at the same time assuring themselves that all these things were being done upon a temporary basis and that the British Government was not responsible for Egyptian internal affairs. A small army of occupation remained in Alexandria and Cairo, Sir Evelyn Wood was sent out as Sirdar to reorganize the Egyptian Army, the gendarmerie was similarly to be reorganized under Colonel Valentine Baker, and a survey of the Sudan was to be carried out by Colonel D. H. Stewart of the 11th Hussars. Gladstone persuaded himself that within a few months Egypt would be a land with an efficient army and free institutions, capable of self-government. In the meantime the British Agent and Consul-General at Cairo, Sir Edward Malet, was promoted to be Minister at Brussels. His place was taken by Sir Evelyn Baring, who has already been glimpsed as Major Baring. He had great experience of the country and some sympathy with its people, although he was convinced that their own interests called for a long period of paternal British rule.

3. Baring at Cairo

It would have been difficult to find a more able man than Baring to fill the post at Cairo. The course of this great administrator's life had been finally decided in 1872 when, as a Captain who had passed through the Staff College and worked with distinction in the War Office, he had been offered the choice between civil and military employment, and had gone out to India as private secretary to his cousin, Lord Northbrook, who was then the Viceroy. When he came to Egypt in 1877 this subtle, intelligent man with the air of conscious intellectual superiority which led enemies to call him Overbaring, had begun the most serious work of his life. Now he was taking it up again. He had a complete grasp of the financial problems which had to be solved if the Egyptian economy was ever to become self-supporting. His urbanity of manner masked a deep and genuine concern for the wretched conditions of the fellaheen and small farmers. All human qualities, however, imply limitations. The rational intelligence of Baring precluded him from any real understanding of the emotional force behind the Arabi revolt or the later revolt of the Mahdi, just as he was incapable of apprehending the irrational power exerted by such a man as Gordon. That corrupt government by one's own people may be preferred to honest administration imposed by foreigners, that appeals can be made which transcend human logic—these were propositions that Baring could understand intellectually, but he never really felt them to be true.

During 1883 Wood and the English officers he had brought with him did their best to train the Egyptian Army. It was not easy. The officers, most of whom signed two-year contracts, found that they had to give instruction by signs, or in bastard Turkish. Progress in drill was slow because the Egyptians seemed unable to understand the concept of a straight line, or parallel and right angles. Many of them could not grasp that a rifle should be fired, and Colonel Stewart thought that they would have been more formidable armed with sticks. He observed too that in the Sudan the troops were greatly hampered by women. 'It may be really said that every regiment of soldiers is followed by an equally numerous regiment of women.' There was much petty jealousy, which was not confined to the Egyptians. It had been originally proposed that Baker should command the

Egyptian Army, but he had been rejected because years earlier he had been found guilty of attacking a girl in a railway carriage. Baker was a talented officer, and there was indignation when he was relegated to command of the gendarmerie, and Wood was brought out from England as Sirdar. There was also some rivalry between Wood and General Stephenson, who commanded the army of occupation, one particularly sore point being the higher pay given to British officers serving with the Egyptian Army. In the course of the year also steps were taken to improve the methods by which taxes were collected, and attempts were made to eliminate the use of the rhinoceros-hide whip called the kourbash. The measures had no great success, and there was general complaint that without the kourbash it was impossible to keep order. Baring did not take up office until September 1883. He found the Cairo Treasury exhausted, and a powerful revolt in progress in the Sudan. Mohammed Ahmed, an apprentice boatbuilder who had proclaimed himself to be the Mahdi upon whose coming the whole world would be converted to the Mohammedan religion, had defeated the Egyptian forces sent against him, had captured El Obeid, and now ruled a considerable part of the Sudan.

It is tempting to say that the Mahdiist revolt was, like Arabi's, essentially an expression of nationalism, one which added to the hatred of Turk and European an equal detestation of the Egyptian ruling class. That is certainly part of the truth about Mahdiism. Very often the troops opposed to him went over to the Mahdi as soon as they had a chance of doing so, and few of them were ill-treated. His chief opponents were the Turkish and Egyptian Pashas and their followers, who had bled the country of money for so many years. But although the effects of Mahdiism were largely political, by intent it was a religious movement which enforced upon its believers a stricter, purer life here on earth. Punishments were severe. Followers of the Mahdi found drinking wine received eighty blows of the kourbash, and those found smoking tobacco received a hundred blows. The Mahdi tried to establish rules of 'morality, obedience and moderation'. Weddings, for instance, were to be as little as possible concerned with outward show. The banquet should not consist of more than one lamb, the trousseau should be no more than two dresses. The money saved 'must be kept to further the Holy War, and must be distributed among the fighting men.' It is true that the Mahdi was often far from conforming to the rules he laid down for others. He accumulated money, he enjoyed the trappings of luxury, and although he confined himself within the permitted limit of four wives, he did so only by frequent divorces and remarriages. Yet the intention was there, and although upon occasion the Mahdi's followers slaughtered the inhabitants of the villages they captured, there were other places where the defeated were incorporated into the army of the victors without bloodshed.

Three days before Baring's arrival at Cairo to take up his appointment, General Hicks left the town in command of an army of 10,000 Egyptian soldiers with the purpose, as it was stated at the time, of protecting Khartoum and clearing the nearby country of rebel bands. Hicks was an Indian Army officer appointed to the staff of the Egyptian Army. In the British Army he was no more than a Colonel, but the Khedive appointed him General and Commander-in-Chief. Hicks, advancing unwisely into the Mahdi's stronghold of Kordofan, was led astray by treacherous guides. His force wandered about for three days without water, and then was attacked and destroyed almost to the last man. The Mahdi captured four Krupp field guns, ten mountain guns, six Nordenfeldts, and some thousands of rifles. News of the catastrophe, which occurred early in November, reached Cairo later in the month, although for some time it was not fully believed.

The Hicks disaster utterly changed the situation in Egypt. During his first two months in office Baring had been working towards Gladstone's end of withdrawing the army of occupation. At the end of October he thought that it would be safe to withdraw from Cairo, leaving a small British force at Alexandria, and Gladstone announced this at the Lord Mayor's banquet on November 9. Within a fortnight the news about Hicks was known, and Baring immediately recognized its significance. There was no effective Egyptian Army, nothing to stop the Mahdi from taking the whole of the Sudan. Were the Gladstone Government prepared to accept that? Or to see the Egyptian Government ask for Turkish troops? Baring's conclusion seems to have a hint of irony. 'It will be very difficult, under the circumstances, to maintain a purely passive attitude, and to give no advice whatsoever.' Granville's reply was for him straightforward, and reiterated the policy of non-intervention. 'We cannot land English or Indian troops', he said, and added that it would not be for Egypt's advantage to bring in Turkish troops. 'If consulted, recommend the abandonment of the Sudan within certain limits.'

Abandonment: the word was out, forced out by the firm logic of Baring, and it expressed correctly Gladstone's desire to have no military involvement in the affairs of Egypt. But during the following weeks it became clear to the Government that to assert disinvolvement is one thing, to ensure it quite another. At every step Granville and his colleagues were reminded that they had obligations to Egypt—well, were they obligations? Perhaps that was putting it too strongly, but there were circumstances that made everybody in the Government uncomfortable. Here were the Egyptians threatening to call in Turkish troops, and although the threat was probably a bluff, Britain would certainly not be pleased to see the Turks back in Egypt. There was Baring sounding off all sorts of alarms, saying that Stephenson, Wood and Baker all thought it impossible to hold Khartoum, and that if Khartoum fell Egypt itself might be menaced. Here was Colonel de Coetlôgon, the temporary commander of the Khartoum garrison, saying that in two months' time there would be no food, and advising immediate retreat. There was another force of 500 Egyptians beaten by the dervishes in the Eastern Sudan, near Suakin. And here again was Baring asking, almost insisting, that he must have definite instructions, and must give the Egyptian Government definite advice.

It was in these circumstances that Granville, casting about for some way of avoiding the cost and responsibility of military operations without cutting too humiliating a figure, suggested the employment of Major-General Charles George Gordon. The name of Chinese Gordon, as he was generally called, was firmly established in that sort of popular esteem which can suddenly convert a fallible human being into a superhuman mythical figure, when the occasion favours the creation of such a myth. Gordon had been a soldier from the age of fifteen, had received his brevet as Lieutenant-Colonel when he was thirty-one, and had been promoted Major-General in March 1882, in his fiftieth year. In army terms his career had been successful rather than remarkable, but the myth of Chinese Gordon rested on what he was rather than on what he had done. In China twenty years earlier he had moulded his force of a few thousand Chinese irregulars into a force that became known as the 'Ever Victorious Army', and it was the inspiration of Gordon's personality that had touched the Chinese and their European officers, changing them from a rabble into an army that in its courage and coherence was the wonder of all who saw them fight. When Gordon left China he declined the large present offered to him by the Emperor, and in the succeeding years he had often shown his contempt for money. In the three years he had spent as governor of Equatorial Africa he had refused to accept more than a small fraction of his £10,000 annual salary, and during his later years in the Sudan, from 1877 to 1879, his primary concern had been to suppress the slave trade. 'When that man comes into the room I feel I am with my superior', the deposed Khedive, Ismail, had said, and during these three years as Governor-General not only of the Sudan but of the Equatorial provinces and the Red Sea littoral, Gordon fought vigorously and with much success against the slave traders. He had said that he would not stay in Egypt if anything happened to the Khedive, and soon after Ismail's deposition he resigned. At the time his resignation had been readily accepted, not only by Tewfik but by the European administrators who found his crusading zeal a frequent embarrassment. He had been replaced by a native Pasha, formerly dismissed by Gordon for cruelty, who was tolerant of the slave trade. It was evidently impossible, however, to tolerate the Mahdi, and if a European was to be sent to the

Sudan who, after all, knew as much of the country—and who was more respected in it—than Chinese Gordon?

Granville's suggestion seems to have had its origin in a letter enthusiastically advocating Gordon's employment in the Sudan written on November 23 by a Colonel who had served with Gordon in China. The letter was written to the Inspector-General of Fortifications, Sir Andrew Clarke, who sent it on with his note supporting the idea to Childers, the Chancellor of the Exchequer. Childers passed the correspondence to Granville, but received a reply that was not encouraging. Nevertheless, Granville pursued the matter. He wrote to Gladstone at Hawarden, putting the pros and cons. 'He has an immense name in Egypt— he is popular at home. He is a strong but sensible opponent of slavery. He has a small bee in his bonnet.' Was there anything to be lost by sending him out? Gladstone thought not, and so did Granville. When the Foreign Secretary telegraphed Baring to ask if Gordon might be useful, however, he received very promptly a negative reply. The Egyptian Government were very much against employing Gordon, Baring said, on the ground that he was a Christian and that his appointment might alienate the tribes that still remained faithful. 'I think it wise not to press them on the subject.' What Baring did not mention was his own dislike and distrust of Gordon. The two men had met briefly five years earlier, when Gordon was Governor-General of the Sudan, and had violently disagreed about the future financial policy of the country. Gordon had noted that Baring had 'a pretentious, grand, patronizing way about him. . . . When oil mixes with water, we will mix together.' Baring's opinion was no more favourable. He felt that Gordon was a man with whom it would be very difficult to work satisfactorily.

This telegram was sent at the beginning of December, and Baring spent the rest of the year in trying to spur the Government to action. Abandonment of the Sudan had been decided upon but how, practically, was it to be carried out? In a private telegram he warned Granville that the Egyptian Government were merely drifting, in an official one he said that the Khedive and his Ministers 'had resolved to place themselves absolutely in the hands of Her Majesty's Government', but that they were again talking about calling in Turkish troops. The final resource of timidity is obstinacy, and the five Cabinet Ministers who met at the War Office to consider Baring's telegram decided pettishly to reiterate what they had said before. Granville told Baring that the Egyptians must do what they wished about the Sudan, but in any case there was no intention of employing British or Indian troops. Baring decided to force the matter further. On December 22 he sent a memorandum from Tewfik's Prime Minister, Chérif Pasha, saying that the Egyptians could not agree to the abandonment of the Sudan. Baring added his own gloss to this. Negotiations with the Turks were bound to fail, it was likely that no Egyptian Government could be found to carry out the policy of abandonment, and the Government at home must face the fact that it might be necessary to appoint English ministers to rule the country. He added that 'it would also be necessary to send an English officer of high authority to Khartoum, with full powers to withdraw all the garrisons in the Sudan.' When the year ended Baring had received no answer to this telegram.

The Government were passing through one of their frequent internal crises. At the end of 1882 Gladstone had proposed to resign on the ground that his 'brain powers would not enable him to face the great measures of construction which are before the Liberal Party.' Even those who found him most infuriating realized that the Government would fall apart without him, and he was persuaded to stay, giving up the post of Chancellor so that he would have more time to concern himself with those great measures of construction. Now, in the autumn session of 1883, the question of the extension of the franchise to the Irish counties as well as to Great Britain was being debated. The absurd position arose that Chamberlain and Hartington made speeches expressing completely opposite views about the franchise, and the accompanying proposed redistribution of seats. Hartington offered, or threatened, resignation. He remained, as his biographer puts it, 'strongly entrenched' at his family seat of Chatsworth, and said that in any case he was sick of office.

Gladstone believed that Hartington was trying to force his own
resignation. Granville acted as man in the middle, attempting to
arrange an accommodation between the dissenting parties. In
the end a compromise was agreed, and nobody resigned, but the
question of the franchise occupied the principal figures in the
Government during December. Egypt had a minor place in
their thoughts, and it was not until early in January that discussions took place at two Cabinet meetings and it was decided
to adhere to the policy of abandonment. The effect of this
decision was that Chérif and all his Ministers resigned. He was
replaced as Prime Minister by Nubar Pasha, a personal friend
and admirer of Gordon. Urged by the Queen and by Hartington, who in turn had been prompted by the Adjutant-General,
Lord Wolseley, Granville again asked Baring about Gordon:

'Would General Charles Gordon or Sir Charles Wilson be
of assistance under altered conditions in Egypt?'

Wilson was a man of very different character from Gordon.
He was by training an engineer and survey officer, by temperament a politician rather than a soldier, and he had never held a
command in the field. During the Arabi revolt he had been
appointed political officer to keep sweet the relations between
the Egyptian Government and British troops in Cairo, and had
done this difficult job with much tact and skill. He took charge
of Arabi when he was made prisoner, and felt very sorry for the
Egyptian nationalist, with many of whose ideas he sympathized.
Perhaps a man with the inspirational qualities of Gordon and
the conciliatory ones of Wilson would have been an ideal choice
for Egypt. Baring talked to the new Prime Minister about both
of them, but Nubar was in favour of sending an Egyptian to
Khartoum as Governor-General. Baring made no attempt to
dissent from this view, which was indeed his own. He told
Granville that he did not think the services of Gordon or Wilson
could be utilized at present.

4. The Choice of Gordon

Gordon, meanwhile, was in a whirl of excitement. He had just

accepted an offer of employment in the Congo made to him by
King Leopold of the Belgians.

Gordon was in Jaffa when he heard from King Leopold. In
January 1880, indignant at the treatment of Ismail, and infuriated
by the financial grip exerted over Egypt by the new French and
British controllers of the economy, he had resigned as Governor-
General of the Sudan. The following years were spent in deliberate obscurity, punctuated by such curious incidents as his
acceptance of the post of private secretary to the new Viceroy
of India and resignation from it within a week. He spent some
time in Mauritius, paid a visit to Cape Town and one to
England, and then left for Palestine. As he grew older, Gordon
found himself more and more absorbed by the desire to investigate further the manifest truths of the Bible, and especially
to make a precise placing of various holy spots. Excited letters
to clerical friends in England, accompanied by elaborate dia-
grams, told of his discoveries. He became certain that he had
found the hill of Golgotha, and felt sure that the burial place of
Jesus Christ was near at hand. His approach was not scientific,
but Gordon would have considered that no criticism, for it was
his endeavour always to push through science to some ultimate
truth about the relationship of the Christian religion to his own
nature. He knew that his discoveries might be criticized, but
what did it matter? 'I do not claim that what I say is always true,
but to me it appears so. *I* see this or that, another does not see
it: I can say no more.' It seemed that the public career of this
visionary man of action was over. This did not disturb him, for
he believed that whatever happened to him was ordained by
God. His fatalism, however, was conditional. 'We have nothing
further to do, when the scroll of events is unrolled, than to
accept them as being for the best', he wrote to his friend the
Reverend R. H. Barnes. '*Before* it is unrolled, it is another
matter.'[1] He was always waiting for a sign that would call him
to further action. Was the invitation from King Leopold such
a sign? Surely it was, for one of his supreme objects in life was
to crush the slave trade. He had gone a long way to doing so

[1] Barnes and Brown, p. 25.

in the Sudan, and now here was a further chance in the Congo.

As he thought about the possibilities, Gordon's characteristic euphoria asserted itself. It was plain that he would be undertaking God's work in the Congo, and although he would be turning his back decisively on his own country, perhaps that would be for the best. 'You know what little rows I get into when in England, and I am far better away', he told his sister. From Jaffa he wrote to the Secretary of State to ask for permission to accept employment with King Leopold, and received a reply: 'Secretary State decides to sangdon your employ on Congo.' He told Leopold that he could go, and was disconcerted a couple of weeks later to learn that the telegraph clerk in the Jaffa Post Office had misread the telegram, and that not only should 'sangdon' have read 'sanction', but that the word 'decides' should have been 'declines'. This meant that he would have to resign from the Army and forfeit his pension rights if he went to the Congo, but although checked he was not dismayed. He went from Egypt to Brussels, and arrived there on New Year's Day. In Brussels he received a letter from the War Office telling him that since he had not been three years unemployed as a general officer he was 'precluded from retiring at the present time with a pension'. The obstacle was quickly overcome when he saw Leopold, for the King agreed to give him a grant of £7,000 to cover his losses. So it was settled. He would go to the Congo. In a ferment of enthusiasm he drew up a memorandum of his intentions, and sent it to the secretary of the British Anti-Slavery Society. He said that he had realized that the idea of doing anything further in the Sudan at the moment must be abandoned, and it was also suddenly plain to him that 'until we cut off the slave trade at the *source* of its *existence*, no measures can be efficacious'. To his sister he conveyed what had happened with the brevity that characterized him when announcing important decisions. 'I have seen the King, he wishes me to go to the Congo. I said I would.'

On January 7 he returned to England. He went to stay with

General Gordon

Gordon's departure from Charing Cross Station. The Duke of Cambridge is helping him don his coat, Wolseley...

his sister at Southampton, and from there posted his letter of resignation to the War Office. The scroll of events seemed to have been unrolled.

*

Baring said afterwards that the movement to send Gordon to the Congo had been engineered by the newspapers, and although this is obviously much less than the truth, two newspapers played an important part in the agitation that took place in the New Year. On New Year's Day, when Gordon arrived in Brussels, a letter from Sir Samuel Baker appeared in *The Times*, urging that Gordon should be sent to the Sudan as British High Commissioner. The importance of the letter lay in the character of the writer. For Victorians, Baker's name was one to set with those of Speke and Stanley. His life had been spent in exploration and big-game hunting (his first book, *The Rifle and Hound in Ceylon*, was published after seven years in that island), and his knowledge of the Sudan and the Equatorial provinces was immense. In 1861 he had set out from Cairo to look for the source of the Nile, and although he had not found it he had discovered the Albert Nyanza, had travelled thousands of miles in the company of slave dealers, and at the end of the eighteen sixties had been appointed Governor-General of the Equatorial Nile basin. His endorsement of Gordon was bound to carry weight, and after the appearance of his letter *The Times* battered away at the subject. On January 5 a leading article headed 'Gordon and the Congo' expressed deep regret that one of the brightest ornaments of the British Army had been allowed to take service with a foreign power.

The press movement initiated by *The Times* was given impetus by W. T. Stead's *Pall Mall Gazette*. Stead was a pioneer of the personal interview which is now a commonplace of journalism, but was then a rarity. He had sent a telegram to Southampton, asking for permission to interview Gordon and to discuss the Sudan problem, and on the morning of the 8th he arrived. He sat on a sofa covered with a leopard skin, and talked to the great man. Captain Brocklehurst, an old friend of Gordon, and one of the two men for whom he prayed every

C

night, was also present. Stead's impression of Gordon was of a slightly built man with a sweet smile and a childish simplicity of speech and manner. 'His face is almost boyish in its youthfulness, his step is as light and his movements as lithe as the leopard's.' Gordon's friends concur in describing him as being of the middle height (in fact he was five feet five inches tall) and strongly built, with powerful shoulders. His face now was furrowed with deep lines, his brow broad, his mouth and chin determined. His voice was pleasing, 'as clear and vibrant as the note of an old Burmese bell', so Colonel William Butler said. Almost everybody was struck by the intensity of his grey-blue eyes, which one friend called delicately expressive, which Butler thought contained within them a depth like that of ocean, and which seemed to Wolseley to search into your inner soul. He had no small talk, but when dealing with a subject which engaged his interest revealed 'a kind of spiritual power which exercised a singular fascination', particularly if the subject was connected with religion. In Stead's presence he held up the *Imitation of Christ* and said, 'This is my book.'

Under the persuasion of Stead—although it is not likely that he needed much persuasion—Gordon talked about the policy that should be pursued in the Sudan. He did not know that abandonment had been settled on by the Government, and expressed himself freely in opposition to the idea. What would become of the garrisons in Khartoum and elsewhere? Were they to be sacrificed? It was all very well to talk about evacuation, but such talk was not practical. 'Whatever you may decide . . . you cannot evacuate, because your army cannot be moved. You must either surrender absolutely to the Mahdi or defend Khartoum at all hazards.' The point of view was clearly and forcibly stated, and Stead, who received a copy of the *Imitation of Christ* upon his departure, gave a page and a half to the interview and printed on his front page a leader, 'Chinese Gordon for the Sudan', in which it was suggested that Gordon should be sent out to assume command, treat with the Mahdi, and—not by weight of troops but through the prestige of his name—bring away the garrisons. Other papers reprinted the interview, and

the demand for Gordon's employment in the Sudan was reiterated in them.

Gordon, oblivious of the storm he had created, went to stay
with his friend Barnes, the vicar of Heavitree in Devon. He had
been in constant touch with Barnes about his Palestinian discoveries, and these were their chief topic of conversation. On
Sunday he received Holy Communion and then drove over
with Barnes to see Sir Samuel Baker at Sandford Orleigh. Baker
pressed on him the idea that he should go out to the Sudan as
Governor-General if he were asked. Gordon said nothing, but
it seemed to Barnes that an eager expression passed over his face
as he listened. Later he came to the vicar's room and said to him
softly, 'You saw me today? That was myself; the self I want to
get rid of.'[1] With the week-end visit over, Gordon returned to
his sister. On Monday a telegram from Wolseley at the War
Office was delivered to Heavitree. It was sent on to Southampton, and reached Gordon on the following day. The telegram
was a summons to the War Office.

Wolseley was moved by feelings and hopes that were quite
the opposite of those entertained in the Government. He had
first met Gordon more than a quarter of a century ago, in the
trenches before Sebastopol, when Wolseley had been a dashing
Captain and Gordon a good-looking curly haired subaltern.
The two men greatly admired each other. Gordon regarded the
victor of Tel-el-Kebir as the greatest soldier of his age. It has
been said that he prayed for two men every night, and Wolseley
was the second. Wolseley on his side said that he was not fit to
pipeclay Gordon's belt, and that Gordon was 'one of the very
few friends I ever had who came up to my estimate of the
Christian hero.' The aspects of Gordon likely to seem absurd or
antipathetic to a modern reader are exactly those which made
many otherwise hard-headed Victorians feel something like
reverence for him. A desire to worship the Hero, the truly selfless
and religious man whose actions were inspired not by greed of
power or money but purely by the love of God, lay deep in the
hearts of many Victorian business men, military men, adminis-

[1] Barnes and Brown, p. 71.

trators: a desire felt all the more strongly because the Hero was by definition unique, and could not be emulated. The Hero served for the Victorians as a scapegoat in reverse, embodying in himself not the guilt but the highest aspirations of his society. Wolseley held a supremely powerful position in the British Army of that time, and Gordon was no more than a Major-General whose active career seemed finished, but the Adjutant-General still felt for his friend a deep and wondering respect, together with a responsibility for getting him out of troubles into which he might be led through sheer unworldliness.

It was Wolseley who in October had told Hartington that Gordon should not be allowed to go to the Congo. 'Looking at the fanatic character of the man, I think it very doubtful whether the permission should be given.' On January 4, in a letter answering one from Gordon which told him of Leopold's offer, he tried to go further. Addressing him as 'My dear Gordon' he mildly rebuked his friend for the formality of calling him 'My dear Lord Wolseley', and went on:

> I hate the idea of your going to the Congo. You have had enough of liver-grilling climates, and the world does not seem bounded with the clear horizons that would warrant—if I may say so to an old friend—our very best man burying himself amongst niggers on the Equator. Of course if you will go there, all will go right for King Leo, and I am anxious his project should succeed, but I think he might attain his end without taking our best man from the English Army. . . . I wish I could have a long talk with you on Egyptian affairs, and hear your views on the Sudan question. . . . To reconquer the Sudan would require an army of 20,000 Indian or Turkish troops. There would be little difficulty about it as a military operation, but money would be wanted, and where is it to come from? The Sultan has not got it, nor could he borrow it, and Egypt is head and ears in debt. Is the English taxpayer to pay for the reconquest of this province? Cui bono?[1]

On Tuesday, January 15, Gordon came to see Wolseley at the War Office in response to his telegram. The ostensible reason for the visit was discussion of his resignation, which had not yet been accepted, but this seems to have been briskly swept aside when the Adjutant-General told his old comrade-in-arms that

[1] Wolseley Papers, Hove.

the claims of his own country must come first if they wished to employ him. It may be asked how such a wish was possible, when Gordon had expressed views about the Sudan that were diametrically opposed to Government policy. The answer to this question, which is at the root of the tragi-comedy of Gordon, rests in the illogic of human conduct compared with the rationality of human thought. His despatch would be a popular gesture, he had worked miracles in China, perhaps the magic of of his name might work a miracle here. Government thinking went little further than this. It may be asked also how Gordon found it possible to consider accepting the commission to carry out a policy with which he did not agree, and the answer is that while talking to Wolseley he had a sudden intuitive understanding that he was called in the Sudan to carry out the work of God. A fortnight earlier he had been able to write to a friend with placid detachment that in Egypt God was 'working out His wonderful embroidery of events', but his heart stirred at the thought that he might have a part to play in that embroidery. For Gordon such perceptions cancelled any conclusion that he might have reached by the process of reasoning. So, now, he did not flinch from undertaking a course of action which he had declared to be impossible.

After the meeting Wolseley set down for Hartington's benefit the views Gordon had expressed. On the subject of evacuation 'he stated most clearly that it would in his opinion be a policy preferable to that of conquering if such reconquest was to entail again handing it over to the government of Egyptian pashas.' He thought reconquest would cost £2 million (a figure which he later modified to £1 million). The Mahdi? 'He had no opinion of the Mahdi's military power' and regarded him as 'a tool in the hands of slave dealers.' Were the garrisons in danger? He thought they 'could always make terms with the Mahdi'. Gordon had referred more than once to his hatred of Cairene intrigues and double dealing, and expressed a strong distaste for going to Cairo. When he said this he was not referring to Baring. 'He spoke in the nicest manner of Baring and how glad he should be to work with and under him', but he was anxious not to be brought into direct contact with the Khedive or his ministers. If he went to Suakin, thus avoiding Cairo, he thought it important that he should have 'some agent in Cairo who would counteract and expose the intrigues of his personal enemies there.' And finally, what would his policy be? Gordon reasonably said that he could not be sure before going out to Egypt. He might find complete evacuation advisable, or he might find it better to restore order and arrange a settled form of Government.

It was agreed that the mission should be one of enquiry, and Wolseley suggested that Gordon should put down a few notes covering his likely activities. He did so under eight heads. Six of them are comparatively unimportant. They dealt with his expenses (passage money, £3 a day for travelling, and £500 to await him at Suakin), the notification of Nubar, Baring and the public, an arrangement for a writer to meet him at Suez, and permission to go to the Congo after carrying out his mission. The two headings of importance are Numbers 1 and 7:

1. To proceed to Suakin and report on military situation of Sudan and return. Under Baring for orders, and to send through him letters, etc. under flying seal.

7. I understand H.M.G. only wish me to report and are in no way bound to me.

It was a mission of enquiry, then, and nothing more, but Granville unintentionally give a different impression to Gladstone when asking for his approval before Gordon saw Wolseley. If Gordon thought he could 'excite the tribes to escort the Khartoum garrison and inhabitants to Suakin', Granville suggested that 'a little pressure on Baring might be advisable.' Gladstone agreed—he was recovering at Hawarden from the nervous condition in which the battle of threatened resignations had left him, and a few days later went to the Riviera to recuperate—and Granville proceeded to apply the pressure. He proposed Gordon once more, and tried to placate Baring by saying that after reporting on the military situation he would return, 'and his engagement towards Her Majesty's Government would cease'. He would take instructions from Baring, and send reports through him. Would Baring accept him? Gladstone approved this proposal, although he was concerned that Gordon's mission should be confined to reporting on the situation, and that 'if he reports what should be done, he should not be the judge *who* should do it, nor ought he to commit us on that point by advice officially given.'

At the same time pressure of a different kind was working on Baring in Cairo. The Egyptian Minister for War, Abd-el-Kader, who had accepted the post of Governor-General, now suddenly changed his mind. It was evident that something must be done quickly, and Baring wired to Granville that the Egyptian Government would like sent out at once 'a qualified British officer to go to Khartoum with full powers civil and military to conduct the retreat'. After sending this telegram, Baring received Granville's third proposal of Gordon. At last he gave way, saying that Gordon would be the best man 'if he will pledge himself to carry out the policy of withdrawal from Sudan as soon as possible, consistently with saving life', and that he would 'rather have him than anyone else, provided there is a perfectly clear understanding with him as to what his position is to be and what line of policy he is to carry out'. This crossing of Granville's and Baring's telegrams permanently confused the purpose of Gordon's mission, although nobody realized this at the time. Baring had been asked whether he would accept Gordon as an agent coming out to make a report. What he asked for was a man to conduct a retreat. By the time Gordon arrived the idea of mere 'reporting' had been forgotten, and it was obvious that he must be the man to conduct the retreat, although the Government were later to claim that in doing so he had exceeded his instructions.[1]

Gordon's excitement had been increased by the interview with Wolseley. From being an unwanted Major-General, his services were demanded by two countries. On the 16th he returned to Brussels. A journalist named Demetrios Boulger met

[1] Mr. Bernard M. Allen's examination of the relevant telegrams in the Public Record Office revealed this misunderstanding, although I think he attaches too much weight to it.

him at Charing Cross Hotel before his departure. Map in hand,
Gordon explained his plans for the Congo but said mysteriously:
'There may be a respite.' The secretary of the Anti-Slavery
Society, who was also at Charing Cross, wrote a letter which
appeared in *The Times*, beginning: 'This morning, at Charing
Cross, I had the melancholy pleasure of saying good-bye to
that great and good man, General Gordon, who has started on
his journey to the Congo.' At Dover Gordon scribbled a pencil
note to Wolseley. If any hitch occurred, he said, 'as my friend,
hesitate not a moment to bury the whole matter of yesterday.
.... I would not have the very slightest flutter of hurt on subject
and would never mention it.'[1] Why did Gordon go to Brussels?
Perhaps he did not know himself. Once there, he waited impatiently for news from London, and on the afternoon of the
17th it came in the form of a telegram from Wolseley calling
him back. By six o'clock on the morning of the 18th he had
returned. By midday he was again talking to Wolseley.

It is obvious that on the 15th Wolseley had been deputed to
find out Gordon's ideas, so that if they were wildly eccentric the
Government remained uncommitted. Since they seemed so
thoroughly reasonable the meeting on the 18th was to be a mere
official rubber-stamping of what had been agreed. But it was
mid-January, and very few Ministers were in town. Granville,
never eager to hurry, had wished to leave a final decision until
the Cabinet met on the following Monday, but it had been
pointed out to him that by then Gordon might have started for
the Congo. The only Ministers who could be found, besides
Granville and Hartington, were the First Lord of the Admiralty,
Lord Northbrook, and Dilke. 'I was summoned suddenly to a
meeting at the War Office, in Hartington's room', Dilke noted
in his diary. Wolseley went over again with Gordon the details
they had already discussed and then went into Hartington's
room, leaving Gordon in the ante-room with the official private
secretary. Standing with his back to the fire, Gordon suddenly
asked: 'Do you ever tell a lie?' Before the secretary could reply

[1] Hove.

Wolseley returned, took Gordon in, and left him with the four Ministers.

We do not know exactly what was said in Hartington's room, but there is an almost embarrassing amount of evidence about what the five people present believed to have been decided. The decision to abandon the Sudan had been made by the whole Cabinet, but only Granville and Hartington knew the increasing urgency conveyed in Baring's telegrams. Nobody seems to have raised any awkward questions about the *Pall Mall Gazette* interview, or to have asked whether Gordon had changed his mind about the impossibility of evacuation. For Northbrook and Dilke the question was simple: if Gordon was the man for the job, send him out. Was he going to report and return, or to try to bring away the garrisons? Dilke put down in his notes that the sole decision taken was that Gordon should go to Suakin, collect information and report, but in the same notes he said without any sense of contradiction that Gordon believed 'he would be able to bring away the garrisons without difficulty'. How could he do this by reporting? Northbrook, writing to Baring on the same evening, defined Gordon's duties as 'to report on the best way of withdrawing garrisons, settling the country, and to perform such other duties as may be entrusted to him by the Khedive's Government through you'. Hartington based himself on Wolseley's notes, which he sent to Gladstone as an account of what had happened. These confined themselves to 'reporting', and although Gordon might 'recommend' withdrawal there was no hint that he would carry it out. Finally, Granville's instructions, which he wrote at the time, confined themselves to the 'reporting' aspect, but added that phrase in Northbrook's letter about Gordon performing other duties entrusted to him. Granville may have felt that he had tied Gordon down as Gladstone had wished, but there was a dangerous vagueness not only in the instructions, but also in the minds of those who gave them. There was one consideration that should have been, but was not, obvious to Granville when he received Baring's telegram asking for an English officer to be sent out to Khartoum with full powers. If Gordon was sent out at all, was it not overwhelmingly likely that the very thing Gladstone feared would come about, and that the man on the spot would turn from an adviser on policy into the person carrying out that policy?

None of these doubts and qualifications passed through Gordon's excited mind. Before leaving he wrote several letters, and although they vary in length, they say much the same thing. The one to Barnes is expressive of them all. 'Ministers said they were determined to evacuate and would I go and superintend it? I said "Yes".' Writing to his sister he struck a characteristic note. 'I go to the Sudan tonight to finish a work, then to the Congo. I am not moved, and hope you will not be.'

It had been agreed at the interview that he would leave that night. He went back to Wolseley's house in Hill Street, and the Wolseleys' young daughter, Frances, shook hands with him. She thought him 'rather insignificant, a shrivelled, wrinkled old man, dressed in a shabby not to say shiny frock coat.'[1] Wearing this frock coat and a tall silk hat he prepared to leave to dine with Captain Brocklehurst at his mess. Wolseley asked what clothes he should send on. Gordon said he wanted nothing.

'But you've got no clothes.'

'I'll go as I am.'

Nothing had been said at the interview about money, and in answer to Wolseley's question, Gordon said that he had none, and that in Brussels he had had to borrow from the King to pay his hotel bill. Wolseley said that he would try to get some and have it ready at the railway station. Such unconcern about money seemed to him quite natural in a hero.

While Gordon dined with Brocklehurst and saw other friends, Wolseley went to several clubs and collected £300 in gold. At Charing Cross station he handed the money not to Gordon but to his companion, Colonel Stewart. In a letter to Granville, Baring had mentioned Stewart as a possible second choice if Gordon refused the mission. Tall, spare and abstemious, Stewart had been chosen to provide a check on possible eccentricities. 'They sent Stewart with me to be my wet-nurse', Gordon said

[1] Hove.

later, and relations between the two men were strained in these first days. Granville bought Gordon's ticket. A nephew arrived, carrying his General's uniform in a metal case. Brocklehurst was there, and so of course was Wolseley, who walked along the platform carrying the handbag which held the rest of Gordon's kit. The Commander-in-Chief of the Army, the Duke of Cambridge, had been notified, and put in an appearance. He held open the carriage door. The story that Wolseley gave Gordon his watch and chain seems to be baseless, as does the tale that the departing hero ordered copies of Doctor Samuel Clarke's *Scriptural Promises* to be sent to every member of the Cabinet. Good-byes were said. The train steamed out of the station.

CHAPTER TWO

ARRIVAL OF A GOVERNOR-GENERAL

THE news of Gordon's departure for Egypt was greeted with great enthusiasm. It had been thought that he was irrevocably bound to King Leopold, and *The Times* expressed the feelings of the whole national press in saying that 'It will be a welcome surprise to the country to learn that General Gordon started last night, not for the Congo but for Egypt.' To have snatched this hero from the arms of King Leopold was a triumphant stroke, and the apparent decisiveness shown was favourably remarked. Yet the step had no sooner been taken than the politicians immediately involved began to feel unhappy about it. 'We were proud of ourselves yesterday', Granville said to Hartington. 'Are you sure that we did not commit a gigantic folly?' Gordon had left London on Friday evening, and a rumour immediately spread that he was going to defend Khartoum. By Monday other members of the Cabinet were becoming alarmed. Childers wrote to Granville that he was being asked questions about Gordon. 'On some I do not mind being ignorant, but I should be glad if I might know, for my own information, what is to be his relation to those in authority in Egypt . . . who will be responsible for him, and to whom will he be responsible?' On the same day Dilke wrote: 'While I was at the War Office I heard nothing of his going to Khartoum, or anywhere except to Suakin.' If Gordon were carried off and held to ransom, Dilke suggested, 'we shall have to send a terrible force after him.' Granville soothed these doubts as best he could, but his own uneasiness was not diminished by the messages he received from Gordon, written on his train journey across France. These enclosed draft proclamations that he thought might be issued on his arrival. One was to appoint him Governor-General, another was a Khedivial announcement granting independence to the local Pashas, others were appeals to the tribes to 'stay your hands and remain quiet'. At a Cabinet meeting on Tuesday these suggestions were considered, and sent to Baring for his comments. He replied at once that they were excellent. Granville must have been relieved, but he still had an intermittent feeling that, as Gladstone was to say later, he and Hartington had let the genie out of the jar.

The genie, meanwhile, was at sea, which he never much cared about. 'It is odd that *tears* are salt like the *sea*, Satan's element', he had written a fortnight earlier to his sister. He occupied himself with writing a long, detailed memorandum to Baring from the S.S. *Tanjore*, in which he said that he hoped to be able to carry out the evacuation without fighting, and suggested that power in the Sudan should be restored to the petty Sultans who had ruled different provinces in the past. The memorandum reassured Baring about the wisdom of Gordon's appointment.

In the meantime it had become obvious to him that Gordon should come to Cairo, not only because it was desirable that he should talk to the Khedive and the British military officers, but because the road from Suakin to Berber was now blocked by rebellious tribesmen, and it was doubtful whether Khartoum could be reached by this route. When S.S. *Tanjore* arrived at Port Said Gordon found waiting for him Sir Evelyn Wood and a friend whom he had known since his earliest days in the Sudan, Colonel Watson. They urged him to come to Cairo. 'Must I see the Khedive?' Gordon plaintively asked Wood, who said that he thought it was necessary. He was met also by a message from Granville, a friendly letter from Baring saying that a discussion at Cairo would prevent any risk of working at cross-purposes, and a letter from another old friend of pre-Crimean days, Sir Gerald Graham, who had commanded a brigade at Tel-el-Kebir, and had afterwards stayed in Egypt as a member of the occupying force. Graham's letter began: 'My dear

Charlie, Do come to Cairo. Wood will tell you much better than I why. Throw over all personal feelings if you have any, and act like yourself with straightforward directness.' Faced with all these exhortations, Gordon went to Cairo. On the way, at Ismailia, he saw his old Egyptian secretary Mahomet Bey Tuhamy, who was now blind, and insisted that Stewart should give the man £100 of the money collected by Wolseley. He arrived in Cairo on the evening of the 24th, six days after he had left Charing Cross, and was taken almost at once to see Baring. The British Resident had a bad sore throat and had almost lost his voice, but it was arranged that on the following morning they would visit the Khedive together. Gordon then returned to Wood's house, where he was staying.

The interview with Tewfik went off much better than anybody had expected. Gordon was, as he said, abject—that is, he apologized for the hard things he had said about Tewfik in the past. The Khedive gave him two firmans for use if and when necessary, one appointing him Governor-General of the Sudan, the other saying that he was going to evacuate the country and establish an organized Government. 'Tewfik gave me the Firman on the same sofa as Ismail gave me the same Firman', Gordon wrote to Brocklehurst.[1] Later in the morning there was a discussion attended by Baring, Gordon, Stewart, Wood, and Nubar, to decide about the further instructions to be issued to Gordon. This meeting was adjourned until the following afternoon, when a draft was hammered out. Apart from providing a credit of £100,000 at the Finance Department on which he might draw they added little to what had already been settled, although any pretence that he had come simply to report was abandoned. It was accepted that he had come out to evacuate the garrisons and establish a settled Government in the Sudan. Baring had no illusions about Gordon. 'A man who habitually consults the Prophet Isaiah when he is in a difficulty is not apt to obey the orders of any one', he wrote to Granville, but still he found Gordon's behaviour during the two days he spent in Cairo depressing. Gordon's conclusions were often as prag-

[1] Brocklehurst Papers.

matic as Baring could have wished, but they were reached by most disconcerting intuitive processes. This was particularly evident in the case of Zobeir Pasha.

In December the Egyptian Government had proposed to send this man to Suakin in the hope that the Bedouins and local tribes would rally to him, and that his influence would be useful to a force of Egyptian gendarmerie who were being sent to that area under Valentine Baker. There was no doubt about Zobeir's influence, or about his ability, but he was a notorious slave dealer, and at the very mention of his possible employment there was such an outcry in England that the idea was immediately dropped. On his way to Egypt Gordon had suggested that Zobeir should be exiled to Cyprus, or should at least be watched to make sure that he did not communicate with the Sudan. Now, however, he met Zobeir for a moment, quite by accident, in the house of the former Prime Minister, Chérif Pasha. In that moment he had a mystic feeling that Zobeir was to be trusted, and should be employed. On the following morning the astonished Baring had delivered to him a long memorandum from Gordon enthusiastically advocating the employment of the slave trader. Zobeir, Gordon said, was the most able man in the Sudan, a capital General, a man who would attract all the followers of the Mahdi. Gordon confessed to admiring him greatly. But what about the slave trade? Baring must have rubbed his eyes as he found it thus casually dismissed: 'I think nothing of it, for there will be Slave Trade always as long as Turkey and Egypt buy the slaves, and it may be Zobeir will or might see his interests to stop it in some manner.' The real question was, would Baring and Nubar feel the mystic trust in Zobeir experienced by Gordon? As far as Baring was concerned, the answer was in no doubt. 'I have no confidence in opinions based on mystic feelings', he wrote later. But there was another, and it might have been thought insuperable, objection to Zobeir's employment by Gordon. Five years earlier Zobeir's son, Suleiman, had rebelled against Gordon's authority in the Sudan. The rebellion was crushed, and Suleiman shot. A letter from Zobeir inciting him to revolt had been found, and ever since then Zobeir had been

under a sort of house arrest in Cairo, with all his property confiscated. All this Gordon brushed aside, and indeed it is likely
that Zobeir's reasons for personal hatred only increased the
power of his mystic feelings.

At Gordon's insistence Baring arranged a meeting between
the two men, which was attended by Wood, Nubar and Stewart,
among others. The proceedings read like a piece of low comedy
for the groundlings in a Jacobean play. Zobeir refused to shake
hands, and asked immediately why his property had been confiscated. Gordon replied that it was because he had written a
letter exhorting his son to revolt, and a long wrangle ensued
about this letter. Produce the letter, Zobeir demanded, saying
that if it existed he also should have been condemned to death.
Where was the letter? A messenger, Major Wingate, was sent
to try to find it. Baring said that it must be in the Government
archives, but it was not there. Produce the letter, Zobeir cried
again, and if it was found put him to death with the sword. The
truth was, he said, that he had entrusted his son to Gordon and
he should have been as Gordon's own son, but Gordon had
killed him. Eventually the exasperated Gordon said, 'Well, well,
I killed my own son. There is an end of it.' There are two versions of the way in which the meeting ended. According to the
official transcript it ended indecisively, but there was afterwards
a unanimous vote against the idea of using Zobeir, primarily
because, as Baring told Granville, 'he is manifestly animated by
a feeling of deep resentment against General Gordon'. Wingate's diary, however, says that when no paper involving Zobeir
could be found, Gordon apologized, Zobeir shook his hand and
said 'I am your slave for life', and the subsequent decision not to
send Zobeir was taken by a majority of one. Wingate was later
for many years Governor-General of the Sudan, and his word
must carry weight: on the other hand, there is no indication
that he was present at the meeting.

In any case, the rejection of his proposal about Zobeir bitterly
angered Gordon. That evening a farewell party had been
arranged for him at Wood's house. Wingate was preparing the
cards to be put round the table when Gordon came in, wearing

(*Illustrated London News*)

Towing whalers through the first gate of the Second Cataract

(*Graphic*)

Men of the Camel Corps having a variety of troubles on one of their first
parades. Fixing the saddles was always a problem

Nile boats, used between Cairo and the Second Cataract, but useless above
that point

Whalers arriving at Akasheh

his little black coat, turned angrily on Wood and said, 'You were one of those who voted against Zobeir, I won't sit down to table with you, I'll have a plate of soup in my room', and stumped out. Here again, Wingate's diary does not accord with the recollection of another guest that evening, who remembered Gordon only as silent and preoccupied. When he left for the station he surprised all the guests by taking off his evening coat and waistcoat and giving them to Wood's butler as a gift, putting on instead other clothes that he had brought in a bag. Graham was going with him as far as Korosko, and they were seen off by Nubar, Wood, Baring and the Khedive's Chamberlain. Gordon was still angry, and was obviously on bad terms with Stewart. His temper may perhaps not have been improved by the arrival of the newly-appointed Sultan of Darfour. There were several members of the former reigning family of the province of Darfour in Cairo, and one of them had been chosen as a first example of Gordon's policy of re-establishing the former local Sultans in power. The new Sultan was, according to Stewart, given ' £2,000 E, a well-embroidered coat, and the biggest decoration that could be found', and directed to accompany the Europeans. It proved, however, that taking the Sultan was not the simple matter it appeared. He had twenty-three wives and a great deal of baggage, and the train had to wait while extra carriages were put on to it. At the last moment there was further delay because his splendid uniform had been mislaid. It was not an auspicious departure.

A couple of days after Gordon had gone, Baring told Granville that it was impossible not to be charmed by the simplicity and honesty of his character. 'My only fear is that he is terribly flighty and changes his opinions very rapidly.' Gordon wrote to Brocklehurst that the talks had been long and wearisome, and to Barnes that he had seen only two pleasant things in Cairo, 'Baring's and Wood's chicks'. To his sister he expressed himself with utter confidence: 'I feel quite happy, for I say, if God is with me, who can or will be hurtful to me?'

*

As he steamed up the Nile the irritations of Cairo slowly slipped away, and Gordon became again the delightful companion Graham remembered. During the course of this week he elaborated a bewildering variety of ideas. He drew up a plan of campaign for smashing the hostile tribes around Suakin, spoke of forming a Sudanese army to replace the Egyptians, wrote a letter to King Leopold, with a neat plan appended, suggesting that he should take over in the King's name two provinces south of Khartoum, evolved a plan to incorporate the whole Sudan into a Belgian Congo state, and sent a dozen or more telegrams to Baring. He refused to listen when Graham tried to talk about the views expressed in the *Pall Mall Gazette* interview, but was more receptive to suggestions about his headgear. Graham urged him to wear a fez, saying that the Egyptians would think that immediate evacuation was intended if two men appeared, 'one the redoubtable Gordon Pasha', wearing English travelling dress without even 'that Turkish symbol of authority, the fez'. Graham's view outweighed Stewart's preference for a solar topee and from this time onwards Gordon assumed and wore a fez. The new Sultan was quickly disposed of. He appeared on deck in his splendid uniform, wearing the grand cordon of the Medjidie, which kept slipping off, pushed past Gordon and Graham and took possession of the saloon. Gordon ordered him out, and then gave him a lecture, saying that he was not to go about in his fine clothes until he obtained his throne. Later the Sultan began to drink heavily, and Gordon left him at Assuan. He hoped that the tribes would rise in the new ruler's favour, and that he would take possession of Darfour province. In fact the Sultan got no further than Dongola, and after staying there for some months returned ignominiously to Cairo.

At Korosko Gordon and Graham parted. Gordon and Stewart crossed the desert to Abu Hamed. A handsome young Arab on a beautiful white camel rode beside the new Governor-General. When they parted Gordon gave Graham a heavy silver-mounted kourbash, as a token that the reign of the kourbash was over, and took with him instead a white umbrella. As he moved farther up the Nile from Abu Hamed, sending daily telegrams and occasional volleys of memoranda to Baring, it must have seemed to him that he had come home. The formality of diplomats like Baring was something that he could never understand, whereas the deviousness of the Arabs touched a well of sympathy in his own nature. Discomfort was his natural element, and the harsh, dry desert held no terrors for him. He was supremely confident of his power over the tribes, and when he reached Berber set up in the town a Council of Notables, which was to meet twice a week to administer the area and settle all differences. He did not carry out a vague suggestion he had made about going to see the Mahdi but, he did write to Mohammed Ahmed, sending him robes of honour and appointing him Sultan of Kordofan. He had written to Baring from Abu Hamed, suggesting that the Egyptian Government ought to maintain its position as a suzerain power in the Sudan, and from now onwards the importance of creating and maintaining a stable Government was foremost in his mind. At Berber he issued a number of proclamations, one wiping off all arrears of taxes and cutting the taxes for the coming year by half, and another saying: 'I give you the right to keep the slaves in your service without any interference from the Government or anybody else.' There was an Anglo-Egyptian Convention which made slave-holding punishable by death, but Gordon justified the abrogation of it by saying with Arabian ingenuity that the Sudan was no longer to be part of Egypt, and therefore was not bound by the Convention.

He also showed the Notables the Khedive's firman, which announced the withdrawal of all Egyptian soldiers and officials from the Sudan. He was trying to induce in them the habit of self-reliance, but it was natural that they should ask who would protect them after the soldiers left, since Gordon brought no forces with him, and expressed his abhorrence of war. The step has been called a death blow to his mission, one that made many sheiks decide to throw in their lot with the Mahdi. 'Why should they remain loyal to a Government which had decided to give up their land? Had they remained faithful, what had they to

expect when the Mahdi prevailed?'[1] Now and hereafter Gordon
put too much faith in the magic of his own name.

Nevertheless, the departure of 'Our Father' from Berber was
witnessed by thousands of cheering and weeping Sudanese, and
his arrival at Khartoum four days later evoked an even more
impressive demonstration. Thousands of natives crowded to kiss
his hands and feet, calling him Sultan, Father and Saviour. His
proclamations, already posted, had been well received, particularly the one permitting the retention of slaves. His flair for
drama manifested itself in other impressive ways. The Government books recording outstanding debts were publicly burned
in front of the Palace. Kourbashes and other whips were placed
on the blazing pile. Dozens of people who had been festering in
prison, loaded with chains, were set free. A Council of Arab
Notables was immediately appointed.

The word *Khartoum* means 'elephant's trunk' in the local dia-
lect, and it has been suggested that the town derived its name
from the shape of the strip of land extending between the Blue
and White Niles on which it stands. Colonel Stewart considered
it a wretched place. 'The town is built on a barren, stoneless and
wide plain', Stewart wrote in a report. It was built on the bank
of the Blue Nile, about a mile above its junction with the White
Nile, which flooded in the rainy season from July to September.
The population fluctuated between 40,000 and 60,000 people,
and Stewart estimated that two-thirds of them were Negro
slaves. Their masters were Syrians, Turks, Copts, Albanians and
Jews. 'Of the floating population, the Copts are mostly employed in Government service or trade. The Turks, Albanians,
etc. are generally irregular soldiers or loafers. The European
element is represented by about a hundred individuals, mostly
Greeks. There are also some Italians, French, Austrians and Germans.' Slavery seemed commonplace to the Khartoumese. The
correspondent of *The Times*, Frank Power, noted that in September 1883, there were 27,000 registered slaves in the town,
many of them well treated and happy, although he bought for

[1] Ohrwalder, p. 139.

four dollars a Negro boy who was beaten daily by his master.[1] Manufactures were confined to mats, cotton clothes, sisal and filigree silver work. There was a considerable trade in grain.

The town's appearance was poor and miserable. Seen from the White Nile it presented a view of a mass of dirty grey houses, with the minaret of the one large mosque standing out. A sterile bushless plain lay between the river and the town. One long narrow street stretched from east to west, lined by mud houses, which were each year plastered with dung as protection against the rains. This was the best street in Khartoum, containing the Governor's house (the 'Palace') and the houses lived in by Turks, Copts and Arabs. There was no restaurant, but alcoholic drinks could be bought in a number of Greek-owned shops.[2] The smells were so bad that Power and the only other Englishman in Khartoum, Colonel de Coetlögon, carried camphor to their noses when they went out. Stewart listed the chief buildings: the Government house, a hospital built by Gordon when he was Governor-General, an arsenal with smithy, carpenter's shop and smelting furnaces, a large mud barracks, a powder magazine and workshop, two mosques, a small Coptic church and a Roman Catholic missionary building. It sounds gloomy enough, yet life was not unrelievedly grim. When Marquet, the rich French Consul, departed in November, he gave a farewell dinner with ten servants in livery waiting at a table on which were cut-glass, silver and flowers. Peas, mushrooms and asparagus grown in his garden were served as part of 'a dinner thoroughly Parisian turned out by his French chef'.[3] There was beauty, too, in the sight of the Nile at early morning crowded with white-sailed ships. A lovely picture, Power called it, 'the village opposite, the fringe of palm trees, a field of durra, and the red desert away into the distance beyond'.

On the night of Gordon's arrival, the town was transformed. The bazaar was hung with cloth and coloured lamps, the private houses were decorated and illuminated, there was even a display

[1] Power, *Letters from Khartoum.*
[2] *Sudan Notes and Records*, 1936.
[3] Power.

of fireworks. On the following day the town was perfectly quiet, for the people believed that Gordon's presence ensured their safety. This feeling communicated itself to Stewart and to Power, who had been feeling gloomy before Gordon came. Gordon himself was momentarily under the same illusion. In a letter telling Colonel de Coetlögon that he could return to Khartoum because his 'services here in a military capacity would be wasted', he went on: 'My belief is that there is not the least chance of any danger being incurred by Khartoum. . . . Rest assured, you leave this place as safe as Kensington park.'

CHAPTER THREE

THE REFUSAL OF ZOBEIR

A S Gordon had begun, he went on. He believed that the people adhered to the Mahdi only because of the wretched treatment they had suffered under the Pashas sent to rule them, and his moves therefore were directed to outbidding the Mahdi by showing that under his régime they would gain more than the Mahdi even promised. Within a few days he arranged a much easier passage into the city for food, by opening two gates in the fortifications that had been closed and by abolishing all market duties. Arabs from the neighbouring villages brought in fruit and vegetables, and market prices dropped by half. Boxes were put in various open places for the receipt of petitions and complaints. The process of freeing prisoners of both sexes, many of whom had been in prison for years on unspecified charges, went on. The joy of those released moved the normally taciturn Stewart. 'I cannot express what pleasure it afforded me to set these poor people free', he wrote. 'It was quite worth coming up here to do so.'[1] Plans for evacuating the garrison were begun. It was Gordon's intention 'to get out the white element, then the whitey brown or Bashi-Bazouks, and to leave the pure black, or Sudanese, to manage their own affairs'.[2] The announcement caused alarm among the Council of Notables, and one or two of them waited upon him to suggest that the Egyptian troops should stay. Before his arrival in Khartoum Gordon had acutely noted that the question of getting out garrisons and families was interlaced with the preservation of the well-to-do

[1] Stewart's Diary, P.R.O. 78/3669.
[2] Ibid.

people of the country, and now these merchants, like those in
Berber, were asking who would protect them when the soldiers
had left? For reply Gordon produced a globe, turned it, and
asked them who was the Lord of it? When they made the
expected reply, he said that his own trust was in God, who
would direct all for the best. With this the Notables were satisfied, for the moment at least. Power wrote that Gordon was a
dictator in Khartoum, and that the Mahdi had gone down before
him.

A strong streak of shrewdness was blended with Gordon's
mysticism. He would often be moved by such feelings to views
which were the embodiment of hard common sense, and so it
was in the matter of Zobeir. The success of these first moves did
not blind him to the fact that there was force in the objections
of the Notables, and that if he were able to evacuate the Sudan
the Mahdi would immediately take possession of it. He saw also
the weakness of his own position. If the mere mention of the
departure of troops alarmed the merchants, what would happen
when the garrisons left? It seemed to him that the solution was
the imposition of government under a strong, generally accepted
ruler. In Berber he had considered the Mudir, Hussein Pasha
Khalifa, but had rejected him as possessing too narrow an influence to play such a part. He saw no other possibility than
Zobeir, and said so to Baring. 'He alone has the ability to rule
the Sudan, and would be universally accepted by the Sudan.
He should be made K.C.M.G. and given presents.' Stewart, who
was asked by Gordon to comment on the suggestion, said that
such an appointment would 'greatly facilitate our retirement
from the country', although he was not yet convinced that
Zobeir was the inevitable choice.

Baring had been doubtful of Gordon's 'mystic influence', but
saw at once the force of his argument. He passed on the suggestion to Granville with his general approval, but made the
qualification that he would be opposed to leaving Zobeir and
Gordon in Khartoum together. 'I would not on any account
run the risk of putting General Gordon into his power.' But
what looked like simple realism in Khartoum and Cairo seemed

almost incredible folly in London. Gordon was a renowned opponent of slavery, Zobeir a notorious slave dealer, and there was strong feeling against African slavery in England. Two months earlier the Anti-Slavery Society had protested strongly when a rumour was circulated that Zobeir had been appointed by the Khedive to command the Egyptian Army in the Sudan. Even *The Times*, which had leaned over backwards to extenuate the proclamation condoning slavery in Khartoum, thought that the suggestion of installing Zobeir could not be contemplated as a serious possibility. The slavery proclamation had come as a shock to many Liberals, and the appointment of Zobeir would have been unacceptable to almost the whole Liberal Party as well as to many Unionists. Several members of the Cabinet felt what Dilke brusquely noted in his diary, that Gordon had lost his senses. Granville was often accused of procrastination—Dilke observed that although they had started a red label system for pressing matters, Granville's room was full of red-labelled notes still untouched—but he replied promptly to this suggestion, saying that the gravest objections existed to the appointment of any successor to Gordon, and that 'in any case, the public opinion of this country would not tolerate the appointment of Zobeir Pasha'.

Gordon's spirits were as mercurial as his ideas. He showed a brave face always in public but Power, who had the next room to him in the Palace, heard him walking up and down his room all night, and thought that only piety carried him through. He sent a bitter telegram to Baring saying that he could suggest nobody other than Zobeir, repeated that once he moved out the Mahdi would occupy the town, and added that if Egypt was to be kept quiet the Mahdi must be smashed up. This, he thought, would be comparatively easy. 'If you decide on smashing Mahdi, then send up another £100,000 and send up 200 Indian troops to Wady Halfa.' Such suggestions served for Gordon rather as expletives do for other men. He meant them at the time, but did not regard them as irrevocable or feel that they must not be contradicted afterwards. He had already said that if 3,000 Turkish troops were engaged in British pay 'that would settle the

affair', and within three weeks of his arrival in Khartoum he
had put his idea about the employment of Zobeir to Baring in
half a dozen different ways, and in a series of telegrams sent
between the 8th and 10th of March had said (i) that the people
paid no attention to his proclamation and that there was no
likelihood of their rallying round him; (ii) that Khartoum was
not in danger and that he did not think the rebels would attack
it; (iii) that Stewart could easily retreat to Egypt via Berber
under cover of 2,000 troops which Evelyn Wood might provide; (iv) that Stewart's retirement would be 'a most difficult
matter'; (v) that 'Wood and his forces' should 'move on Dongola'; (vi) that if the immediate evacuation of Khartoum irre-
spective of other towns was decided upon, he would resign his
commission, take all steamers and stores up to the Equatorial
and Bahr-el-Gazal provinces and 'consider those provinces as
under the King of the Belgians'; (vii) that 'if we get hemmed in
and you shall send an expedition Indian troops, Mussulman,
then proclamation liberation of slaves'.

These telegrams, and the opinions expressed in them, are mere
samples of the dozens that Baring received. It is not surprising
that he afterwards counted these first three months of 1884 as
the most difficult of his life, involving a continuous strain on his
nerves, mind and temper, nor that he wrote to Gordon that
'while anxious to help and support you in every way . . . I find
it very difficult to understand exactly what it is you want'. In
desperation he appealed to Stewart, who replied that Gordon
telegraphed as soon as an idea struck him, that there was no use
in trying to stop him, and that it would always be a good thing
to wait for a few days before acting on any telegram 'unless the
subject matter is so evident that there can be no doubt about it'.
Baring felt that it would be dangerous to follow this advice
literally, but he put the batch of telegrams that awaited him each
morning on one side until the afternoon, by which time more
had arrived. He then compared them, tried to discern what
Gordon really wanted, and passed on the sense of the telegrams
to Granville. Some apologists for Gordon have said that this
process of filtering the telegrams through Baring was partly

responsible for Granville's failure to catch the note of urgency that ran through them, but the truth is that such telegrams sent verbatim would have created alarm and confusion at the Foreign Office.

One theme ran through all except the wildest of them, the importance of sending Zobeir. Stewart had become convinced of this, and Baring was now convinced of it too. He felt that Granville's negative should not be taken as a final answer, and made detailed proposals for Zobeir's employment, suggesting that he should be given a lump sum of money to begin with, and thereafter a subsidy of £50,000 a year for five years which would 'enable him to maintain a moderate-sized army'. But now an incident occurred which put paid to all hope of Zobeir's employment. Gordon had meekly said in one telegram that he would accept any Government decision about Zobeir as 'ruled by a Higher Power' and as basically caused by his own inconsistency, so that 'I should bear the blame if Zobeir is sent, and should put up with inconvenience if he is not', but within a couple of days this meekness was replaced by extreme irritation, coupled with a mistaken belief that Baring was not supporting him with sufficient energy. Gordon therefore deliberately gave an interview to Power which appeared in *The Times*, making public the fact that it was vital for him to have Zobeir. The effect of this disclosure was not to enlist support for Gordon, but simply to shock public opinion further. Granville had already replied to Baring with an acid refusal. It was with feelings akin to despair that the British Resident read this stiffly-worded message which asked, 'how you reconcile your proposal to acquiesce in such an appointment with the prevention or discouragement of slave-hunting and Slave Trade, with the policy of complete evacuation, and with the security of Egypt.'

Yet Baring still persisted, and the question was discussed again in the Cabinet. Gladstone, whose Christian intuitions like Gordon's very often accorded with practical considerations, had become a strong convert to the idea of using Zobeir, but he was ill in bed, and the other Commons members of the Cabinet were unanimous in feeling that no government could sanction the appointment because they would be defeated in the House of Commons. Hartington was sent down to tell Gladstone, and on his return reported: 'He thinks it very likely that we cannot make the House swallow Zobeir, but he thinks he could.' Granville embalmed the idea in a long conciliatory letter to Baring, but before receiving this, on March 17, Baring had told Gordon by telegram that all hope of using Zobeir must now be finally abandoned. By this time, however, the telegraph line had been cut, and Gordon never received the telegram.

*

The process of evacuating the garrisons began by the despatch of some four hundred sick soldiers, with their women and children, by boat from Khartoum to Berber. They got through safely, but there were rumours that the whole country was in a state of revolt, and it seemed unsafe to send any more evacuees down the Nile. The Egyptian commander of a post half-way between Khartoum and Sennar sent in a message to the effect that the people thought Gordon's proclamations were not worth the paper they were written on. With the intention of testing local feeling, and also of distributing the proclamation more widely, Gordon decided to send out expeditions up the Blue and White Niles, the first on foot, the second by steamer. The first expedition was cancelled because an attack on Halfiyeh, a few miles north of Khartoum, was said to be imminent. The steamer expedition was carried out, with Stewart in command of it. There were several steamers at Khartoum, most of them strongly resembling the penny steamers that plied up and down the Thames, and it was two of these that went along the river.

Although Stewart's intentions were pacific, and he was equipped with a supply of white flags, the steamers each carried one gun and 110 Sudanese soldiers, who were protected from possible fire by a thick breastwork of biscuit sacks. They were received with cautious friendliness in the vicinity of Khartoum where, as Stewart sardonically noted, the natives appeared to fear both the Mahdi and the Government, but as they got farther from the town, hostility become apparent. At a village about forty miles up the river the villagers fled, and the local sheiks were hostile. Twenty miles farther on, a crowd estimated at fifteen hundred armed men were drawn up to oppose any attempt at landing. Some of the sheiks offered appointments as Mudirs by Stewart refused to accept them, obviously thinking that the honour was an empty one since the British planned to leave the country. No shots were fired on either side, but the general effect was far from reassuring, and on his return Stewart sent a bleak letter to Baring. When the natives saw that he had no force at his command and said they would be obliged to join the Mahdi, what could he reply? Stewart, like Power, disliked and despised the Egyptian ruling class. In his report on the Sudan written a year earlier he had suggested that it might be a good thing if the Mahdi or some other leader drove the Egyptians back into Egypt, and now he expressed himself in the same way to Baring, saying that the only people who would suffer when the Government forces withdrew were the rich Arabs and the Greeks, and that he had no sympathy for either group. As for the so-called towns, Sennar, Kassala, Berber, Dongola, what were they but collections of mud huts which if burnt one day could be rebuilt the next?

> No one will be more glad than I am when this miserable business is over and when we have seen the last of the Sudan. The country is only intended by nature for nomad tribes and a few settled Arabs along the banks of the Nile. It annoys me greatly to see blood and treasure wasted on it.[1]

During the uneasy days of early March, Gordon and Stewart were busy. Colonel de Coetlögon had done a good deal to put the town into a state of readiness to resist attack. It was protected on the north and west by the Blue and White Niles, but on the south and east sides there stretched an open plain running directly up to the fortifications. Coetlögon ordered a deep ditch to be dug in front of these fortifications. The bottom of this ditch and the side of the fortifications were paved with spearheads, and in front of these were broken bottles and caltrops, or as they were popularly called crows' feet, spiked iron balls that lodged firmly in the ground wherever they were placed. Biscuit

[1] Ibid.

boxes filled with powder, nails and bullets were put a couple of feet underground, with electric trip wires attached to them. The effect of these precautions was limited by the fact that there were only 2,000 men to man four miles of earthworks, and that many of the Arabs in the town sympathized with the Mahdi. Gordon inspected the fortifications, beginning at Fort Buri on the Blue Nile and going along the whole line to the White Nile, changing the dispositions of the men at various posts. Some of his moves were dramatic window-dressing, like the occasion when the troops were paraded outside the fortifications and then marched through the town to the central square, where Gordon stood to receive the salute. He made a careful examination of the stores, and recalled workmen to the arsenal, which was placed under the guard of a company of reliable Sudanese troops. Stewart began the armouring of the penny steamers with boiler plate, and their protection above the deck by the erection of a wooden bullet-proof turret which contained the gun. At the foot of this turret was the cooking place, where slave girls baked bread. A bucket-like arrangement was slung to the foremast for a look-out man and the boiler, which was partly above the deck, was protected by wooden logs.[1] The wooden barriers could not of course withstand shell fire, but they were excellent against the rifle fire to which they were generally exposed.

These measures gave great encouragement to the inhabitants. Power thought that 'there is not the least risk now', and that the effect of Gordon's presence was quite miraculous, but Gordon himself was not deceived. On March 12 an attack was made on Halfiyeh by the son of the Sheik El Obeid, and although steamers sent up there were able to effect the release of the garrison, the net was closing in. Rebel armies estimated variously to number between three and six thousand men arrived on the right bank of the Nile, opposite to the Palace, and maintained a frequent although not particularly effective rifle fire. They sent a message to Gordon saying that the Mahdi had ordered them to lay siege to Khartoum, but that his life would be spared if he surrendered. Gordon replied that he would recognize the Mahdi

[1] *Sudan Notes and Records*, 1936.

as Sultan of Kordofan, nothing more. 'As to my surrendering to you, that I shall certainly not do as long as your heads are on your necks. You shall be surrounded by brave troops, before whom you will not be able to stand.'

On March 16 the bravery of the troops was put to the test. Four companies of Bashi-Bazouks, under the command of two black Pashas, advanced upon the rebel columns in the direction of Halfiyeh. Whether through treachery or inefficiency the Pashas halted the advance, and killed two of their own men who disobeyed their orders by attempting to continue it. Gordon, watching through his telescope from the roof of the Palace, saw the Mahdi's horsemen gallop forward and his own troops flee in utter disorder. About two hundred of them were killed, and the transport camels carrying ammunition and water were captured. Power, who had always stressed the cowardice of the Egyptians and Bashi-Bazouks, said that it showed their utter uselessness. 'Today they had every advantage on their side, yet 60 horsemen without firearms signally defeated 2,000 men armed with the best European weapons' he wrote in *The Times*. The two Pashas were tried by court martial, found guilty of treachery and murder, and executed. The speed with which this was done was a measure of Gordon's resolution, his order that anybody found out of his house two hours after sunset would be shot and his property confiscated, convinced the people of his power. There was plenty of food, plenty of ammunition, but from this day onwards Khartoum was undoubtedly besieged.

CHAPTER FOUR

THE TRIUMPH OF GLADSTONE

OF all the people who wished to see Gordon sent to the Sudan, there was only one who anticipated the likely result, that Britain would be compelled to exert a decisive influence over Egyptian affairs. This was Wolseley, who had been for years undoubtedly the most famous living British soldier. His admirers compared him to Wellington and Marlborough, and certainly his victory at Tel-el-Kebir had been won with marvellous speed, and marked by intelligent planting of misleading information. He was a prominent Army reformer, and had made many enemies among the old guard of British officers. The nominal Commander-in-Chief, the Duke of Cambridge, had opposed but was unable to resist his appointment as Adjutant-General in 1881. Those who disliked Wolseley accused him of being arrogant, a destroyer of regimental tradition, and an Anglo-Irish snob.

All of the accusations were true. Arrogance was manifest in his sarcastic memoranda, disrespect for tradition in his merging of regiments under the localization scheme and in his frequent flouting of ceremonial, snobbery in the love of a lord and often-voiced respect for the aristocracy shown by this son of a Major who had sold out his commission because he was too poor to buy a promotion. These defects of character and feeling did not prevent Wolseley from being an excellent organizer and administrator, in days when these qualities were almost unknown in the Army. He was also the first intellectual to occupy a seat of power in the War Office. Since the Duke of Cambridge concerned himself chiefly with parades and ceremonial, the Adjutant-General's influence was very great, and he was necessarily much in contact with politicians of the governing party. For these politicians Wolseley felt no emotion but contempt, bearing in mind the day when Froude had taken him to see Carlyle, and the sage of Ecclefechan had said that there was one more way in which the modern Cromwell could serve his country—he could send the people in *that place* (there must have been a gesture towards the Houses of Parliament) about their business.[1] Wolseley never went beyond making rash sharp-tongued speeches about the military unpreparedness of the country and the way in which soldiers were hamstrung by politicians, but these were enough to make many politicians reciprocate his distrust and dislike.

So far as Wolseley could find tolerable any civilian authority at the War Office, he accepted Lord Hartington, who was the heir to a Dukedom and who consulted him at every turn, regularly sending him Baring's letters and memoranda. Dilke observed that Wolseley influenced Hartington, and Hartington brought pressure upon the flexible Granville. The final moves in sending Gordon came, as has been shown, largely through the activity of Wolseley, and while to the Liberal politicians who knew Gordon slightly or not at all it may have appeared that he was a popular tool to use for the work of evacuation, Wolseley must have known how likely it was that his friend would act by the light of his conscience in a way that would make military intervention inevitable. Within a month of Gordon's departure, while he was still on the way to Berber, there came news of another defeat for Egyptian arms. Valentine Baker had been sent from Cairo with a force of the gendarmerie he had under training, to relieve the garrisons of Sinkat and Tokar, both some fifty miles from the port of Suakin, which was the British and Egyptian base on the Red Sea. When attacked by a small group of Mahdiists under a local leader, Osman Digna, the Egyptians fled at once, and did not respond to Baker's attempts to rally them. More than two thousand were killed, and one result of this ignominious defeat was that British officers,

[1] Hove, letter from Froude.

from Wood to Wolseley, became convinced that Egyptians
were useless in battle. The immediate problem, however, was
that Osman Digna was left rampant in the Eastern Sudan.
Was the whole country to be left at his mercy while the British
naval force at Suakin stayed idle? On February 8 Wolseley sent
Hartington a wonderfully perceptive memorandum about the
new position created by Baker's defeat. He forecast that 'unless
"something" is now done, and done at once', Gordon would be
permanently shut up in Khartoum, the tribes all over the Sudan
would rise, and the Egyptian garrisons would be forced to surrender and be slaughtered, one by one. What was the 'something' that might stop this? He proposed that Gordon should
announce Britain's retention of the Sudan, which would
in future be ruled by Sudanese under British officers, and that
to give force to this statement of intention a British brigade
should be sent to Wady Halfa and reinforcements to Suakin.
The end of the memorandum was prophetic. Wolseley had
spoken of the force of public feeling:

> This feeling that something should be done, like a rolling snowball, will
> go on increasing until the Government will be forced to adopt measures
> to save the Khartoum garrison. A small, but determined and well carried
> out, effort on our part, if made now, would in all probability enable General
> Gordon to treat with wavering chiefs, and so to become master of the posi-
> tion at Khartoum, but if nothing is done that place will be besieged, and
> we shall be, in my humble opinion, faced with a war on a large scale.

Wolseley must have known that he was beating the air, and
that the Government would not be moved from its policy of
disengagement and disinvolvement. They were to be driven
eventually to acceptance of his logic, but during the next months
it was to be their invariable practice to do no more than seemed
essential to relieve immediate anxieties.

So it seemed to them now that the only point of urgency was
the need to deal with Osman Digna. For this purpose three
battalions of the British Army in Egypt were put under the
command of General Graham and sent down the Red Sea to
Suakin. At the end of February and in early March Graham
twice fought and defeated Osman Digna at El Teb and Tamai.

The Arabs' losses were estimated at some 4,000 men, those of the British at less than a tenth of that number. Osman Digna retreated, and the road from Suakin to Berber was reopened. But this success presented the Government with just that decision relating to the employment of force to support Gordon which they were unwilling to face. Graham asked whether he might be permitted to advance on Berber. Gordon accepted enthusiastically the idea of sending 'a small force up to Berber', and said that his steamers would come down from Khartoum to meet it. Baring also supported it. Against this, however, was the view of Stephenson and Wood that an advance on Berber involved great risks, because of the lack of water on the way.

Against it too—and this is what was decisive—was the deep suspicion now felt by some members of the Government about the whole Gordon enterprise. The original vagueness about the object of his mission, well put in that question of Childers', 'Who will be responsible for him, and to whom will he be responsible?' had now become apparent. After a Cabinet meeting on February 8, Gladstone consulted Gordon's memorandum, and noted with satisfaction: 'My belief that Gordon has a perfect freedom of action under our last telegrams is confirmed by a reference to his own memo, which does not quite correspond with some recollections of it expressed by the Cabinet yesterday.'[1] But what did 'perfect freedom of action' mean? Gordon had been sent out with what most of the Cabinet believed to be perfectly clear instructions about evacuating the Sudan. Now he was talking about smashing the Mahdi and asking for all kinds of troops, and in addition there was a suggestion that a considerable force should force its way to Berber to help him. Was this the effect of what they had been assured would be the magic of Gordon's name? Might not the whole thing be a plot devised by Wolseley? Might it not, even, be a good thing if Gordon were cut off and so unable to send these disturbing telegrams through Baring to London? Granville at least suggested as much to Gladstone.

The question of giving military help to Gordon, whether

[1] Gladstone Papers, 44147.

through Graham or in some other way, split the Cabinet. Granville, the most extreme opponent of any sort of expedition, wanted to recall Gordon immediately on the ground that he had ignored his instructions. Gladstone had supported the idea of sending Zobeir, but he too was altogether opposed to making any attempt to succour a man who had recently said he was as safe as in Kensington Park. Hartington of course favoured some sort of expedition, and so did the two Radicals, Dilke and Chamberlain. Lord Selborne said that he would resign if an expedition were not sent—in the autumn. Sir William Harcourt immediately countered by saying that he would resign if one *were* sent. But even for the advocates of an expedition, the idea that they would send out troops in the autumn made any immediate action seem very much less urgent. Nobody, not even Wolseley, was prepared to say during March that it was essential to save Gordon by sending British troops, nor did most of his own messages give support to such a view.

So Baring was told that there would be no advance on Berber, and that the Government were 'averse to further military operations being undertaken without any definite object'. When he suggested that the situation had changed, and that the problem now was how to get Gordon and Stewart away from Khartoum—and that it must be remembered that they would not willingly abandon the garrison and the Government officials —he received a sharp reply. Granville spelt out the message for him with inescapable plainness: 'The Government have no intention of sending British troops to Berber.' He was to tell that to Graham, and also to Gordon. As for getting away from Khartoum, the Government would 'leave full discretion to General Gordon to remain at Khartoum, if he thinks it necessary, or to retire by the southern or any other route which might be found available'.

When Baring received these instructions he says that he found it difficult to preserve 'diplomatic calm', and his reply shows a generous indignation at what he felt to be the callousness shown in London, and also a determination to make them understand the likely consequences of inaction. His telegram begins: 'I cannot say whether it will be possible for me to communicate your Lordship's message to Gordon, but in any case I cannot reconcile myself to making the attempt to forward such a message without again addressing your Lordship.' The telegram, he said, meant that Gordon and Stewart were virtually being abandoned. If nothing was to be done at once, then at least let Gordon be told that an expedition would be sent to relieve him in the autumn. He ended by saying: 'Having sent Gordon to Khartoum, it appears to me that it is our bounden duty, both as a matter of humanity and policy, not to abandon him.' Granville later described this telegram as 'a heavy cannon-ball', and it was certainly the heaviest Baring could fire short of resignation. A similar protest from the Queen was joined to it. Gladstone and Granville, however, were adamant. Gladstone pointed out to the Queen that what Baring proposed was a reversal of policy, that Wood and Stephenson both thought that a move by Graham on Berber involved 'extraordinary risks', and that there was no evidence of Gordon being in immediate danger. In accordance with this policy Graham's force was withdrawn, a small garrison being left at Suakin.

Baring sent on to Gordon the message from Granville, which he had hopefully held back, but it never reached him. He had, however, received a brief message sent early in March which broke the news that so far as Baring knew the Government did not mean to send troops to Berber. To this Gordon responded with a blistering reply, brought by messenger from Berber.

> I consider myself free to act according to circumstances. . . . I shall hold on here as long as I can, and if I can suppress the rebellion I shall do so. If I cannot, I shall retire to the Equator, and leave you indelible disgrace of abandoning the garrisons of Sennar, Kassala, Berber and Dongola.

This was accompanied by messages from Stewart and Power, saying that although Gordon had suggested that they should go to Berber they preferred to remain with him, and would retreat with him to the Equator. 'I shall follow the fortunes of General Gordon', Stewart said, and Power added: 'We are quite blocked on the north, east and west.' Baring passed on this telegram to the Government in the middle of April.

As communication between Khartoum and Cairo became more difficult, misunderstanding grew, partly because the break was never quite complete. For some weeks Baring did not realize that Gordon was not receiving his messages, and Gordon's own letters filtered through to Cairo only after considerable delay. As the months of March and April passed, what was actually happening in Khartoum corresponded less and less with the picture believed in London to be the truth. If Gordon did not answer the messages and questions sent from London, was it not plain that he was ignoring them because it suited him to do so? Granville, for one, was convinced of this. In the absence of direct news from Gordon, it was an additional irritation that some of Power's despatches to *The Times* got through, and were printed with the smug but accurate editorial comment that the Government appeared to be largely dependent upon their Khartoum correspondent for information. It was through Power that people in Britain learned of the 'serious reverse' suffered in that disastrous sortie, of the intermittent fighting and the successful engagements fought by the armoured steamers, and it was through Power that they read on April 1 (the despatch was dated March 23) of Gordon's plight and of his hope:

> We are daily expecting British troops. We cannot bring ourselves to believe that we are to be abandoned by the Government.

The emotion caused by these despatches was profound, for many people thought with Power that Gordon's desertion could not be contemplated, and that something should already have been done to help him. It was possible, however, to read these despatches with a different, a Governmental, eye. Since Power had raised the alarm as long ago as November, saying then that Khartoum could not hold out for more than a couple of months, was he not plainly an alarmist now? And did not his despatch of April 2 (printed on April 17) show that there was no immediate danger? 'The rebels, being gradually emboldened, are approaching the town on all sides. Khartoum for the present is safe, and pretty well provided.' Some members of the Government regarded Gordon as a conjurer who was refusing to do his trick out of malice, others felt that they had washed their hands of responsibility by the terms of the agreement under which he had been sent out. It was this attitude that was expressed by Gladstone when he returned to the House of Commons after his illness, in a speech on April 3 which shattered his Parliamentary opponents. Hartington, in a very long answer to a question, had taken refuge behind the fact that they were still ignorant of Gordon's intentions, and did not know what he would do now that his request for Zobeir had been refused. Sir Stafford Northcote, the leader of the Tories, then made a speech in which he quoted from Power, and said that the House was entitled to more information. Gladstone was withering. This was the seventeenth night, he said, upon which the House had been introduced to an Egyptian debate. Was such insistence on the Opposition's part beneficial to the country, and was Northcote saying that the gallant General had failed?

'Is that the way in which those who claim to themselves a monopoly of the terms "loyal", "constitutional" and "patriotic" justify their claims?' Such suggestions were irresponsible and mischievous. Gladstone's own view was very different. 'The charm of the Mahdi's success' had been broken, 'the counter attraction of General Gordon's great name' had prevented any dangerous combination from forming in Egypt. There was, undoubtedly, an unfortunate lacuna: they did not know what substitute Gordon might have found for Zobeir or what precisely he meant to do, but was that a reason for saying that he had failed? And, with a reference to the Franchise Bill which was still agitating Hartington he went on, 'We are sometimes told that, having regard to Egyptian affairs, the Franchise Bill ought not to go forward. Why, Sir, when the great Reform Bill of 1831-2 was carried through Parliament there were questions . . . ten times more formidable for the people of England than the questions now raised in Egypt and the Sudan.' He finished with a contemptuous reference to the Opposition attempt to use Power's views as 'an official declaration probably conveying the mature conviction of General Gordon', which he described as farcical. His personal irritation with the whole Gordon affair showed in his last phrases that 'the debates thus constantly renewed are out of all proportion to the pressure and urgency of the question, and have the effect of offering immense obstructions to important public business'. That, he hinted, was the real object of the Opposition.

This 'angry and almost infuriated harangue', as one member of the Opposition called it, seems today an exercise in evasion, but at the time its effect was overwhelming. Harcourt, who was far from uncritical of Gladstone, said afterwards: 'They thought that they could play tricks with the sick lion: but they were mistaken. He just put out his paw and there was an end of them. It was a wonderful scene. I have never seen the like of it in my political life.' The motion was withdrawn, and Gladstone was able to return for a few days to the problem of reconciling the diverse views of Chamberlain and Hartington upon his Franchise Bill. On April 21, when Parliament reassembled after the Easter recess, he replied to a number of questions less angrily, but with one of those very particular uses of words that dismayed his friends almost as much as they annoyed his opponents. Khartoum, he confessed, was undoubtedly hemmed in, 'that is to say, that there are bodies of hostile troops in the neighbourhood forming more or less of a chain around it'. But, he went on, 'I draw a distinction between that and the town being surrounded, which would bear technically a very different meaning.' He was surprised by the laughter on the Opposition benches, and by the way in which the phrase ('He is hemmed in, but he is not surrounded') became a bitter joke.

All Parliamentary triumphs are transitory. Less than a week after he had crushed the Unionists in the House, Gladstone was being worried by Hartington. Baring had received some thirty telegrams from Gordon, all of them considerably delayed in transit, and in one of them he had said that 3,000 Turkish infantry and 1,000 Turkish cavalry could crush the Mahdi in four months. 'We can scarcely say any longer that we know he does not want troops', Hartington wrote to Gladstone. 'I presume that he would prefer British to Turkish.'[1] He went on to

[1] Gladstone Papers, 44147.

say that Wolseley had prepared a sketch of an operation, and to suggest that perhaps the time had come when they should consult Stephenson and Wood. Gladstone was dismayed by Wolseley's sketch, for it suggested that two brigades of infantry and nearly a thousand cavalry and mounted infantry, some 6,500 men in all, should be sent to Shendi, and that these troops should be exclusively British. Granville had at last asked Baring to speak to Stephenson and Wood about a possible movement of troops already in Egypt as far as Wady Halfa, but this was a far more ambitious project.

Wolseley was a man who liked to know what was happening to the Army, even in regions where it was beyond his direct control. In February he had received a letter from General Dormer, Stephenson's Chief of Staff in Cairo, dealing with the delicate situation that existed between the Sirdar, Evelyn Wood, and the commander of the British troops, General Stephenson:

> Evelyn Wood has gained complete ascendancy over the other Evelyn on all military matters, and is his sole adviser. These two lay their heads together, and concert measures and arrange plans for sending Egyptian troops to Assuan or elsewhere, without any but a nominal reference to General Stephenson.[1]

Stephenson, Dormer said, was a man of immense tact, which was often sorely tried. Had not the time come for disbanding the Egyptian Army, or putting it under Stephenson's command? '(He) is far too modest to insist on his claims to be heard, though he has thoroughly mastered the whole of the details of the situation and has very clear ideas and views of what is to be done.'

This letter, together with the wretched performance of Baker's gendarmerie, strengthened Wolseley's feeling that only British troops would be of any use for serious fighting. In reply to protests made by Wood through Baring, he insisted that 'the only way in which Wood's army could be employed with safety would be in holding strong points on the lines of communication'.[2] In several biting memoranda he prodded forward

[1] Hove.
[2] War Office Records.

the uncomfortable Hartington, saying after Gladstone's speech that 'the Government should at once determine upon the line of action or inaction it means to pursue, and Gordon should be immediately informed of the determination arrived at'. And he proceeded to fill in details of the 'sketch'. The force could go to Suakin, and from thence across the desert to Berber. Sir Andrew Clarke, the Inspector-General of Fortifications, had said that a railway from Suakin to Berber could be begun on July 1 and should reach Berber on November 1. On this basis Wolseley gave Hartington on May 20 detailed arrangements for the supplies to be provided along the route, much of which was waterless desert. From Berber, the troops would go by river and 'we should therefore at latest reach Khartoum on December 15.'[1] This date, however, was based upon Clarke's calculations about the speed with which the railway could be laid, and Wolseley made it plain that he thought them optimistic, and that he strongly favoured sending the force the whole way up the Nile, from Cairo to Khartoum.

All this was deeply disturbing to Hartington. He circulated Wolseley's memoranda to the Cabinet, but dissented pettishly from their assumption that an expedition was to be sent, telling Granville that he did not know on what the Adjutant-General founded such an inference. 'I may have indicated my own opinion that this will have to be done, but I have not the slightest idea what the Government at present proposes to do.' This sort of refusal to accept responsibility was basically what divided the Cabinet. At meeting after meeting the question of Gordon and Egypt was discussed, without any decision being reached. Hartington and one or two others were in favour of an expedition being sent at once, and accepted the idea that once British rule was established in the Sudan it would have to be perpetuated. The Radicals, Chamberlain and Dilke, were in favour of an expedition, but not of subsequent occupation. Through April and May the bitter wrangling went on, and Northbrook thought the Cabinet would probably break up on

[1] War Office Records.

it, for nearly half its members were ranged against these strange Liberal Imperialist and Radical allies.

Nearly half: but this is misleading, for the true determination not to send an expedition began and ended with Gladstone. Had the Prime Minister admitted that troops might have to be sent, had he even been neutral, some of his followers would have wavered, but as the weeks passed the People's William felt more and more repugnance to the idea of sending British troops to Khartoum. He was able to point to details in almost every message received from Gordon which made it seem that his situation was far from desperate. It was true that he had asked for Turkish soldiers—and had gone on asking for them with tiresome iteration, saying that the Turks were Hobson's choice, that they would get both the Government and him out of their troubles, that the Sudan had better be given to the Sultan with a subsidy—but had he not said in the very same telegram that the revolt was a trumpery thing which 500 determined men could put down? The insistent jarring tone of newspaper comment, the nagging editorials in *The Times*, the bellicose messages from the Queen, the merely lukewarm support of half his own party and the trembling moral indignation of the Opposition, all made Gladstone more determined not to be caught in a confidence trick of which Wolseley was the engineer, Gordon the expositor, and Hartington the dupe. To defeat them he employed his immense Parliamentary skill, his flexibility in evading an issue while appearing to deal with it, and above all his prestige as the coagulant without whom the Liberal Party would dissolve into half a dozen quarrelling groups. In Cabinet meetings he used every chance of engaging in almost metaphysical discussions about the precise shade of meaning that might be attributed to any particular phrase. When, after long indecisive discussions in April, Hartington said that he thought they had decided 'practically to do nothing and make no preparations, and this I cannot acquiesce in', Gladstone was ready with many qualifications and hesitations to moderate such bluntness and to delay the necessity of action. He was in favour of making all kinds of enquiries, about the navigability of the Nile and what boats were

available to move up it, he thought that a telegram sent to
Stephenson should refer to Gordon's 'removal' and not to his
'relief', and also that it should 'ask whether any, and, if so, what
preparations (as distinguished from inquiries) should be made
immediately'. Early in May it became known that Sir Michael
Hicks-Beach had put down a motion of censure, and Gladstone
drafted the Government amendment to it again and again,
finding each time a new phrase to include or reject. It was said
in one draft that the Government would 'carefully (and promptly)
employ the best means of securing his (Gordon's) safety if need
should arise', but Gladstone must have thought this far too
definite, and it had been dropped by the time that the motion
was debated. On one of the drafts Gladstone noted: 'The whole
discussion is premature'[1] and in the debate he used another phrase
which was to become famous, when he declared that an expedition must involve 'a war of conquest against a people struggling,
and rightly struggling, to be free'. His critics pointed out that
Gladstone's feelings had been less tender when the Arabi revolt
was suppressed, and W. E. Forster, a Liberal who had become
thoroughly disillusioned by Gladstonian subtleties, said that the
Prime Minister could persuade most people of most things, and
could persuade himself of almost anything. The Government
majority dropped to twenty-eight on a division, and it was
thought that they might actually have been defeated but for a
winding-up speech by Hartington in which, although visibly
battling with his conscience, he supported his chief.

Hartington grumbled, he defended the Government clumsily
and with bad grace, but in practical terms he did acquiesce in
doing nothing, and nothing had been done when news came
that Berber had been stormed, and that a massacre of the
Egyptian soldiers and townspeople had followed. The fall of
Berber gave new impetus to the demand for an expedition to be
organized, and lent fresh passion to the arguments about which
route it should take.

[1] Gladstone Papers, 44768.

CHAPTER FIVE

THE BATTLE OF THE ROUTES

THERE were two routes by which an expeditionary force might reach Khartoum. It could use as a base the Red Sea port of Suakin and then cross the desert to Berber, a distance of some 245 miles. Or it could go by railway and river up the Nile to Wady Halfa, and then continue in boats to Khartoum. The distance from Cairo to Wady Halfa was 760 miles, and from Wady Halfa to Berber was a further 666 miles. There were other possibilities, like that of using the Red Sea port of Massowa as a base, but it was behind Suakin-Berber and the Nile route that the partisans lined up. The arguments about the route began in April and continued until, and even after, a decision was reached in August. The fact that expert opinion was so completely divided gave Gladstone another reason for postponing any definite action, by suggesting that more people should be consulted.

The opening shots were fired by Wolseley in the long memoranda of April 8 and 14 already mentioned. He expressed himself decisively against Suakin-Berber primarily on the ground that the distance between the wells were so great 'that not more than 300 Cavalry or 400 Infantry could move along it daily between the several places where drinkable water is at present obtainable ... the last 100 miles before reaching the Nile at Berber, is across a desert where water is to be found, one may say, only at the half-way station of O-Bak.' More wells could be sunk, but this would be difficult because of the hostility of the tribes, who had been only temporarily subdued by the defeats inflicted on them by Graham. If the road were safe the force could be pushed over

65

it in small detachments, but as things were the men would have to fight their way right across the first 150 miles from Suakin to Ariab. Between these points they would sink wells and establish fortified posts, but they would still have to make a dash across the desert for nearly a hundred miles, and Wolseley assured the Cabinet that 'British infantry could only get safely across that desert in the month of October if carried on camels'. As he totted up the number of troops needed, Wolseley made it come to nearly 11,000. Losses would be heavy, because of the violent heat and lack of water. They would not be able to manage with less than 4,000 camels, and losses in camels would be heavy too. Altogether it was an extremely dangerous and difficult operation, and 'nothing short of an absolute necessity should cause us to undertake it'.

About the Nile route he wrote in very different terms, and if his description of the perils of Suakin-Berber sent a shudder up the Cabinet's collective spine, they may have detected in relation to the Nile route a light of passionate feeling in Wolseley's single eye. (He had lost the other eye in the Crimea.) Fourteen years earlier Lieutenant-Colonel Wolseley had been the leader of a small expedition that went 600 miles in boats up the Red River in Canada, guided through the rapids by the expert local boatmen known as voyageurs. They had carried provisions for three months, and had supported themselves through desert regions destitute of supplies. The Red River exploit had first won fame for Wolseley, and he proposed now to repeat it upon an immensely larger scale. It would be an exercise in logistics of a kind that had never been attempted before, an operation worthy of Gordon and, more important still it may be thought, worthy of Wolseley. When Hartington questioned whether the Nile Cataracts were not formidable, and asked also if there might not be some point between Wady Halfa and Berber where progress in boats became impossible, Wolseley reassured him:

> To those who do not know what was done by the men of the Red River Expedition the possibility of reaching Berber in boats may well be doubted. Sir Redvers Buller took part as a Captain commanding a com-

pany in that expedition; tell him to study this question and state his opinion.

The cataracts? Without having seen them, Wolseley still felt able to say that they were only what would be called rapids in Canada, although 'without doubt very serious and very difficult rapids'. On the Red River Expedition they had ascended and descended not only rapids but waterfalls, one a few feet higher than Niagara, and they had not lost a man drowned. If there were places where the boats could not be taken up the cataracts they would be portaged (carried round) 'as we portaged our boats dozens of times in 1870'. Further than this, there would be camels with the force who would take the stores round any rapid, while the boats and small steamers were hauled over on rollers. And for this route, of course, a significantly smaller force would be needed, since Wood's Egyptian troops could be used on the line of communications.

Wolseley's prestige was immense, but his preference was expressed with such force that in some minds it raised doubts. Was it really true that a land march of 250 miles presented such frightful difficulties and dangers compared with a rail and river expedition that was nearly six times as long? Were the Cataracts as easily negotiable as he said? The Government decided to consult Stephenson and Wood, saying with some understatement that 'information here as to Nile navigation is imperfect'. During May a considerable body of opinion from men on, or at least reasonably near, the spot became available, almost all of it opposed to the Nile route. Stephenson responded briskly in a telegram: 'Propose Suakin route. Wood prefers Korosko desert. Nile throughout route impracticable.' A memorandum followed, embodying his objections. Up to Wady Halfa the Nile was navigable at any season of the year. So far, so good. Beyond it, however, and particularly for the 180 miles between the Second Cataract at Wady Halfa and the Third at Hannek, it was 'according to the best accounts, practically unnavigable at any period'. Stephenson therefore assumed that the 860 miles between Wady Halfa and Khartoum would have to be undertaken by marching, and said that there would be insufficient food for camels and horses, it would be difficult to dispose of the sick, it would take at least four months to reach Khartoum, and altogether 'I consider this route quite unsuited for the purpose intended'. What of Suakin-Berber? When in March it had been suggested that Graham might push a few hundred men across the desert, Stephenson had opposed it as too risky because of the lack of water. Now he had changed his mind. He thought that the problems of getting from Ariab to Berber were not insuperable, and that Khartoum could be reached in nine weeks. Wood's suggested Korosko route also involved a desert march, and was never considered seriously.

A paper was prepared by the Intelligence Department, which considered no less than seven routes. The Nile route was dismissed as impracticable because of its great length, the lack of sufficient native and other boats, and the problems presented by the Cataracts, and Suakin-Berber was favoured. The Assistant Quartermaster General, when forwarding the report, dissented from its conclusions, and said, 'The Nile route is, in my opinion, the best one as a main line of advance for a large force.' Other advice was not lacking, like that of Sir Samuel Baker, who favoured columns advancing along three routes, Suakin-Berber, Korosko-Berber and up the Nile, and offered suggestions about carrying water on camels in galvanized-iron barrels and placing 2,000-gallon tanks at various points in the desert. Other travellers gave their unsolicited views. Wolseley wrote to General Sheridan to ask whether he had encountered any similar difficulties during the American Civil War. The General replied: 'I can only say that in the United States there are no such desert conditions as those to which your letter refers', and added that they rarely had to consider the question of carrying water supplies for more than two or three days.[1] Sir Andrew Clarke, the Inspector-General of Fortifications, prepared a paper about the construction of a railway across the desert from Suakin to Berber. He estimated the cost at £1½ million, and although he had never seen the area thought that the platelaying could be carried on at the rate of two miles a day, 'thus requiring a total of 130 days'.

[1] Hove.

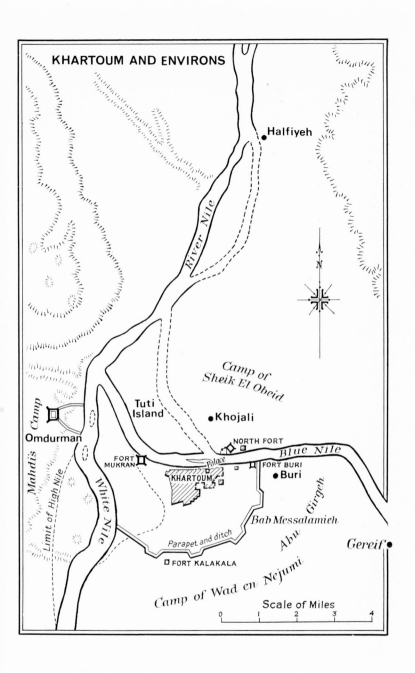

KHARTOUM AND ENVIRONS

Halfiyeh

River Nile

N

Camp of
Sheik El Obeid

Tuti
Island

Khojali

NORTH FORT

Mahdis Camp

Omdurman

Blue Nile

FORT
MUKRAN

Palace

FORT BURI

Buri

KHARTOUM

Girgeh

Limit of High Nile

Bab Messalamieh

Abu

White Nile

Parapet and ditch

Gereif

FORT KALAKALA

Camp of Wad en Nejumi

Scale of Miles

0   1   2   3   4

Clarke admitted that 'a railway cannot compete with other modes of advancing in point of speed alone', but pointed out that when it had been completed all the subsequent problems of supply disappeared. The idea of the railway was greeted enthusiastically by the military authorities at Suakin, and although Wolseley later called it a mad idea that had sprung from the brain of a man who was a politician rather than a soldier, it was accepted by the Government. A sceptical and sulky Wolseley prepared plans for the railway to be begun by July 1, and it seemed that the last had been heard of the Nile route.

The railway was never begun. Hartington's slowness, Granville's weakness, Gladstone's procrastination, combined to make any speedy action impossible. Thus, Clarke's memorandum was dated May 19, but it was not until nearly four weeks later, on June 14, that Stephenson was told of the decision to 'take some preliminary steps to facilitate the construction of a railway', and asked to send a company of Engineers to Suakin. But the railway, which would have been immensely useful when Graham's troops were controlling the area round Suakin, was no longer a practicable proposition. The fall of Berber on May 26 was confirmed in London some three weeks later, and by the time Hartington sent his telegram to Stephenson the whole country round about was in the hands of the Mahdi's men. In a long memorandum on July 19 the wounded Wolseley set out the lack of progress made through (it was implied) the decision to choose the wrong route. When Suakin-Berber was settled on, he had at once withdrawn his own plan. But what was the position now? 'It is quite certain that all possibility of completing a railway between Suakin and Berber, in time to carry a force to the latter place for an advance upon Khartoum is out of the question.' He went on to maintain that the route itself, 'with or without the construction of a railroad', was now quite hopeless. 'If Berber be held in any force by the enemy, how are we to get a column of troops of sufficient strength across that 100 miles of almost waterless desert to enable us to sweep away all resistance we should encounter when debouching from that desert?' He savagely pointed out that 'no preparations whatever' had been

F

made for carrying out his Nile plan, and that the operation was now much more difficult.

Wolseley's object was to bury Suakin-Berber finally, and to force the Government's hand, but acceptance of his own plan was checked by yet another report. In March Vice-Admiral Sir John Hay, in command of the naval contingent at Suakin, had had a report prepared on the Nile from Cairo to Wady Halfa, the part of the river navigable throughout the year. Several officers had examined parts of the Nile, and had reported on the numbers of steamers and other boats available, their character, and the nature of likely obstacles. This report, completed by the end of April, was succeeded by another, prepared under the Vice-Admiral's instructions by Commander Hammill. Sections of this second report filtered through from May onwards until mid-July, and they were not encouraging to the Nile route. After a detailed analysis of all the Cataracts, Hammill concluded that the area between the Second and Third Cataracts was supremely difficult for navigation, and that 'it would be next to impossible to get steamers and cargo boats of any size down the principal rapids, and the effort to do so would probably cost more than they would be worth at the end of the journey'. And as for their return down the river, 'that I do not think would ever be likely to be attempted'. The Admiralty obligingly prepared a précis of the difficulties involved as described by Hammill, the Intelligence Department of the War Office, John Mason Cook of Thomas Cook and Sons, who had been called into consultation because Cook's had been granted by the Khedive exclusive control of all passenger steamers on the Nile, and others. The précis summarized also the remarks of various travellers, from Sir Samuel Baker in the eighteen sixties onwards, on the times at which the Nile was navigable for steamers and other boats. The various authorities differed about the exact period of high Nile, but they agreed that between Wady Halfa and Hannek, where the greatest difficulties would be encountered, high Nile came in June or July, and that after about three weeks the river began to fall and was totally unnavigable.[1] Finally (as they must have thought) the Admiralty embalmed the whole project in a report made in July which said that the difficulties of passing the Cataracts were so great that it would not be possible to rely on water transport as the sole means of taking a force up the Nile. Portaging boats of any kind round the Second Cataract was flatly declared by Hammill to be impracticable, and getting boats of any size up the principal rapids would be next to impossible. As a kind of consolation prize this report added that Hammill thought it possible 'for a small force to proceed *by land* to Dongola'. Hay added that in any case it was now too late in the year for an expedition, because of the falling Nile. The infuriated Wolseley noted on Hay's letter: 'This is very amusing—an Admiral who knows as little about war on land as I do of war on sea, lectures me on a boat expedition up a river—he has had no experience of such expeditions, but *I have*.'[2]

In reply he contented himself by saying that he and Hay were looking at the operation from different points of view. Hay was talking about large steamers and the native craft called dahabeahs; he himself was talking about rowing-boats like those used in the Red River Expedition. The Admiralty replied sharply that it would take two months to build the 400 boats mentioned in Wolseley's letter, and another month to get them to Alexandria. To get them from Alexandria to Wady Halfa would, they reckoned, take another 2½ months, so that nearly six months would pass before they were ready to start up the Nile from Wady Halfa. It was implied, although not actually stated, that this could be of no possible help to Gordon, and the Admiralty pointed out too that the boats would need a skilled coxswain and bowman, as well as native pilots. Where were the

[1] In fact they were all wrong. The Nile at high Wady Halfa was at its lowest in May and June, after which it rose steadily. A height of 15 metres 17 centimetres was recorded on 6 August 1884, which had risen to over 16 metres by 27 August. It first fell below 16 metres on 11 September, but at the end of September was still nearly 15½ metres. (War Office Records.)

[2] War Office Records.

men to come from? 'The most serious question for the consideration of the Admiralty is, if all these steamers, Nile boats, row-boats and steam launches are engaged, from whence are their crews to come? To man 24 Nile steamers, 1,000 Nile boats, 400 row-boats, and, say, 20 steam-launches, would require a very large number of men, probably from 5,000 to 6,000', and perhaps a third of these would have to be seamen. The Admiralty washed their hands of attempting to do more than passing up the Second Cataract and distributing in the reaches above it 'as many steamers and boats as can be got up whilst the Cataracts are passable'. The responsibility after that rested on Wolseley.

There was no prospect that he relished more. His suggestion about obtaining a report from officers involved in the Red River Expedition had at last been acted on. None of the three officers reporting, Major-Generals Sir Redvers Buller and Sir John McNeill, and Colonel William Butler, had any personal knowledge of the Nile, but after reading all the papers they expressed the opinion (to nobody's surprise) that the operation was perfectly practicable, that the boats could be built more quickly than the Admiralty suggested, and that they 'did not contemplate the employment of any sailor of the Royal Navy', but would rely on native pilots.

There was something unreal about these passionate arguments in relation to an expedition which remained unsanctioned by the Government. Now at the end of July, with the War Office and the Admiralty wholly at odds, the deadlock between them was broken by the pressure exerted on the Government by news from Khartoum. On July 31 Hartington once more offered to resign, and this time it was not in relation to the Franchise question nor to Ireland, but to Gordon and Khartoum. The offer took on almost the tone of an ultimatum.

CHAPTER SIX

KHARTOUM AND LONDON: MAY TO JULY

1. Gordon in Khartoum

THE Mahdi was not impressed by the letter which appointed him Sultan of Kordofan. He regarded Gordon as a cunning unbeliever who was making promises which he had no intention of keeping, in order to gain time. 'He could not understand how it was Gordon came to offer him what he already possessed some time ago; and he remarked that the very ground on which Gordon was standing was practically in his hands.'[1] In reply he sent messengers with two letters, one long and one short. The long letter was a general expression of goodwill, an assertion that the writer was really the promised Mahdi, a man without pride, a lover of poverty and the poor, a humble servant of God. It called on Gordon to deliver himself up and become a follower of the true religion, and said 'Our pity for you has induced us to write you this letter.' The short letter came with articles of dervish clothing, a dirty patched coat, a turban, cap, girdle and beads. 'If you truly desire to come to God and seek to live a godly life, you must at once wear this suit and come out to accept your everlasting good fortune.' Gordon threw the bundle containing the coat across the room, and refused to have any further communication with the Mahdi. He had persistently underestimated the Mahdi's influence and intelligence, but this insult at least forced him to realize that no accommodation with the enemy could be expected. Khartoum was already under attack when Gordon received this letter on March 22, and a fortnight later the Mahdi himself moved out of

[1] Ohrwalder, p. 111.

73

El Obeid. His progress towards Khartoum was leisurely, and he stopped at Rahad where his forces tried to subdue the Nubas, the black mountain-dwelling tribes of Kordofan. He delegated to a former Nile pilot named Abu Girgeh the task of taking Khartoum, and on April 15 the Mahdi's lieutenant appeared before the town with a force that included four companies of Egyptian and Sudanese soldiers, armed with rifles. He also brought two guns, a rocket battery, and plenty of ammunition. With his arrival the siege began in earnest.

Gordon excelled in this kind of situation. His nature was autocratic, his mind ingenious, and he enjoyed fighting against odds. No combination of qualities could better have fitted him to defend Khartoum successfully. He had telegraph stations placed at all outlying posts, communicating with a central point, and the defences were strengthened by placing more wire entanglements outside the lines, and by putting beyond them mines made of old water tins filled with dynamite, in a chain extending from the Blue to the White Nile. The fort at Omdurman was also strengthened by mines and wire entanglements, and mines were put at the village of Khojali and on Tuti Island. These percussion mines were much feared by the Arabs, and the defenders were convinced of their effectiveness when an engineer officer, after putting down a mine containing 78 lb. of powder, trod on it and was blown to pieces with six of his men. A new and stronger fort was built on the eastern edge of the defences at Buri, and since this was thought to be a weak point, a chain was stretched across between the fort and the Nile, with a number of mined boats attached to it. The houses of the several thousands who had fled to the Mahdi were destroyed, and the wood they contained chopped up for the steamers. The ammunition was removed from the magazines, where it might easily have been blown up, and stored in the stone Roman Catholic church. Four armed steamers patrolled the Blue and White Niles beside the town at night. Dummy wooden figures were made, and placed on the east bank of the Blue Nile as targets for the enemy.[1]

[1] *Sudan Notes and Records*, 1930.

Many of these purely military preparations were in the hands of Stewart. Gordon himself was even more concerned with administering the town, and creating in it a miniature state. The money given him had unfortunately been left at Berber, and the Treasury was empty. Gordon borrowed from some of the merchants, and also established a paper currency, lithographing bonds for sums from 5 to 2,000 piastres, sealed and signed by him. The greatest single proof of his personal power is that the people accepted and used this currency, and that the troops willingly took their arrears of pay in Gordon paper notes. Cloth was bought, and trousers, tunics and greatcoats were specially made for the soldiers. No system of food rationing was put into force, but some prices were fixed, including that of bread. Power noted at the end of April that food was very dear. Frequent searches were made for food hoarders, and when found they were severely punished. Upon the whole the people, whose number was variously estimated between 40,000 and 60,000, were satisfied with this rule: or, if satisfied is the wrong word, they endured it without much complaint because of their faith in Gordon. Notices were published frequently to the effect that large English armies were at Dongola and Kassala, and these helped to maintain morale. When these notices proved to be diminishing assets Gordon drew pictures of different soldiers on tissue paper, and said that they had been sent to him by post. Decorations, cast in a special mould, and inscribed 'The Siege of Khartoum 1884' provided a further stimulus. They were made in silver gilt for officers above the rank of Major, in silver for Majors, and in tin for Captains, Lieutenants and other ranks. Civilians could buy a decoration for ten pounds, paper money. Music was also provided to lift low spirits. A band played in the square on Fridays and Sundays after sunset, and battalion bugles performed a variety of pieces, always ending with the Khedivial salute.[1]

During April and May the town was invested, but there was no sense of urgency in the Arabs. Abu Girgeh had forts constructed along the Blue Nile, which protected his men from the

[1] *Sudan Notes and Records*, 1930.

attacks of the patrolling steamers, and the forts were armed with guns and rockets. These occasionally shelled the town, and the defences were exposed to continual rifle fire. Attacks were made on Khojali, where a number of Mahdiists were killed by the mines. Gordon on his side ordered several daring raids, in one of which a thousand cattle were captured and brought back into the town. The steamers maintained control for several miles down the river, and his Krupp 20-pounder was thought to be causing havoc among the Arabs. Early in May three of the steamers raided another fort constructed by the dervishes on the White Nile, capturing the gun that manned the fort and a quantity of arms.

No serious attempt was made to take Khartoum, but the other Government garrisons in the Sudan fell one by one before the Mahdi. At El Fasher the Austrian governor Slatin Pasha saved his life by becoming a Muslim, the province of Bahr el Gazal surrendered at the end of April, and before the end of May came the fall of Berber. All this bad news became known gradually to the defenders of Khartoum, as rumours which were denied and then confirmed, and which were blended with many other rumours, including a persistent one that a British relief force really was on its way. Before the end of June the Nile began to rise, and the spirits of those besieged rose with it. Gordon was surprised and annoyed that the dervishes continued to attack him during Ramadan, and after some sporadic engagements in early July he launched an attack on their positions opposite Fort Buri, by land and river. The attack, spearheaded by the steamers *Bordein*, *Telehawieh*, *Mansurah* and *Abbas*, was a complete success. One of the dervish forts was destroyed, their losses were reckoned at 800 killed, and a quantity of arms and food was captured. Abu Girgeh retired to Gereif, and asked the Mahdi to send reinforcements. A little flotilla of five steamers and four armoured barges sailed up and bombarded Gereif for eight hours, disabling the cannon of the two forts there. These attacks greatly eased the position, and at the end of July the town seemed no nearer to falling by assault than it had been in April. Yet on a longer view there was little room for optimism. Power, in the last despatch from him received by *The Times*, written on the last day of July but not received by them until late September, summed up the situation:

> Since March 17 no day has passed without firing, yet our losses in all at the very outside are not 700 killed. We have had a good many wounded, but as a rule the wounds are slight. Since the siege General Gordon has caused biscuit and corn to be distributed to the poor, and up to this time there has been no case of any one seriously wanting food. Everything has gone up about 3000 per cent in price, and meat is, when you can get it, 8s or 9s an ober. . . . When our provisions, which we have at a stretch for two months, are eaten we must fall, nor is there any chance, with the soldiers we have, and the great crowd of women, children, etc. of our being able to cut our way through the Arabs. We have not steamers for all, and it is only from the steamers we can meet the rebels.

Power commented once more on the failure of the Egyptians as soldiers, and said 'The Negroes are the only men we can depend on', but this last despatch was resigned rather than bitter. The last words in it were: 'I am quite well and happy.'

2. The View from London and Cairo

After the telegraph line between Berber and Khartoum had been cut, messages could be sent from Cairo only as far as Berber, and had to travel the 200 miles on to Khartoum in the hands of Arabs, who might be captured by Mahdiists. On April 25 Cuzzi, Gordon's agent at Berber, said that the situation was desperate, and that it was impossible to send on letters or telegrams to Khartoum. Perhaps he did not greatly trouble himself to find messengers, perhaps they were caught, but in any case only one of the many messages sent from Cairo between the end of March and the end of July got through. Gordon was more successful in sending his own messages through the Mahdi's lines, and it was natural for the authorities in Cairo, and still more for the Government, to think that since Gordon's messages eventually reached them, their telegrams must also be reaching him. The misunderstanding, already referred to, ceased after the fall of Berber, because by then it was obvious that ordinary communication had become impossible.

Before the end of April Baring was called to London, primarily to advise the Government in connection with a conference on the finances of Egypt. He did not return until September, and for that time his place was taken by Edwin Egerton, who although a diplomatic official of considerable experience had only been in Cairo for a few weeks. The change was important, for where Baring often expressed himself in terms decided enough to convey his own interpretation of events, Egerton was for the most part little more than a post office between London and Khartoum. In this capacity he sent on telegrams, from which Granville and Hartington had to discern for themselves the real situation. Two sent early in April said that Khartoum had plenty of provisions, and added that the Mahdi evidently distrusted the rebels surrounding Khartoum and would send them no help. On April 10 there arrived in Cairo a telegram from Gordon to Zobeir, sent in ignorance of his final rejection, appointing him sub-Governor-General of the Sudan, and asking him to come out to Berber. This was blocked by keeping a watch on Zobeir to prevent his escape. A day or two after sending this telegram Gordon received the one already referred to, in which Baring had told him that there was no intention of sending troops to Berber. His reaction was to send a telegram to Sir Samuel Baker, making one of those suggestions which made even some of his friends wonder if he was entirely sane. Since no British troops were to be sent, he asked whether 'an appeal to the millionaires of America and England for the raising of £200,000 would be of any avail', and suggested that the Sultan might agree 'on certain terms' to send up troops who would 'settle our affairs here, and also do for the Mahdi'. Gordon revived this suggestion in different forms, perhaps without ever intending it to be taken quite seriously, but it produced a bad impression in London.

During May Granville peppered Egerton with telegrams which were to be sent on to Gordon, telling him that no Turkish or other forces would be supplied for offensive purposes (May 1), and asking him to report upon 'or, if feasible, to adopt', measures for his own removal and that of the Egyptians at Khartoum who had served him faithfully, by any route he wished, making 'free use of money rewards or promises at his discretion' (May 17). The original plans for evacuating the Sudan had been dropped, Granville said, and repeated that 'aggressive measures cannot be undertaken'. There is a note of desperation about this telegram, which is reinforced by Granville's further suggestions. Would it not be possible, he asked Egerton, to make sure by 'a liberal supply of money' that a message reached Gordon? Could not Zobeir or some other influential Arab arrange it? Zobeir offered to find a man who would go to Khartoum for £50 down and another £400 if he brought back a reply within fifty days. Granville immediately agreed, and said that the money would be doubled if he came back within thirty days. On June 2 he was impatiently asking from what date the messenger's departure was to be reckoned and was told, from May 21. Thirty, forty, fifty days passed, but there was no word out of Khartoum from Gordon or Stewart, and no despatch received by *The Times* from Power, after those printed in April which had caused the Government so much trouble.

There was plenty of other news of a cheerless kind, which Egerton passed on without comment, including the fall of Berber and the surrender of Slatin Pasha at El Fasher. Osman Digna had lifted over 1,000 sheep belonging to the Suakin townspeople, and by the end of June more than 5,000 Mahdiists were reported outside Suakin. It must have been apparent to Egerton that the revolt was spreading, but he made no attempt to impress this upon Granville, perhaps feeling that the news spoke for itself more strongly than any possible comment. Was there no light in the darkness? According to the Mudir of Dongola a new Mahdi had arisen who claimed to be able to fly through the air on his bed. He had many adherents, and had said that the so-called Mahdi Mohammed Ahmed was only one of his dervishes. There was a report also from Suakin that pilgrims who had left Khartoum on May 23 had said everything was well there, food plentiful and the garrison strong. For such chips of comfort Granville was no doubt grateful.

3. Military Activity

At the end of March it had been decided to send two British officers on a kind of scouting mission among the tribes near Dongola and Berber. The choice for this assignment fell on a Major of Engineers named Horatio Herbert Kitchener, who had recently composed two reports on the state of the roads in a region of Upper Egypt which had much impressed Granville, and had also pleased Wolseley. Kitchener had attracted less favourable notice six years earlier, when Wolseley was Governor of Cyprus. He had tried then to make an elaborate survey of the island when only a rough one was called for, and showed open mortification and surprise when told that Wolseley was Governor, and meant to have his orders obeyed. Since then Kitchener had advanced from Lieutenant to Major, but he was anxious to remove any lingering cloud of Wolseleyan displeasure, and seized this chance of doing so.

Early in April, taking as assistant Major Rundle, he left Cairo for Assuan and Berber. It proved impossible to reach Berber, but during two months at Assuan, Kitchener organized a group of 1,500 irregular soldiers. ('I have got 1,000 Bedouins under my command and expect 1,000 more, all mounted on dromedaries', he wrote early in May.) At Assuan he obtained a good deal of information about the likely loyalty of the tribes, and then in June moved to Korosko. He was asked to negotiate with the chief of the Kababish to see if he could be bribed to advance on Khartoum and relieve Gordon. The amount of the bribe was to be £10,000, or 'if it were considered absolutely desirable, double that sum'. The project failed, and on a further instruction he crossed the desert, wearing Arab dress and accompanied by twenty tribesmen, to talk to the Mudir of Dongola. His first opinion of the influential Mudir, who was coquetting with an offer by the Mahdi to make him an Emir, was favourable. 'He assures me forcibly of his loyalty to the Government, and implores that soldiers may be sent', he wrote to Evelyn Wood, to whom he reported daily. He soon changed his mind, however, and decided that the Mudir was not to be trusted. In August he disguised himself as an Arab, and personally reconnoitred some of the routes leading to Khartoum.

Kitchener spoke Arabic well, and the information he sent back was useful. He also sounded a note of assurance which was very welcome in Cairo, not only to Egerton, but also to the military commanders. There was considerable confusion about the exact responsibilities and areas of authority belonging to Stephenson and Wood if any serious military activity was ordered. Hartington summed up the situation in a note to Granville when he said that there were boats patrolling the Nile under the orders of an Admiral, Kitchener's Bedouins 'wandering about somewhere in the desert', Egyptian troops at Assuan and Wady Halfa under the orders of Wood, and the British troops under Stephenson. Should not Stephenson have complete control, and should he not see the reports of Wood's officers on frontier questions? In June this was done. Stephenson was confirmed as supreme commander in Egypt, and Wood was told to his chagrin that 'no orders should be sent by Sir E. Wood or any of his officers south of Cairo except those relating to the interior economy or general administration of the native troops, without the authority of the general officer commanding Her Majesty's troops in Egypt.' Dormer's letter had had its effect. The order no doubt made for military efficiency, but it did nothing to soothe the feelings of the British officers in the Egyptian Army, who felt themselves very shabbily treated.

In June also certain troop movements were carried out. As the revolt spread, Stephenson became alarmed about the safety of Egypt itself, and in June the 1st Battalion of the Royal Sussex were sent to Assuan, and another battalion were stationed at Keneh, farther down the Nile. Stephenson asked for a battalion to be sent out from Britain, and added that he would probably want 'one battalion more', because by pushing British troops up the Nile he was denuding the garrisons of Cairo and Alexandria. This request was denied by Hartington on Wolseley's advice. They already had two battalions up the Nile, Wolseley said, and 'if you send a third, you will certainly be asked to send a fourth, a fifth and so on, until a large British force will be employed upon what one may almost term police duties'.[1] Further representations by Stephenson, who said that there were considerable desertions from the Egyptian Army near the frontier, induced Hartington to send a battalion from Malta to Egypt. Nothing more than this had been done—and the force on the Nile could do no more than fight a holding action if they were attacked—when on July 20 the Mudir of Dongola received a scrap of paper from Gordon. The message was dated June 22. It said that Khartoum was still holding out, and asked 'the place where the expedition from Cairo is, and the numbers coming'.

This was the first message from Gordon for three months, and those words asking 'where the expedition from Cairo is' precipitated the end of Gladstone's resistance.

4. Hartington's Ultimatum

For a day or two it seemed that the plea in Gordon's message would have no effect. The immediate result was an ungenerous and unimaginative telegram sent by Granville to Egerton, asking that the messages already given should be repeated, and affirming in general terms an interest in Gordon's safety. It seems likely that Hartington was not consulted before this telegram was sent. He must have disapproved of its sharp and patronizing tone, and probably it played a part in helping him to decide that he could not continue as a member of the Government.

Hartington's frequent perturbations of conscience have been noticed, and there were many more of them than have been mentioned here, but it cannot be said that they seemed to be gathering strength with the passage of time. In early July he was complaining, as he had complained in May and June, that he was continually put off, that he got only five minutes at the end of each Cabinet for discussion of Egypt, and that he could not be responsible for military policy under such conditions. Then suddenly these subterranean grumbles turned into something like a roar. Gladstone must have felt as if he had been bitten by

[1] War Office Records.

a sheep. Prodded on by two long memoranda from Wolseley, one of which ended, 'At any rate, I don't wish to share the responsibility of leaving Charlie Gordon to his fate', Hartington circulated his own memorandum to the Cabinet. By now Wolseley, furious with frustration, was prepared to promise almost anything to obtain firm approval for an expedition, and he suggested that they might perhaps need to send only 'a small, cheap expedition' as far as Dongola, where the moral effect of their presence was presumably to make the Mahdi's adherents melt away. Hartington rehearsed Wolseley's arguments in favour of the Nile route, proposed that a brigade should be sent out as soon as possible from England to Dongola (not to Khartoum), and said that the War Office estimate for this operation was £300,000. (This did not include the cost of the rowing-boats, nor of transport to Egypt.) The memorandum made some impression on his colleagues, for Dilke noted that at the Cabinet of July 25 there was for the first time a large majority in favour of 'sending some sort of British force to or towards Dongola', a phrasing which correctly reflects the vagueness felt by the majority about the object of the expedition. The voting was 9 to 3 in favour of an expedition, but Gladstone was one of the three and, as Dilke puts it, 'by the stoutness of their resistance the three for the moment prevailed over the nine'.[1]

But not for long. Gladstone wrote one more of his judicious delaying minutes, and this proved too much for Hartington. He wrote to Granville: 'From what he has written . . . I infer that his mind is made up and that nothing is to be done. This is a conclusion which I do not think it is possible for me to accept. . . . It is a question of personal honour and good faith, and I don't see how I can yield upon it.' He was supported by the Lord Chancellor, Lord Selborne, and their resignations were in the balance. Selborne's could have been survived, but Hartington had a symbolic importance which had little connection with his ability, and his resignation would have brought down the Government. Gladstone's refusal to send help to Gordon had by now become an obsession, and he was not moved by the

[1] Gwynne & Tuckwell, *Dilke* ii, p. 60.

evidence of increasing danger for Khartoum, any more than by
the hissing and booing he received in public, or by the white
feathers stuck on cards which were widely circulated and called
'the Gladstone primrose'. He was sustained, like Gordon, by a
total certainty of his own rightness that could not be affected
by mere logic. He saw that he must yield, but he gave as little
ground as possible, reproachfully commenting on the fact that
Hartington had presented his ultimatum at a time when the
Government had two crises on their hands (the Franchise Bill
and the international Conference on Egyptian finance, which
had occupied a great deal of Cabinet time). He continued with
typical obscurity:

> It is a difficult but paramount duty for each one of us to ask himself
> what he can contribute towards meeting the present emergency. Un-
> doubtedly I can be no party to the proposed despatch, as a first step, of a
> brigade to Dongola.

Was this a downright refusal, then? By no means, for

> There are, however, preparations, perhaps, of various kinds which
> might be made, and which are matters simply of cost, and do not include
> necessary consequences in point of policy. To these I have never offered
> an insuperable objection.

These grudging words meant that he was prepared to move
in Parliament, as he did during the following week, for a credit
not exceeding £300,000 to 'undertake operations for the relief
of General Gordon, should they become necessary'. During
August he fought a rearguard action every step of the way,
saying that a movement to Dongola by Stephenson's troops
was a step of great political importance which must be referred
to the Cabinet, questioning whether in any case Gordon would
come to Dongola, suggesting that the Mudir might take over
Khartoum, 'so putting an end to this most perplexing and dis-
tressing affair', implying that Hartington was imposing a cruel
burden on a sick old man. Hartington commented bitterly that
continual consultation with Gladstone was 'a pleasant way of
doing business when every hour may be important', but for the
most part he played the Gladstonian game of let's pretend,

stressing that the force being sent out to Egypt was not an expedition. (What was it then?) 'I wish to explain very distinctly that I do not propose to send Wolseley to *command an expedition*', he wrote on August 22.[1] Yet all this was a game, because both Gladstone and Hartington knew that the absurdly inadequate credit would be ignored, and that the troops sent out would not stop at Dongola. On the day that Gladstone had moved the vote of credit, preparations for the relief of Khartoum began on a scale that made the figure he had named seem trivial. Four days later the Confidential Mobilization Committee was meeting at the War Office, attended by representatives of several departments, under the Presidency of Wolseley.

[1] Gladstone Papers, 44147.

G

PART TWO

MOVING UP THE NILE

CHAPTER ONE

PREPARATIONS

1. The Question of Command

STEPHENSON was the obvious overall commander for an expedition, but his appointment would certainly be a further blow to Evelyn Wood and to the other British officers in the Egyptian Army, who already felt themselves ignored and slighted. At a conference in Hartington's room the Duke of Cambridge asked that the officers already in Egypt, both in the British and Egyptian armies, should receive particular consideration, and suggested that command of the troops actually advancing to Dongola should be given to General Earle, who had been in command of the Alexandria garrison for the past two years. The Duke hoped to check Wolseley's custom of appointing to important posts the officers who had accompanied him in the Ashanti War of 1873, and who because of the favour subsequently shown them were known as 'the Wolseley Ring'. Wolseley reacted strongly, asking Hartington to disregard 'the sentiments of personal vanity and ambition of the few superior officers in Egypt to whose feelings H.R.H. referred so frequently yesterday'. The expedition would be a serious trial to all concerned. 'It will be no ordinary parade, and if its execution is committed to ordinary parade officers, please don't turn round by and bye on me if it comes to grief.'[1] And what folly it was to think of appointing Earle!

To select for the command of this contemplated expedition General Earle, of whose capacity for command we know literally and absolutely

[1] War Office Records.

nothing, and whose name is totally unknown to the Army and will not therefore impress our rank and file with confidence, whilst you could give that command to General Buller, whose name is known to every bugler in the Army, who has proved his capacity as a leader in war. . . . This is a policy that is incomprehensible to me. How many of our worst disasters are traceable to the adoption of such a policy.[1]

Buller had a great reputation, gained largely in Africa, as a dashing and fearless cavalry leader, and he had commanded a brigade with conspicuous success in Graham's recent excursion to Suakin. He had been with Wolseley on the Red River expedition and in Ashanti, and was one of the most prominent members of the Wolseley Ring. 'A stern-tempered, ruthless, saturnine man, with the gift of grim silence not less than a gift of curt, forcible expression on occasion', one war correspondent called him.[2] He was notable also for his extremely red face ('as red as a Red Indian', Wolseley said), his fierce manner, his liking for food and drink. The unfortunate Hartington was bound to disoblige either the Adjutant-General upon whom he so greatly relied, or the Royal Commander-in-Chief. The Duke liked and admired Buller, but he was very much junior to Earle, and it was one of the Duke's chief complaints against Wolseley that he was always trying to promote junior officers over the heads of those with more service. Hartington's compromise solution was to appoint Earle as commander of any force that had to go south of Wady Halfa, with Buller as his chief of staff.

But the overall command itself was then called in question. The battle of the routes was not resolved by agreement. The Government preferred Wolseley's assurance of success to the Admiralty's certainty of failure, and once the vote of credit had been passed never afterwards questioned that the Nile route was the right one. With acceptance of the Nile went of necessity acceptance of the small rowing-boats to pass up the Cataracts, but Stephenson was firmly convinced that these would be of no use. When on August 9 Hartington asked whether he wanted the boats 'proceeded with and sent to Egypt', he flatly replied:

[1] Ibid.
[2] Forbes, *Memoirs of War and Peace.*

'Small boats proposed not suitable', adding that he could obtain water transport locally, and emphasizing the importance of getting as many boats as possible past the Second Cataract by mid-September because of the falling Nile. A week later the point of complete disagreement had been reached. Hartington's telegram of August 19 has an ominous sound:

> It is desirable to avoid any misunderstanding. Her Majesty's Government wish to be in a position to send a force this season to Dongola, and if necessary to Khartoum. The force to be so equipped, that it shall be able to return from Khartoum this winter. . . . In the circumstances we are organizing an expedition in small boats, propelled by their crews beyond Wady Halfa. You disagree, but what do you propose?

Stephenson did not delay his reply. He said that it was impossible to send an expedition to Khartoum and get the troops back during the winter, and expressed once more his preference for the Suakin-Berber route.

The disagreement was decisive. It was obviously impossible to employ a commander who had no faith in the success of the expedition, and Hartington's mind turned inevitably to Wolseley. The plan itself was Wolseley's, he was accepted by everybody as 'our only General', and so was the obvious candidate. Opposition could, however, be expected from the Radicals in the Cabinet as well as from the Duke, who thought with good reason that Wolseley was always managing to circumvent his authority, and from the Queen who disliked Wolseley's vanity and felt that it was a bad principle to place so much reliance upon one man. In the event Hartington got his way with less trouble than seemed likely, although the Queen expressed herself as 'decidedly opposed to the practice of sending out the Adjutant-General to a distant command'. The Duke also complained. Wolseley wrote to a friend that 'H.R.H. rushed back from Scotland in a devil of a rage, and so hot has been his head and his anger that I am sure he will have a bad attack of the gout.' If only the Duke could be locked up for a year or more, he thought, it would be of the greatest benefit to the public service. Granville thought that Gladstone would never consent to Wolseley's appointment because it would be an acceptance of the fatal word, *expedition*, but the Grand Old Man was soothed by the explanation that the object of his appointment was to smooth out the 'cross purposes here and in Egypt as to the plan of operations on which our preparations are based'. He replied on August 22 by telegram: 'I think I understand now and I agree.'[1] Soothing letters were written to Stephenson by Hartington and by Wolseley, who said that he might have felt as Stephenson did but for his experiences on the Red River. Wolseley had served under Stephenson long ago, and there were rumours of a resignation, but they did not come from the commander in Egypt, who accepted a decision that cannot have been unexpected.

There was a good deal of ironic comment in the press. *Vanity Fair* printed a comic opera, in which Wolseley's success was seen as assured, and reference was made to his liking for honours:

> Then, when the Prince of Men
> Travels back home again,
> He'll be made Duke of Khartoum, we know.

In the opera Wolseley advanced with the aid of a Giraffe Corps and a Tiger Brigade, only to find that Gordon had freed himself and had a plan for sending out Gladstone to take a turn in Khartoum. Wolseley then upbraided Gordon for not waiting be rescued:

> Think, Gordon! Had you only waited
> What pictures in the Illustrated!
> What rapture from my Fleet Street friends!

For Wolseley it was the fulfilment of a dream. In youth he had often wondered whether he would be content to die unnoticed if by doing so he could benefit England, and had persuaded himself that he would, but as he grew older he longed for some achievement that would finally establish him as a great captain, a campaign that would be not only successful, but unique. In July, during one of his frequent periods of gloomy introspection, he wrote to his wife:

---

[1] Gladstone Papers, 44147.

Now I am getting old. I have struggled hard, make hundreds of mistakes, many of which I fall into from never having had a father or someone in a father's position to take council with. I was always too self-contained, and never felt inclined to consult others, this has been a great drawback to me during my career. If I had a youth to instruct who was imbued with my notions, with the thoughts and ambitions which haunted me as a boy and as a young man, I am sure I could mould him into a great man.[1]

Surely the Nile expedition—when had an army been sent such a distance by river before?—was the great opportunity of his lifetime? This intellectual soldier, who was so deeply conscious that slackening concentration accompanied the advance of age, became obsessed with re-creating on a bigger scale the trivial Red River Expedition undertaken when he was at the peak of his powers. To employ the same boats, and even the same boatmen, became for him a consideration of vital importance.

Wolseley always chose his subordinates with care. Buller was already Chief of Staff, and two of his most devoted adherents were appointed to posts of considerable importance. Colonel Henry Brackenbury, who was given the position of Deputy Assistant Adjutant and Quartermaster General at Cairo, was the most effective army organizer of his time, although the fact was not fully realized until the South African War, fifteen years later. Brackenbury, yellow faced and morose, had been under a cloud ever since he had resigned from a post in Ireland two years earlier. He was no soldier in the ordinary sense of the word, and it is typical of him that when he complained to Wolseley that his military ambitions were thwarted he should have meant that 'Never once have I been asked to serve on a Committee or a Commission, or in any way whatever to help in the work of organization or administration of the Army.' Sir Herbert Stewart had met Wolseley in 1879 during the Zulu War when, disgusted by the poor prospect of promotion, he was considering retirement from the army. Wolseley made him his Military Secretary, advanced his career when the war was over, and after the campaign against Arabi said that Stewart was one of the best

[1] Wolseley Papers, R.U.S.I.

staff officers he had ever known. He was now chosen to accompany the expedition with the idea that he, rather than Earle, might be given command if it became necessary to make a dash across the desert. Stewart had the dash appropriate to a Hussar officer, but his range of interests was unusually wide for an active soldier of the period. They included engineering and architecture, and he had spent twelve terms as a student in the Inner Temple, feeling that a knowledge of law would further his ambitions. There is one more appointment that must be particularly mentioned, that of Sir Charles Wilson to take charge of the Intelligence Department. Wilson's wide knowledge of Egypt and sympathy with national aspirations qualified him particularly for dealing with the Sudanese, and Wolseley wrote to him that 'I know of only one man to fill (the) office'[1] of Intelligence Officer, and that Wilson was the man. He accepted the appointment with alacrity. It was to prove a disastrous one for him.

Some appointments that Wolseley had hoped to make were frustrated by the Duke. The most important of these was that of Colonel Burnaby of the Blues, who had offended the Prince of Wales by making unsuitable jokes at the expense of the Prince himself and his friends. There was much that failed to accord with military convention about Burnaby, his ascent in a balloon unauthorized by the authorities, his famous ride to Khiva which had prompted a peremptory telegram from the Duke of Cambridge ordering his return, his bohemian way of life. His great height and bulk distinguished him in any company. This most engaging of Victorian military adventurers had raised great enthusiasm by putting to a Birmingham audience the simple question: 'Is Mr. Gladstone's Government to live or Gordon to die?', and in the early summer he had volunteered, with Colonel Sterling of the Coldstream, to raise 2,000 volunteers, half each from the infantry and the cavalry, who would go out and save Gordon. They would obtain 3,000 camels from the Berber district, and make a forced march from Suakin to Khartoum, where they proposed to kidnap Gordon forcibly into safety. Buller is said to have commented sourly that the

[1] War Office Records.

man was not worth the camels, but the scheme met official disfavour, and must have confirmed the Duke's view that Burnaby
was a bad fellow. He implored Wolseley to take him on the
expedition, claiming that as he was 'the only officer who has
been to Khartoum by the Suakin and Berber route—returning
by the Korosko route',[1] he must surely be of use. Burnaby had
the kind of recklessness Wolseley admired, but the Duke placed
a veto on him. 'I expect that my *friends* have ignored your
application', Burnaby wrote darkly. He later asked for leave of
absence to take a trip to the Cape, and joined the expedition, on
which he was to meet his death.

There was a flood of applications. The Prince of Wales had
hoped to accompany the expedition but, no doubt to Wolseley's
unspoken relief, Queen Victoria refused to consider the idea.
'You know how gladly I would accompany you—as to see service with our troops has been the one ambition of my life', the
Prince wrote to Wolseley, adding that he had no idea of the size
of the force because 'I am always systematically kept in the dark
by the authorities as to what goes on.'[2] He went on to ask that
Wolseley should take Lord Charles Beresford as his Naval
A.D.C. and added: 'May I bring Stanley Clarke's name to your
notice? You are I know well aware of his capacities as an officer
—his only misfortune is that he has never seen active service.'
He did not mention that Clarke had been away from any kind
of military service for six years. They were both employed,
Beresford as A.D.C. and Clarke as commander of the Light
Camel Corps, an appointment which Wolseley was to regret.

After the appointment there was a week of bustle, which
included a visit from the explorer, H. M. Stanley, who pleased
Wolseley by saying that he had used river boats on the Congo
and thought them 'the most rapid, safest, cheapest and most
comfortable way of moving troops'. Then he left on September 1, in the company of Lord Northbrook, who was being sent
out to confer on Egypt's financial position. Wolseley was made
wretched by parting from his wife. He wrote to her in the train

[1] Hove.
[2] Ibid.

on the way to Dover, telling her that he was glad she had not come to see him off:

> I should have broken down altogether—as it was, I was not fit for the occasion when I reached the platform and had to say goodbye to so many so-called friends.

He grew fonder of her, he said, in middle age. 'I love you far more intensely now than I have ever done.'[1] He had made varying predictions about the date on which a force could reach Khartoum, based of course on the different starting dates proposed for an expedition. Now, with the date at last fixed, he wrote on September 13 to say: 'I ought to shake hands with Gordon near Khartoum about the 31st January next.'[2]

Among the many letters received by the Wolseleys after his appointment there is one which seems worth quoting, because it is so characteristic of its writer. Henry James had been a friend of the Wolseleys for several years. On September 3 he wrote to Lady Wolseley:

> I have indeed both to congratulate and to condole with you, but I have thought it better to wait until Lord Wolseley had left these shores and the tossed-up waters of your fate had begun to subside. Now (unless you spend all your time in reading his missives—though they will hardly as yet have begun to pour in) I suppose you are accessible to a word from an old friend who would like you to know that he appreciates both your glory and your gloom.[3]

James and the Wolseleys had been guests at a house party a couple of weeks earlier, and curiosity about the command had been insistent. He had admired Lady Wolseley's skill in fencing off questions, but

> Now that we are all in the secret, I can say that we all *did* suspect it, and can pretend that my discretion (even amid the co-operative familiarity of the gooseberry-picking) was almost as great as yours.

2. Men and Equipment

It has sometimes been said that the expedition was carried out

---

[1] Wolseley Letters, R.U.S.I.
[2] Ibid.
[3] Hove.

without any attempt having been made to discover the prevailing local conditions and possibilities. That is far from the truth. The exhaustive examination of the different routes has already been indicated (the Intelligence Department prepared a large-scale map of Suakin-Berber showing the size and positions of all the wells), but the War Office authorities had also at their disposal notes on various desert routes prepared by Kitchener, a nine-page report made by the Intelligence Department in January on possible lines of retreat for the garrisons, a detailed account of the caravan routes from Egypt and the Red Sea to Berber and Khartoum, a paper on the treatment and management of camels, and much other material.[1] All of this information was available to the Confidential Mobilization Committee which sat, first with Wolseley as President, and later under the Presidency of the Quartermaster General, Sir A. J. Herbert. Little of it, however, was directly relevant to the problems of moving up the Nile in boats to Dongola. (It is important to remember that the objective acknowledged by the Government was Dongola, and that only in case of necessity was a force to be sent on to Khartoum.) The problems peculiar to an expedition that placed so much reliance on row-boats were the weight of the stores to be carried in them, the use of the existing railways, and the organization of camel transport where boats could not be used.

Buller had prepared a memorandum in which he was insistent that supplies to be carried in the boats should be packed in cases not over 60 lbs. in weight, and not more than eight inches in height. Each boat was to take nearly 800 lbs. of corned meat and 200 lbs. of preserved fresh meat, 168 lbs. of bacon, 770 lbs. of navy biscuits and 240 lbs. of cabin biscuits, 200 lbs. of flour, 240 lbs. of sugar, together with quantities of cheese, pickles, tea, jam, marmalade, preserved vegetables, rice, oatmeal, lime juice, tobacco and soap. The list is not exhaustive, and the rations were calculated to last the crew of twelve for a hundred days. The total weight of the rations and stores for each boat was to be between 6,000 and 7,000 lbs. It was laid down that each boat

War Office Records.

would be complete in itself, and that the boats would be 'the unit of any expedition beyond Wady Halfa'.

There were three stretches of railway that would be used, one running from Cairo to Assiut, the second running nine miles round the First Cataract from Assuan to Philae, and the third beginning at Wady Halfa and running for thirty-three miles, past the Second Cataract, as far as Sarras. Very little was known by the Committee about the condition of the railway, and nothing had been done to make sure what burden could be borne by the track and the existing locomotives. On September 23, Sir Andrew Clarke had given a warning that 'serious blocks are inevitable as soon as the full strain of heavy transport is thrown upon them',[1] but by that time it was too late to do anything to remedy whatever weaknesses might exist. It would in any case have been difficult to improve them, because the Cairo-Assiut line was worked under the Egyptian railway administration, and the other two lines were controlled by the Sudan government. Wolseley had asked repeatedly for the Wady Halfa-Sarras narrow gauge railway to be extended for another sixty miles, but the engineers in Egypt had said that the ground was difficult and that too much cutting was involved for the work to be done quickly. By September, nothing at all had been done.

Orders were given that a transport corps of 1,200 camels should be collected, and this instruction was passed through to Wood. Of the several miscalculations made in planning the expedition this was the most serious and the least excusable, for more than 8,000 camels were eventually used, and even this number proved insufficient. The camel equipment also proved to be sadly inadequate, and here the main fault rested with the army in Egypt. On August 18 the Committee minuted that Stephenson was to be asked whether he could supply pack saddles and kavajahs. In reply, he asked for head collars, head and heel ropes and nosebags, but was reassuring about saddles, saying that 500 were being carefully made and would be completed in about a month. It was wrongly assumed, both in

[1] War Office Records.

Egypt and in London, that there would be no difficulty in obtaining more camels, and saddles for them, whenever they were needed.

All of the troops were British, but the force sent out came from Bombay, Gibraltar and Malta, as well as from England. The 1st Battalion of the Royal Irish Regiment and the 2nd Battalion of the East Surreys came from Bombay, the 1st Battalion of the Berkshires from Gibraltar, a battalion of the Yorkshire Regiment from Malta. From England came various infantry drafts, a telegraph section, engineers, commissariat and transport companies, troops of the ordnance corps and a naval contingent. The first soldiers reached Egypt in August, the last by the end of September. What clothing were they to wear? Khaki was generally worn by the Indian Army, and three years earlier the Duke of Connaught had said that it was the only thing for troops in action, but there was strong resistance throughout the army to this idea. When, early in 1884, Wolseley had staged a demonstration of khaki uniform before the Queen at Windsor, her opinion was expressed through Sir Henry Ponsonby:[1]

> The Queen thinks the karkee clothing hideous and hopes she may never see it in England—we sent the men off a little distance with a red Highlander—but their white belts would have attracted attention anywhere. And the Karkee shows out very vividly against a green background.[2]

The 1st Berkshires were already equipped with khaki serge and the 1st Yorkshires with red serge frocks and khaki drill, but at their meeting on August 18 the Committee decided that the troops going up the Nile were to wear their red and blue Mediterranean serge frocks. The Assistant-Director of Clothing noted: 'I propose to take no more steps to provide a reserve either of khaki drill such as was recommended by the General Officer Commanding in Egypt in his telegram of the 12th inst., or of khaki serge such as was recommended by the Adjutant-

[1] It should be understood that 'khaki' referred to any uniform made of drill or holland, and not to the mud-coloured clothing we now associate with the word. This particular khaki was brown and gold, with a white belt.
[2] Hove.

General . . . but to send out instead as a reserve 5,000 red and 2,000 blue serge frocks, and 10,000 pairs of blue serge trowsers.'[1] Nor were thin shirts sent, in spite of a recommendation in their favour from the Army Medical Department. Since 'blue union flannel shrinks a good deal and will not stand rough wear, it would be best, in view of the men having to wear their shirts for six months, to adhere to the pattern now in wear in Egypt, i.e., that of grey flannel'.[2]

There remained the question of transporting men and stores from Alexandria to the Second Cataract at Wady Halfa. The Admiralty, sloughing off as much responsibility as possible, suggested that the transport on the Lower Nile should be handled by Thomas Cook's, since they had so much experience of the river. John Mason Cook realized the strength of his position and, as he put it, 'the Government must either buy me out or give me the work'.[3] The remark should not be taken as an unfavourable reflection on Cook's patriotism. After Tel-el-Kebir the firm had taken the sick and wounded from Cairo to Alexandria with no charge except that involved in running the steamers, and they had transported Gordon to Korosko very efficiently earlier in the year. When Cook was called in during April to advise on the problems of taking boats up the Nile, he had quickly realized that 'no one could give the slightest information as to the difficulties we might expect to meet between the Second Cataract and Dongola or Hannek'. This was true in April, not so true after Hammill had made his report, although Cook noted that since he had gone up the river in April and May, whereas the expedition would move up it in October and November, much of what he said must be conjectural. Cook's own opinion was that the whalers would be useless and that the thing could not be done, but that was not his concern, for he was asked only to provide for the passage of about 6,000 men and between 6,000 and 8,000 tons of stores from Assiut to Wady Halfa, and to take 400 boats by rail from Alexandria to Assiut

[1] War Office Records.
[2] Ibid.
[3] 'Mr. John M. Cook's Visit to the Sudan.' (Cook Archives.)

and then on by steamers to Wady Halfa. The agreement with Cook was made by a civilian named Baughan, acting for the Director of Transport. The tender submitted on July 1, and accepted, was said afterwards by the War Office to 'show a very large profit to that firm'. Under this tender the price agreed was £21 for every passenger taken from Cairo to Wady Halfa, £16 per head for those taken from Cairo to Assuan, and £12 per head from Assuan to Wady Halfa.[1] This was the first and last time in British history that a commercial firm was given a contract to convey an army, and it led to a good deal of recrimination. At the time of placing the order, however, both sides were happy. Cook said that he would send up between 8,000 and 10,000 tons of coal to Assiut immediately, and that he would have no trouble in hiring local labour at half a crown a day. He received final instructions on September 2.

3. The Boats and the Voyageurs

'Who among us is without his anniversaries? What fly on the big wheel of life does not find himself brought round again to some particular spot on the Sun-circle, where, when leaves were green or trees were bare, he once felt the sunshine of success, and knew a day or an hour to be marked henceforth as a folded leaf in memory.'[2] For Lieutenant-Colonel William Butler, August 4 was such a day. On this day in 1870 a small birch-bark canoe from the Canadian North had met a larger one which had come a long way in the opposite direction. The large canoe held Colonel Wolseley, leading the Red River Expedition. In the smaller one were five Indians and an intrepid scout who had been sent on a special mission to find out the state of affairs in the Red River Settlement. The name of the scout? Captain William Butler. Now, on 4 August 1884, Colonel Butler received a telegram from Wolseley at the War Office which ran: 'I want to see you here to-morrow.'

Butler was one of the most eccentric and engaging of

---

[1] War Office Records.
[2] Butler, *The Campaign of the Cataracts*, p. 9.

Victorian soldiers. Irrepressibly loquacious and indiscreet, he was
an Irish patriot who combined keen enthusiasm for Home Rule
with a detestation of Jews that was outstanding in an army
where anti-Semitism among officers was a commonplace. His
later career was to be marked by an official report on the state of
the ordnance stores so intemperately phrased that it had to be
suppressed, and by an attempt to support the Boer cause when
he was acting High Commissioner in South Africa which led
to his resignation. Yet Butler was energetic, inventive and ingenious, and possessed, Wolseley said, the quality of imagination
that was 'so much above the other gifts required for excellence
in military leaders'. Wolseley's telegram was prompted by a
memorandum submitted by Butler headed 'Notes on the Advantages of the Use of Small Boats for the Ascent of the Nile.' His
notes were meant as a counterblast to the adverse Admiralty
reports, and although Butler handsomely admitted that 'I have
not seen the Nile above Cairo and its neighbourhood, and, so
far, I labour under a disadvantage in writing these rough notes',
he did not hesitate to controvert the views of Commander
Hammill. 'Water is water, and rock is rock, whether they lie in
America or in Africa', and he calculated the fall of the Nile,
came to the conclusion that it was far less than the fall of the
Winnipeg River at certain points, and triumphantly pointed out
that 'it was this last-named river up which the 60th Rifles
worked their way in September 1870, at the rate of sixteen miles
a day', lifting their boats out of the water and re-launching them
twenty-seven times in one short piece of river. With boats from
twenty-six to thirty-two feet long, of six to seven foot beam,
and with a draught of only eighteen to twenty-four inches, he
thought it would be possible to go up any river, using sails,
oars, poles and track-line.

Sanction for ordering these boats was not given until August
12, but nearly a week before this Butler and another Red River
comrade, Lieutenant-Colonel Alleyne, were asked to find suitable boats and get them made more quickly than in the Admiralty's specified two months. There were no designs or
specifications, and it was apparent after a day's investigations

conducted, as Butler says with characteristic floridity, in 'the highest office of Naval Administration in Whitehall, the humble building-yards of Lambeth Wharf, the city offices of Glasgow shipwright firms' and elsewhere, that no existing boats in the fleet, the dockyards or the merchant navy were of any use—and apparent also that by putting out contracts to a number of commercial firms, 400 boats could be built in four weeks if price was not the main factor. The boats had to be strong enough to withstand the Cataracts, light enough to be portaged, able to sail well, pull easily, and draw only twenty-two inches of water with a four-ton load. This last was the most vital point, and it seemed to Butler and Alleyne that there was nothing for it but to get together the exact load for a hundred days, biscuit, meat, groceries, arms and all, and test them out in boats. It does not seem to have occurred to them that dummy boxes of an appropriate weight would have done as well, and some delay occurred because biscuit is a navy issue, and the Navy victualling authorities refused to sanction so large an issue of biscuit without knowing its precise use.

On the hot summer afternoon of August 7, Butler and Alleyne, in company with some of the principal local boat-builders, wandered about the boat lofts of Portsmouth Dockyard, looking at ship's cutters, jolly-boats, life-boats and various clinker-built craft. They were walking through a shed full of old disused boats, when Butler spotted something that looked suitable. When taken down from the crossbeams it proved to be a whale gig, twenty-eight feet long, five and a half feet in beam, and about two feet deep. The food and equipment, which had now all arrived, was loaded up, twelve dockyard men took their places in the gig, and it was successfully floated out into the centre of the basin. After this elementary test, it was decided that these whalers, slightly modified in size, would be suitable. Each of the boat-builders present said that he could build ten in a month, and there ensued a flurry of drawing up specifications, sending out circulars and obtaining estimates from firms at some twenty ports all round the country. The work was done with extraordinary speed, both on the War Office's and the boat-builders' sides, and within four days estimates were in which made it clear that 400 boats could be ready in a month. On August 12 Butler was called to the office of a 'high Government official', who wrote upon a half-sheet of paper: 'You may proceed with the preparation of 400 boats.'

The decision, when publicly known, was greeted with comments that ranged from the ironic to the savage. The idea of sending boats from England for use in distant Egypt seemed ludicrous to many. It was said that they would arrive too late, and that even when they did arrive they would crack and warp so badly as to be unusable. The comment in the *Army and Navy Gazette* was typical:

> A more wicked waste of money was never perpetrated, a more silly quackery was never devised, by any public department than that of which Lord Hartington and the Duke of Cambridge, representing the War Office and the Horse Guards, have really and truly been guilty in ordering that monstrous armada of boats, that unfloatable flotilla for the Nile! Burn them for firewood! Send them to Jericho, to play on the Palestine canal of the future! Make matches of them—do anything with them! Put men in them, and try to send them up the Nile cataracts—never, we beg of you!

There was a body of expert opinion against use of the boats, and almost the only voice raised in their favour was Stanley's. Butler consoled himself with the test of the first whaler at Portsmouth. This boat, built in seven days, was loaded with all the boxes from two large service wagons, and under its total load was sailed, rowed and tracked very easily. As Butler stood looking down from the wharf, the romantic Irishman saw in his mind's eye a distant picture:

> It was of a great river flowing through a desert world, with buried temples and ruined tombs of forgotten kings standing at long intervals on sand-swept wastes. And, sailing there I saw this frail boat, and scores of others like it, with sails and oars flashing in sunlight, moving on through that immense land in the grandest effort our generation had seen—the saving of the noblest knight among us all.[1]

The reality was to be in several respects sadly different.

By the first week in September, 100 boats had been shipped

[1] *The Campaign of the Cataracts*, p. 33.

for Alexandria, together with the first of two stern-wheel steamers built by the Yarrow firm for use on the difficult part of the river above the Second Cataract. These stern-wheel steamers were built because Wolseley recalled seeing boats of this kind on the Mississippi when he had paid a visit to the United States during the Civil War, and wrote in April to General Beauregard asking for details of them. All 400 whalers were sent out from England by the middle of September. By this time the size of the project had swelled, and before the end of August another 400 boats had been ordered. The last of them left England on October 3. The building and shipping of the boats in so short a time was a notable feat of organization, but the chief architect did not stay to see the end of his work. In mid-September Butler left England, travelling via Trieste to avoid the quarantine cordons in France and Italy, and thence down the Dalmatian coast, where he took refuge in the forecastle from the aggressive North Germans, cosmopolitan Pashas scenting a sutlers' harvest in the Sudan, and 'Jews of all nations but a single type' who crowded the after-deck. In the forecastle he found sailors, a Franciscan friar, an old Albanian chief, 'immensely nicer and more interesting people, whose pecuniary resources only permitted them a second-class passage'. He arrived at Alexandria on September 24, to see light-coloured boats, looking very small and slight, held high in the crane slings as they were swung from the decks of the steamers to the trains that stood ready to receive them. He thirsted to be with them on the Nile.

*

It was not until August 20, eight days after the placing of the order for the boats, that the Colonial Secretary, Lord Derby, sent a telegram to Lord Lansdowne, Governor-General of Canada, saying in part:

> It is proposed to endeavour to engage 300 good voyageurs from Caughnawaga, Saint Regis, and Manitoba as steersmen in boats for Nile expedition—engagement for six months with passage to and from Egypt.[1]

[1] *The Nile Voyageurs*, P.R.O., W.O. 32/124.

The idea of using the voyageurs sprang, of course, from Wolseley, and it is difficult to see why the request was delayed until August 20. Butler suggests that it was because originally great stress had been placed on Indian boatmen, and that just as a century earlier Chatham had protested against the employment of Indians in the War of Independence, 'so now it was thought necessary to safeguard the Arab of the Sudan against the savage proclivities of the French-Canadian and half-breed voyageur'. Whatever the reason, the delay created problems, for within a week Wolseley was asking what number of boatmen would be ready to embark at Quebec about September 10, and demanding an immediate reply. In fact a party of 386 men was despatched on September 14, in less than a month from receipt of the original request, and this too represented a great deal of hard work and excellent organization. On August 27 an advertisement headed IMPORTANT TO BOATMEN, and asking for 'Good boatmen to accompany English Expedition up the Nile, to steer boats through the rapids and do all necessary portaging', appeared in the *Ottawa Free Press*[1] but a great deal more than mere advertising was involved.

Most of the work fell on Lansdowne's Military Secretary, Lord Melgund, and as he observed in a report made after the men had gone, the original request presented the particular difficulty that Wolseley was harking back to the past. The old voyageurs had in many districts become extinct with the spread of the railway, and it was decided that the best available substitutes were lumbermen who felled timber during the winter and in the spring ran logs and rafts down the rivers, working their way up again with provisions for their shanties. Melgund made a contract with an Ottawa lumber broker, who did a good deal of the actual recruiting work, and then travelled about the country himself, interviewing people in Caughnawaga and Saint Regis. The final roll shows that about half of the men came from Ottawa, and fifty-six Indians from the Iroquois community of Caughnawaga. About half of the Ottawa men were French-Canadians, and in addition thirty-nine villainous-looking but as it proved reliable French-

[1] *The Nile Voyageurs.*

Canadians came from the Three Rivers district. The request for men from Manitoba seemed at first impossible to fulfil, because it was so far from the despatch point of Ottawa. However, a telegram from Derby saying 'decidedly give preference to Iroquois and Winnipeg voyageurs' led Melgund to telegraph yet another old Red River hand in Manitoba, Lieutenant-Colonel Kennedy. The results were unfortunate. Wolseley had in mind Indians from the Winnipeg area, but although Kennedy engaged about thirty Indians, he also took on what Melgund called 'a certain number of men of a better class who have been employed in surveying but are accustomed to boat work'. These were young business and professional men, with eight lawyers among them, and they proved quite unable to cope with the problems of the Cataracts.

The status of the voyageurs and of their commanders was curious. They were the first group from the self-governing Colonies ever to assist Britain in an overseas war, but the contingent had no military status, and in fact it was thought unwise to stress the military character of the expedition in case they were scared off. The expedition was Canadian, but it was paid for wholly by the British Government. Major Denison, the commander of the voyageurs, held his rank in the militia, and was not a professional soldier. He was a Toronto alderman, had a law practice in the city, and was thirty-seven years old. Of the five other officers appointed, two were militia Captains with experience in river work, one was a priest and another a doctor. The last was Colonel Kennedy, whose determination to go to Egypt presented the difficulty that he was Denison's superior in rank. The problem was solved by Kennedy's embarkation as an unpaid foreman. In Egypt he dropped his militia rank and was appointed Paymaster, while Denison received the brevet of Lieutenant-Colonel. 'The Red River men naturally are rather past their prime, and have mostly settled into some profession', Melgund wrote to Lansdowne, but Denison and the doctor, Surgeon-Major Neilson, as well as Kennedy, had been associated with the Red River expedition.

The voyageurs travelled in the *Ocean King*, 'a staunch iron steamship', as a local newspaper called it, and it is surprising that only two of these rough semi-literate diamonds (on the engagement forms that still exist, nearly half of the men made their mark instead of signing) deserted on the voyage. One of the Manitoba Indians died. Otherwise the contingent was at its full strength, and in fact had picked up one recruit further, when the *Ocean King* reached Alexandria on October 7. They left by train for Cairo on the following day.

CHAPTER TWO

———

WOLSELEY IN CAIRO: SEPTEMBER

A NY long contact with politicians lowered Wolseley's
spirits, and his journey to Egypt with Northbrook was no
exception to this rule. They stayed a day at Vienna, he
told his wife, because Northbrook had never been there, wanted
to see the city, and 'did not see why he should knock himself up
by unremitting travel at the beginning of his mission'.[1] A few
days later he wrote from on board H.M.S. *Iris*, amplifying this
unfavourable impression:

> Northbrook is a very weak man, you must be with him to realise how
> weak and impulsive he is. . . . If his grandfather had not been a successful
> tradesman he would now most probably be a Brevet Major in a regiment
> at the Hague or keeping a second rate money changer's stall at Hamburg.[2]

Nevertheless, the two men were still on good terms when they
arrived at Cairo on the following day. Wolseley remained there,
quartered in the Kasr-el-Noussa Palace, for nearly three weeks.
The palace was surrounded by pretty gardens, and the weather
was fine. His day began every morning at 5.30, and was divided
between organizing the expedition, soothing the ruffled feelings
of local officers, and engaging in discussions with Baring and
Northbrook.

A war correspondent on the Nile once asked Wolseley why
he had never met a reverse. 'The reason is that I never fight
unless I know that I am certain to win', he replied.[3] This passion

[1] Wolseley Letters, R.U.S.I., 3.9.84.
[2] Ibid., 8.9.84.
[3] Villiers, *Peaceful Personalities and Warriors Bold*.

for certain victory can be seen in the new arrangements he now proposed, which he sent to the Duke of Cambridge while on board the *Iris*, and elaborated in a despatch to Hartington as soon as he reached Cairo. There were nearly 11,000 troops in or on their way to Egypt, including 13½ battalions of infantry—more than enough, it might be thought, for an expedition on which serious fighting was not expected. When, however, the battalions which must be left to garrison Alexandria and Cairo and the men needed to guard important points along the route had been deducted, he reckoned that only three battalions would be available to go on to Khartoum. He asked for two battalions of infantry from Malta, and—this was the crux of the matter—for a Camel Corps of some eleven hundred men to be formed by taking forty men each from the sixteen regiments of cavalry of the line at home, a hundred from the three regiments of Household Cavalry, and forty each from the seven battalions of Foot Guards and from the two battalions of the Rifle Brigade at home. Two officers would be selected from each regiment, and they would be joined by a hundred marines to form Heavy, Light and Guards Camel Regiments. These picked men would form a flying column which could make a dash across the desert if that should prove necessary. He ended with one of those warnings which so much disturbed Hartington. 'I should be wanting in my duty if I did not point out in the clearest terms that, unless the force in Egypt is augmented forthwith to the extent I have proposed, we shall not be able to relieve General Gordon this year if the force now surrounding him remains where it is.'

Gladstone had delayed the expedition for months and Wolseley was, it might be said, taking his revenge, for now that the affair was launched it was almost impossible to deny his request for more men. The strongest protests came not from the Government, but from the Duke of Cambridge. His shooting in Scotland had already been interrupted once by Wolseley's appointment to the command, which had brought him back to London, and now the Adjutant-General was stealing another march on him. The new suggestion gave the greatest offence to his sense of military propriety and regimental tradition, and if it

had been made while Wolseley was in England he might have
worked for its rejection. As it was he saw nothing for it but to
agree, while telling Wolseley that the men chosen were 'the
life's heart and blood' of the regiments from which they would
be taken, that the principle was unsound and destructive of
esprit de corps, and that the Commanding Officers would be
'disgusted at seeing their best men taken from them, and themselves being debarred from sharing in the honours and glories of
the service'. His letter to the Queen was even stronger, and he
was not placated by Wolseley's assurance that the Camel Corps
would be 'in reality, the very finest troops in the world', and
that where supply problems were acute 'the cheapest result and
best plan to adopt is to use selected corps like this Camel Corps'.
The Camel Corps embarked on September 26.

On the day after Wolseley's arrival a list of appointments was
published. Those of Buller, Wilson and Brackenbury have
already been mentioned, but elsewhere there was some re-
shuffling. Earle's appointment was changed to command of the
troops at Wady Halfa, and Stewart was given command farther
up the Nile at Dongola. If, therefore, a column struck across
the desert, Stewart instead of Earle would be its commander.
Stephenson, whose occupation had really gone, was fobbed off
with the command of the troops north of Assiut, and Evelyn
Wood was put in charge of the line of communications south of
Assiut. The list did not give much joy to the resident officers.
Colonel Ardagh, in Cairo, wrote of the bitter feeling between
the old garrison and the new arrivals, and Wolseley told his
wife that when Dormer gave him dinner, 'I wonder there was
no arsenic in it, for I am sure he hates me because I have not
included him in the list of those to go up the Nile.' After dinner
they went to a musical party in the next flat, where six or eight
grass widows entertained them, 'a larky lot—some of them, I
should say, bound to come to grief'.[1] Wolseley was surprised by
the looseness of manners and conversation in Cairo, and a week
later wrote that he thought 'society has now come to allowing

[1] Letters, 20.9.84.

men and women to discuss the most minute details of sexual
intercourse in the most open and unblushing manner'.[1]

He received a visit from Admiral Hay, who was much concerned to know whether Wolseley 'was Commander-in-Chief
or General Commanding-in-Chief', and told him with relish
that the first steamer to be passed through the Second Cataract
had stuck.[2]

Wolseley was determined not to have with him in any important post those officers who had expressed total opposition to
the Nile route, but before he left Cairo he tried to ease some of
their grievances. Ardagh, for instance, was appointed Commander of the Base, where he did much good work. The expan-
sion of the expedition made it possible to fit in almost everybody,
but also made it more likely that the organization would crack
at the seams. This was soon realized by Buller, who had reached
Cairo a week before Wolseley, after a voyage part of which had
been spent in trying without much success to master the Arabic
alphabet. He was alarmed by the increase in the expedition, and
depressed by the calculations he had made about stores. 'What
we want is to have supplies for 10,000 men for 100 days at
Dongola. Of course we also have to supply the 10,000 men from
other stores on their way up to Dongola. . . . We have only
supplies for 10,000 men for sixty days in the country: most of it
is, I am glad to say, at or about Halfa, but all the rest has to go
up. Now one day's supply for 10,000 men weighs about 17 tons,
so 120 days will weigh 2,040 tons. . . .'
Buller was not an easy man to get on with, and a quarrel soon
developed between him and Wood, which smouldered throughout the expedition, so that Wood was later to complain that
Buller had tried to interfere with his authority 'to the detriment
of the Public Service'. The cause of the quarrel illustrates a basic
problem. The whalers were to carry both men and stores, but
until they were in use it was a question which should have pre-
cedence. Wood insisted that until more supplies were sent up,
there was no point in having troops sent forward to eat the

[1] Ibid., 27.9.84.
[2] Wolseley Papers, R.U.S.I. Unpublished autobiography.

rations stored at Wady Halfa and Dongola. He was intent to pass up the local water transport above the Second Cataract before the Nile fell too low to make this possible. The transport consisted of nuggers, each of which could take 400 tons of supplies, and native boats which were named broad arrow boats, taking over 150 tons each. By getting work out of these boats during the short time before the Nile fell too much to make their use practicable Wood was able to pass up more supplies, but he delayed the progress of the troops. He also passed through the Second Cataract two Egyptian steamers, one of which—as Admiral Hay had told Wolseley—was wrecked.

Other immediate difficulties arose in relation to camels and railways. The original order for 1,200 camels had not taken into consideration the needs of a Camel Corps, and this order was raised to 4,000. It did not prove easy to buy these camels, although from the middle of September onwards agents were at work in Upper and Lower Egypt. The price began to rise and the quality of the animals offered to deteriorate. On September 18 Buller noted that out of 1,200 baggage camels needed only 200 had been bought, and out of 1,700 riding camels only 329. Wood reported from Wady Halfa that it would be difficult to buy more than 200 a month, and Kitchener from Debbeh that 'riding camels are scarce at present'. The full extent of the need for camels had not yet been realized, but by the end of September it was apparent that they would play a much bigger part in transporting men and supplies than had been expected. Some of the camels were required for a transport train, which would accompany the projected flying column. The Director of Transport, Colonel Furse, commented that this 'was so unexpected that no provision had been made for a large supply of saddlery'.[1] The idea that saddles would be easily obtainable proved quite unfounded. By the end of September only 500 baggage and 150 riding saddles had been supplied, and at this stage and thereafter all sorts of unsuitable saddles had to be used, from old gun saddles to those of the Egyptian Army pattern which enveloped the animals and rested on the bones of their

[1] War Office Records.

backs. Many of the saddles caused open wounds on the baggage camels, and these were neglected although a paper on the treatment and management of camels had been circulated by the Commissary-General. No special tools or repair materials had been sent, so that when the lashings and leather straps broke, repairs had to be improvised.

The railway position was equally unsatisfactory. When stores arrived at Assiut, as they were doing every day in large quantities, it proved impossible to unload them at once because of the lack of proper sidings and wharfage facilities. The rate of forwarding stores from Cairo had to be deliberately kept down. On the vital stretch of railway from Wady Halfa to Sarras the position was even worse. When a detachment of the Royal Engineers arrived at Wady Halfa they found the four engines in a broken-down condition, and early in October only one train a day was running. On October 8 'the returning engine had to be pushed by sixty men of the Staffordshire Regiment round a difficult curve'.[1] All the surplus railway plant had been sent back to Assuan, and it was thought more important to move stores up the river than to bring it back.

At the end of September, however, these seemed no more than minor inconveniences. The whalers, upon which so much depended, were arriving and being unshipped, and more than a dozen depots had been established at various points on the Nile, each with its hospital or rest camp, its postal and telegraph or heliograph station, and in most cases with its wood supply. Several of these were food depots, which in the words of the official history 'may be compared to a number of reservoirs, placed successively at decreasing levels and connected by overflow pipes', so that as one filled up the surplus was taken to the next. These depots were garrisoned by Egyptian troops and commanded by Anglo-Egyptian officers.

The question that loomed largest for Wolseley was that of discovering the urgency of Gordon's position. The long silence from Khartoum was over, and from mid-August onwards notes, letters and telegrams came almost in profusion, many of them

[1] War Office Records.

repetitions of a message given to several emissaries in the hope
that one might get through, some sent to Baring, some to the
Khedive, some to the Mudir of Dongola. All of the messages
took a long time to reach Cairo, many made it distressingly clear
that no news was reaching Gordon through Kitchener, and that
a variety of wild schemes were still chasing each other through
his mind. At the end of August, Kitchener at Dongola received
no fewer than five letters from Gordon sent on July 13, all saying
that they were well, and could hold out for four months. On
September 20 Wolseley told his wife that they were 'inundated
with curiously worded messages'. Most of them had been sent
to the Khedive, but the one addressed to the authorities in Cairo
must have made Baring's heart sink for it repeated, with varia-
tions, many of the old suggestions long since denied, and added
some new ones. Gordon made elaborate calculations of the
British Government's debt to the Egyptian soldiers in the Sudan,
and worked it out at £300,000. He told them that Stewart had
been sent with troops to take Berber, but that since it would be
difficult to hold the town he had been instructed that it should be
burned and that Stewart's expedition should return to Khartoum. Almost as an afterthought, he added: 'If the Sultan's
troops come, they should come by Dongola and by Kassala.
You should give them £300,000.' His telegrams to the Khedive
were to much the same effect. They asked also for decorations
to be given to Power and the Austrian Consul in Khartoum,
Hansall, and said that a reply should be sent in Arabic so that
the people could read it. 'The telegrams which come in English
cypher do not state what are their intentions, and only ask us for
information and waste time.' Several references in the telegrams
made it clear that he knew of no plans for relief from England.

Northbrook was dismayed by these telegrams. 'Northbrook
and Baring both hate Gordon, and never lose any opportunity
to denigrer his talents and his worth', Wolseley wrote. 'They
call him mad because he does not worship the party Gods whom
Gladstone and Co have set up.'[1] The point of most importance,
however, was the time limit implied in the messages to Kitch-

[1] Letters, 1.10.84.

ener. If Gordon could hold out no longer than four months, he could not possibly be reached in time. But in relation to this there was nothing practical to be done, and Kitchener was told to make fresh efforts to get messengers through to Khartoum and obtain up-to-date information.

The routine of life in Cairo was almost as exacting for Buller as for Wolseley. He detailed his day: 'Up at 5 a.m., and out riding at 6 a.m. to inspect a regiment, back by 7, work till 11, breakfast till 12, work till 5 p.m., then out for a ride on my camel, which I have got quite fond of. It is capital exercise and rather fun.' Lord Charles Beresford had bought a camel named Bimbashi and Buller, whose sense of humour was not subtle, 'used to laugh till he nearly fell out of his saddle', when Bimbashi ran away with Beresford, 'through and over foot-passengers, donkeys, carriages and dogs'. These innocent amusements ended when Beresford was ordered up to Wady Halfa to oversee the arrangements for water transport. He made the 330-mile journey up river to Assuan in a Cook's steamer which had, he said, the appearance of a boat and the manners of a kangaroo. If anybody touched the helm or walked from port to starboard the boat listed violently, shooting Beresford off the locker on which he was trying to sleep. The mosquitoes were a great source of irritation, and Beresford's only comfort was a pneumatic life-belt which he used as a pillow. A few days later Wolseley and his staff entrained for Assiut, and then had their first taste of the Nile.

UP THE NILE AND THROUGH THE GATE: OCTOBER

THE train journey to Assiut was intensely hot and uncomfortable, but thereafter Wolseley's party travelled in
comparative luxury. The Khedive had made available one
of his yachts, the *Ferooz*. Cook's supplied the food and linen, for
which they charged £1 a day, and Wolseley was housed in a
large, spacious cabin. There were thirteen passengers on board,
including four A.D.C.s, Buller, Brackenbury, and the artist of
the *Graphic*, Frederick Villiers. Wolseley's attitude to war correspondents was ambiguous. Years earlier he had described them
in his *Soldiers' Pocket-Book* as a race of drones, an encumbrance
to an army, who ate the rations of fighting men and did no work,
yet one of them noted acidly that he took considerable pains to
be spoken of by the profession he so much despised. On this
journey he talked with his habitual politeness to Villiers. The
little party looked at the preparations being made along the Nile,
and with particular interest at the lines of whalers, the first of
which had been loaded into barges and slowly towed up the
river. Otherwise there was little to do except try to keep off the
flies, play shilling whist in the evening, and contemplate the
Nile, the mud villages, the pigeons in the Coptic towers, the
fields of waving dhurra, the water-wheels, the date palms, the
whole memorial to a vanishing way of life.

Buller was at first impressed by the strange colour of the
water, but later became bored with the sameness of the scenery,
'the same large richly coloured muddy river, the same sand and
rock mountains on each side with the same very green strips of

vegetation between them'. He felt a sympathy for the Egyptians eking out a wretched existence beside the shore which reflected the paternal care he gave to the tenants on his own Devon estate:

> The more one sees of the system of cultivation in Egypt, the constant labour at the water-wheel and the canal banks, and the really small return made by the soil for the labour expended, one feels how wicked it is to have any land tax at all, and how much these poor devils could do were they not ground down with the tax.

They passed by Luxor and the temple of Karnac, but neither General thought highly of them, Buller feeling that he would rather see an English cathedral than all the ruins in Egypt, and Wolseley being disturbed by their pagan unlikeness to Gothic, 'which breathes of a spiritual religion, of a pure, refined faith in things not seen'.[1] Like Buller, he found that the sight of Egyptian temples gave strong retrospective appeal to York Minster and Lichfield Cathedral, 'and when I am told such or such a mono-lith was erected by Rameses the 3rd of the 18th dynasty, it is gibberish to me; it recalls nothing I take any interest in or care to investigate'. He tested himself by giving up smoking for a month. His eating and drinking habits were ascetic, unlike those of his subordinates. He wrote a long letter to Northbrook ex-horting him to stand by 'my hero Charlie Gordon', and cast a disillusioned eye upon one or two of his companions, in particular Brackenbury:

> Brack has not improved in beauty. I think he has become yellower and certainly much uglier than ever. He has already the broad expanded figure of middle age, and as he grows older his legs seem to become shorter.[2]

He read a life of Cicero and was reminded of Gladstone by the flexibility of the Roman who 'pandered to the whims of the mob to gain and retain power'. He also read a book about the Great Pyramids, by a man with the exotic name of Piazzi Smith.

At Assuan they reached the First Cataract, and Buller was cheered by the sight of it, remarking that in Canada it would not even be considered a rapid, and that if it was a fair specimen

---

[1] Letters, 1.10.84.
[2] Ibid.

of the other cataracts they would have little difficulty in getting up the river. But he knew that it was not a fair specimen, for Hammill's report had stressed that the difficulties arose at the Second Cataract, past Wady Halfa. At the head of the First Cataract the party transferred into two large dahabeahs, again provided by Cook's. When they reached Korosko Buller wrote home, with a characteristic mixture of modesty and self-satisfaction:

> This climate is delightful, my work is interesting, and Wolseley allows me as much responsibility as I choose to accept. I think that I have the situation that really about suits me best, one, that is, involving all the responsibilities of execution without those of invention and preliminary organisation. I never have credited myself with much ability on the inventive side: all mine, if I have any, is on the executive side, and possibly if I have a strong point it is resource.

They reached Wady Halfa without incident on October 5, to find awaiting them a telegram which said that the last of the 800 whalers had left England.

*

Difficulties had arisen in relation to the whalers before ever they attempted to ascend a cataract. They had been sent from England in nineteen ships, and as each ship arrived at Alexandria the whalers were taken over by Cook's agent there. Workmen repaired damage done during the sea voyage before putting the boats on to the Egyptian Railway into trucks which had been specially prepared to receive them by having sacks of coal placed along their sides, with a lining of chopped straw within these sacks and on the floor. They were also covered with matting as a protection from the sun. Unfortunately the gear for the boats, which had been carefully packed in England, became mixed up in Alexandria, partly because the work was not properly supervised and partly because Cook's maintained that their contract provided simply for the delivery of boats and said nothing about gear. The gear, which had been numbered for individual boats, was therefore separated from them and sent up independently. There was a great deal of gear—Wolseley had said when looking at the list presented to him by Butler, that the only thing missing was a service of plate for each boat. Each boat had twenty-six articles of gear, including two masts, two sails and yards, twelve oars and rowlocks, rudder, yoke and tiller, which fitted only boats by the same maker, and there were forty-seven different makers. In consequence, although an average of forty boats was sent off daily by train to Assiut, and there was little delay in taking them up the Nile to Wady Halfa, they arrived in a state of great confusion. An immense amount of work was involved in readjustment and refitting of boats. In some cases gear, in particular sails, had been stolen, and new sails had to be made.

Butler reached Assuan and the First Cataract on October 7. He watched eagerly as the first dozen whalers were taken in tow by a launch and then handed over to a local sheik who was waiting with a hundred men to pilot them through.

> Then began a curious sight. In the twinkling of an eye the naked Arabs were on board, and the boats were out in the rushing stream. If there had ever been a doubt in my mind as to the practicability of our craft to cope with a Nile rapid, that doubt would have been dispelled, for the Arabs, utterly disdaining ordinary methods of hauling from the shore, began to shove the boats forward, sometimes in them and often out of them, swimming, poling and diving as easily as a lot of laughing children would slide straws along an English brook.[1]

By the evening a convoy of thirty-two whalers had passed up without trouble, and the exultant Butler was fully able to appreciate the beauty of the scene, 'the palms and colours of the sacred island, Philae the Beautiful . . . and beyond all, boats, ruins, rocks and desert, the saffron afterglow was in its glory'. Having seen more than 200 whalers past Assuan, he went on to Wady Halfa in a steamer which was towing two dahabeahs and fourteen whalers. Unlike Wolseley and Buller he delighted in the ruined temples, the vestiges of towns and fortresses, the lonely towers standing in the desert, and above all in Abu Simbel, with its four gigantic figures carved out of rock expressing the 'vast immovable calm' that seemed to him the essence of Egyptian art. On the evening of October 19 he reached Wady Halfa,

[1] Butler, *Campaign*, p. 110.

where he found to his indignation that because of Wood's insistence on sending up native transport, not one of the hundred and twenty whalers which had arrived there had passed up the Second Cataract.

*

Wady Halfa, like any military camp, presented an appearance of confusion. 'Horses, camels, steam-engines, heads of departments, piles of food and forage, newspaper correspondents, sick men, Arabs and generals, seemed to be all thrown together as though the goods station of a London terminus, a couple of battalions of infantry, the War Office, and a considerable portion of Woolwich Arsenal had all been thoroughly shaken together, and then cast forth upon the desert.'[1] Wolseley was still there, housed in the dahabeah that had brought him up from Assuan, and Buller was in another dahabeah. Wood and Earle were on shore, living in tents. Beresford lived in a small bell tent close to the river, furnished with a penny whistle, a photograph of his wife, letters from home, and 'a stag beetle big enough to carry me to hounds'.[2] At this moment Wady Halfa was the nerve centre of the expedition. It could be reached easily enough from the north, by rail and river. South of it were those reaches of the Nile said to be impassable, and a few miles beyond them lay Dongola, where Stewart and Wilson were already stationed with a detachment of the mounted infantry and the 1st battalion of the Royal Sussex. And beyond Dongola were hostile tribes to be dispersed or defeated, then more rapids, then Berber, then Khartoum.

And now the collapse of the Wady Halfa-Sarras railway was really felt. In theory this railway should have been able to carry the whalers, and a large quantity of stores, round the Bab-el-Kebir, 'the Great Gate'. In fact it was almost useless. The rolling stock had become a sand-covered wreck. 'Engines on wheels and off wheels, tanks and tenders, bolts and boilers, lay around, while the walls and chimneys of buildings that were to have

[1] Ibid, p. 119.
[2] Beresford, *Memoirs.*

formed the terminus and storehouses of the railway stood un-
finished in the desert.'[1] The wheels of the locomotives were
dangerously worn, and their crank pins were out of centre. The
old-fashioned engines became quickly clogged with sand, and
they were so constructed that none of the vital parts could be
reached except from a pit. The use of the railway had to be
confined solely to the movement of stores, and it was inadequate
even for this. During October only a little more than 1,000 tons
of stores were moved by the railway, and although this figure
was more than doubled in the following month, the railway
never gave the help it might have done in moving supplies. 'No
train ran to-day, there being no locomotive in working order',[2]
the Chief of Staff's diary noted on October 19, and on the
following day the engine which had taken a detachment of
troops to Sarras could not draw back the empty trucks. It was
rarely that more than one train a day ran during October, and
on the 28th Wolseley stopped the extension beyond Sarras that
had been begun, feeling that the line would not be completed
in time to be of use, and that the Egyptian labourers could be
better employed on other work.

The failure of the railway meant that all other transport must
be carried or portaged round the Bab. On the evening of his
arrival Butler dined with Wolseley, and heard about the difficulties of the 'belly of stone', as the natives called it. Ten of the
native boats taken through had been completely lost in the
rapids, and several others had been wrecked. Butler went with
Earle to look at it, and his description is as vivid as any:

> It was a very ugly-looking, deep, and steep chasm, between black rocks,
> through which passed an enormous mass of water with a fall of many feet
> in a distance of some sixty or eighty yards. A circular bay at the head of
> the Gate, fed by two arms of the river, collected a great body of water
> immediately above, and made the pressure through the narrow gorge one
> of immense force.[3]

Was there anything as formidable on the Red River? Perhaps

[1] Butler, *Campaign*, p. 120.
[2] War Office Records.
[3] Butler, *Campaign*, p. 125.

not, but Butler was not dismayed by the Nile craft that lay wrecked on the shores, nor by the mishap he saw when the boat that was being steered through by the native Reis Koko lurched and foundered, nor by the fact that the furious roar of the torrent compelled the men of the Naval Brigade, who stood on surrounding rocks to tell the natives when to pull upon their hawsers, to communicate by semaphore. He told Wolseley that with six sailors and a hundred natives he would take at least thirty whalers through it each day, using ordinary two-inch ropes. He added that if the method of using long hawsers was employed, he thought there would be heavy losses. In this he was running counter to the views of Beresford, who had been taking through the native boats. Before Wolseley's arrival Commander Hammill had been in charge of this work, but had been replaced because of his evident lack of confidence. When Beresford was asked by Wolseley whether he could do what had been called impossible by hauling up steamers, he replied that he would admit the impossibility when he had smashed up two steamers, and that if he smashed the first the experience gained would no doubt be useful with the other. The steamers, protected from the rocks by timber and mats along their sides, were successfully hauled up. Beresford, who was perhaps not mathematically accurate, says that 4,000 natives hauled up the first one, which got stuck in the middle of the gorge, and had finally to be dragged through by 1,500 soldiers.

Perhaps Beresford realized that there was force in Butler's criticism of the long hawsers in relation to the whalers. At any rate, he evolved a different method for hauling them through. A warp was rigged up, as nearly as possible at right angles to the boat that had to be hauled, and secured to a rock or tree. One end of a short hawser was then hooked to this warp, and a block tackle secured to the other end, with a towing rope through it which was attached to the boat. At certain points variants of this system were used, and as the course of the river shifted almost daily, the position of the warp had to be moved frequently. The system worked very well, but it took a considerable time to set up, and the impatient Butler, after spending a whole day at the

Bab watching sailors and natives laying lines and stretching hawsers, decided to take a boat up on his own. A promise of two hundred piastres induced Koko, who had survived the destruction of the native boat, to track up the rapid from the shore by means of one two-inch line in the stem of the boat and another steadying rope in the stern. Koko did not trust himself to the boat but assigned this position to a nephew while he guided operations from a rock. They succeeded in bringing the whaler up the three lifts of the Bab. Butler had one bad moment when, at the steepest ledge, the boat and the native in the bows vanished from sight, but then the bows came up again, looking as though the boat was being lifted perpendicularly, and 'with one great pull her centre passed the edge of the fall, and she struck down in her entire length upon the smooth surface of the bay, safe and sound over the Bab-el-Kebir.'[1]

This was the first whaler through the Bab. It was a triumph for Butler, and after it Wolseley viewed the more elaborate arrangements of the sailors with disdain. 'They are right good fellows at sea, and could, I have no doubt, haul an ironclad up a hill, but they have as much idea of working boats in rapid waters as my big boot has', he wrote. 'Having worked for hours at these preparations, they began about 1 p.m. trying to get a boat up, and a pretty mess they made of it. The boat, having shipped some water, was at last got up, but I thought she must have been wrecked, so badly was the affair conducted.' According to Butler, Koko was afterwards given the exclusive working of the Gate.

This may be true, but it is true also that as the Nile rapidly fell, and the rocks showed through the surf, it became necessary to portage the whalers. They had to be carried about a mile and a half from the entrance to the Bab, where they were hauled on shore. Masts, oars and poles were used as bearers, other men giving support by resting thwarts and gunwales on their shoulders. Forty men were used to portage each boat, and the boats had to be handled with care because the matting inside was infested with scorpions. Of the 800 whalers, more than three-

[1] Butler, *Campaign*, p. 134.

quarters were portaged in this way. Only three of them were smashed, but this does not mean that they were ready at once to go on the river. They had by now come a long way and had changed hands several times, and several had been damaged in passing through other cataracts. At Gemai, just above the head of the Second Cataract, a repair dockyard was set up, with first Butler and then Colonel Coleridge Grove in charge of it. Here the whalers were repaired and re-equipped. The beach at Gemai was divided into three parts, a receiving point where the boats were brought on shore and their gear removed, a painting slip and carpenters' beach. The dry climate had opened their seams and made the planks of many extremely brittle, but the longest job was fitting them out again with gear, replacing missing masts and sails, and allotting the proper gear to each boat. Finally the immense mass of 'Woolwich Equipment'—tents, cooking utensils, axes, knives, tool chests, tow ropes, etc.— which had been brought up from Wady Halfa by rail, was unloaded and packed into the boats. When everything had been put in, men were marched down to the shore, told off in tens, and got into the boats, with one voyageur to each boat.

The voyageurs had arrived on October 26, and since then had been occupied in ferrying the whalers through the rapids below the Bab. On October 30 a short trial trip was made by six fully-loaded whalers manned by thirty-five voyageurs, under the command of Alleyne. They travelled four days up the river and returned in a day, the Caughnawagas shooting the rapids without trouble on the way back, although one of the most expert voyageurs was drowned on the day of departure. The men were full of praise for the behaviour of the whalers, but there was an ominous side to the trip, for they had had to fight their way up successive cataracts where the boats were tracked and the stores unloaded and portaged on camels. It seemed that, as Hammill had warned, the stretch of river between the Second and Third Cataracts contained very little clear water, and these rapids were to be encountered not as on this trial run by skilled boatmen, but by soldiers who were far from finding water their natural element, and many of whom did not know how to swim.

The accuracy of Butler's planning was remarkable. On August 10, before the boats had been ordered, Wolseley had asked him to submit a calculation of the date on which they would be ready to start from Sarras. Butler had replied that 200 boats should be at Sarras by October 25, ready to start on November 1 after repairs. In fact, 130 boats were at Wady Halfa by October 18, but were then held up by Wood's insistence on passing through native craft. Nevertheless on November 1 five whalers left Sarras containing half a company of Engineers, with one voyageur in each boat. On November 5 thirty-two boats left, and another thirty-three went on the following day, carrying the 1st Battalion of the South Staffordshires. Wolseley and his personal staff left for Dongola on October 28. He had seen that the whalers could go through or round the Second Cataract, he had established the dockyard at Gemai, and he was chafing to get nearer the scene of possible action and to talk himself to the Mudir of Dongola, who had received Stewart and Wilson with a casualness that at times approached absolute incivility. More worrying messages had come from Gordon. They were dated July 30 and 31, and contained savage comments on one of those Gladstone-inspired telegrams which asked why he was staying in Khartoum. 'You ask me to "state cause and intention in staying at Khartoum, knowing Government means to abandon Sudan", and in answer I say we stay at Khartoum because Arabs have shut us up and will not let us out.' He said that any relief expedition should come by the Nile route, but added that he feared it must now be too late.

In any case, Wolseley was tired of Wady Halfa. 'My days are very monotonous', he told his wife. 'I eat, drink, sleep and ride, and write a good deal. When waiting for the supplies for an Army to be collected, the temper is apt to be a little short.'[1] His temper was not improved by the attacks of the flies, which got into the cabin even when all the windows had been filled with wire gauze, nor by the furious dust storms which covered every surface thickly. He expelled bad humour partly by going about a great deal on horseback—he rode twenty-eight miles one day,

[1] Letters, 22.10.84.

trying to get rid of his 'disgusting and superfluous fat'—partly by expressing himself ironically about the other commanders, in particular Evelyn Wood. Although only in his late forties, Wood was already very deaf. He had been taken on the Ashanti Expedition in 1873 as a special service officer, and felt an often-acknowledged debt of gratitude to the man who had given him his start, but he had negotiated the terms of settlement with the Boers after the defeat of Majuba, and had never been forgiven by Wolseley for what he regarded as an ignominious surrender. Wood regretted accepting the post of Sirdar, and was eager to give it up and return to a command in the British Army. 'There is command in the clear blue eye', a war correspondent of the time noted. 'The sweetness of his smile goes to your heart and stays there.'[1] Wolseley, while doing his best to keep the peace between Wood and Buller, commented ironically on the 'inordinate vanity' which seemed to him Wood's most striking characteristic, and remarked that he had already begun to roar at everybody else after shouting at Wood. He was the only senior officer opposed to the Nile route who had been given an important command, and Wolseley was at first inclined to think that his support was not whole-hearted. After a few days, however, he said that Wood was working cordially now, having made up his mind to quit the Egyptian Army and 'throw in his lot with this expedition'. He liked Butler's earnestness and the way in which he ignored red tape, but thought that he did not work well in a team. Brackenbury, as often, was the butt of his humour. 'Brack's voice becomes deeper, his tail squarer, his legs shorter, his calves thicker, his hair thinner, his stomach larger and his complexion yellower every day.'[2] Perhaps it was as well that he was leaving these various irritants and going to see the Mudir, whom he thought vain and pompous but also able and energetic. He borrowed Buller's decoration so that he could make the Mudir K.C.M.G., and set off.

The journey was made by camel. Wolseley did not look forward to the idea of camels as mounts, and the reality proved no

[1] Forbes.
[2] Letters, 22.10.84.

better than his expectation. 'I cannot say that I at all enjoyed it', he wrote to his daughter after his first camel ride at Wady Halfa. 'I never knew what the brute was going to do next, or whether it would not lie down suddenly at any moment. It grunted and made a sort of gurgling noise in the throat all the time I was on its back.'[1] But although he did not like camels he enjoyed the silence and remoteness of the desert. The party made very good time, travelling often at night, and averaging about thirty miles a day. They made what was reckoned to be an eight-day journey to Dongola in seven days. At one point they met a group of officers, and Wolseley stopped to talk to them. When they made a move again, his camel swerved suddenly and he fell off. Remounting, he looked hard at the war artist Melton Prior, who had witnessed the scene. Prior dutifully said, 'I did not see you fall, sir', and received the General's thanks.[2]

*

Now there came a strange and astonishing delay. For five days no troops moved from Sarras. There were whalers ready, but no men to embark in them. The supply of coal bringing steamers—and men and supplies—from Assuan to Wady Halfa had run out, and on October 23 the steamers ceased to run.

The delay sprang from the carelessness with which the original contract agreed with Cook had been drawn at the War Office. It was understood by Buller, who had overall responsibility for the supply side of the expedition, that Cook's had contracted to deliver men and supplies as far as Wady Halfa at a certain rate. He expected that they would continue to work the steamers as long as they were needed, and had no idea that there was any limitation of numbers. Cook, however, viewed the agreement differently, as providing for a specified number of men, stores and boats. The Admiralty had reckoned that he would need 12,000 tons of coal, and he had ordered about 20,000 tons to be on the safe side. But in the event, he was being asked to carry more than double the original numbers—11,000 English and

---

[1] Hove, 12.10.84.
[2] Prior, *Campaigns of a War Correspondent*.

7,000 Egyptian soldiers, nearly 40,000 tons of supplies and 30,000 tons of cereals, and 800 whalers. To move all these he had had to use a fleet of nearly 700 sailing boats and 27 steamers, and a small army of 5,000 men and boys. 'The military had everything that they required, splendid rations and plenty of them',[1] and Cook felt injured by the suggestion that he had failed to fulfil his contract. The situation was complicated by the fact that John Mason Cook himself did not arrive in Egypt until late in October, and that in the meantime matters were handled by the firm's chief Egyptian representative, Rastovitch, who speedily became on bad terms with the Generals.

The first warning was sounded in Buller's Diary very late, on October 18. 'It appears that no contract has been made for the delivery of any given quantity of coal above Assuan. Cook says that he undertook to deliver 300 tons at Korosko at £4 a ton, and 800 tons at Halfa for £4 8s. a ton. This has been delivered. All that at Korosko has been used and about 500 tons remain at Halfa. Cook wants 10/- a ton more for future supplies.'[2] Yet Buller does not seem to have realized the danger that the pipeline of the expedition would be blocked unless urgent action was taken. Three days later he was engaged in a barren discussion with the Senior Commissariat Officer, Lieutenant-Colonel Hughes, about the terms of the contract. He was not himself in possession of the facts, he said, 'but I know that the War Office guaranteed Mr. Cook the sum of £30,000 against possible loss on coal, which would seem to represent an implied contract for a much larger supply than has been delivered. Anyhow, we want at least 1,000 tons at once between Philae and Korosko, and must get it at any price. Please ascertain what amount is on the way to Assuan, and arrange that we do not run short.'[3] Two days after this the steamers had stopped, and Buller noted that 4,000 tons of coal were required immediately. An arrangement to obtain coal from a local sugar factory collapsed when the coal proved to be useless and a new contract was signed on the

---

[1] Cook.
[2] War Office Records.
[3] Ibid.

terms demanded by Cook's, but it was several days before troops and supplies began to flow freely again. On November 1 Buller noted that the difficulty was still serious and that there was coal left for only one steamer, and it was not until November 10 that the delay was completely cleared.

The incident meant, as nearly as one can estimate, a delay of ten days for the whole expedition, and must have brought home the bitter truth that if there was a block anywhere along the huge pipeline of the Nile, it was likely to affect movement throughout the whole distance from Cairo to Dongola. In this case the blockage was most vital at Gemai and Sarras, where only the Staffords left between November 1 and 11, but because of it Assuan became choked with men and supplies, and movement halted everywhere along the river. Who was to blame for the delay? Buller afterwards drew the moral that 'if you do employ a contractor make sure that he thoroughly understands (i) what it is that you require, (ii) what it is that he contracts to do'.[1] Yet whether blame in the first instance rests with Cook or with the War Office, there can be no doubt that Buller failed to show any sense of urgency when he was fully seized of the situation on October 18. He seems to have kept the reason for the delay from Wolseley as long as possible. When the Commander-in-Chief learned what had happened he blamed himself for leaving the coal question to Buller instead of investigating it personally. But the failure was less that of any individual than that of an organization. The idea of staff work in a modern sense hardly existed in the British Army of that time, and the respect felt for Wolseley by his subordinates was so great that often they hesitated to make personal decisions. As one commentator has said in relation to the handling of the whalers at the Second Cataract: 'One is impressed by the strong element of improvisation in the transport arrangements, and the number of decisions with respect to them that were made by the Commander-in-Chief personally.'

[1] War Office Records.

CHAPTER FOUR

THE CAMEL CORPS MEET THEIR CAMELS: OCTOBER–NOVEMBER

ON October 8 several units of the Camel Corps arrived in Cairo. Instructions were given 'to encamp them at the Pyramids if possible, in order to avoid the risk of venereal disease',[1] a precaution reflecting the rank and income of the officers rather than their superior virility over the men in other regiments who had stayed in Cairo. The Corps was divided into a Heavy Camel Regiment, drawn from the 1st and 2nd Life Guards, the Blues, the 2nd, 4th and 5th Dragoon Guards, the 1st and 2nd Dragoons and the 5th and 16th Lancers, a Light Camel Regiment which came from several Hussar units, a Guards' Camel Regiment from the Coldstream, Grenadier and Scots Guards plus a detachment of Royal Marines, and a Mounted Infantry Camel Regiment made up of twenty-five men each from a number of Infantry Regiments together with men from the King's Royal Rifle Corps and the Rifle Brigade. The names of the officers reflected their social position—Captain Lord St. Vincent, Captain Lord Cochrane, Lieutenant Lord Rodney, Lieutenant Lord Binning, Lieutenant Count Gleichen. Most of these young and courageous aristocrats had little knowledge of actual fighting, and regarded the expedition as a tremendous lark. Colonel Stanley Clarke, for whom the Prince of Wales had spoken, was appointed to command the Light Camel Regiment, to the indignation of Lieutenant-Colonel (later Sir) Hugh McCalmont, who had been promised the command and characterized the appointment as a piece of job-

[1] War Office Records.

131

bery. Each little detachment had its own officers and N.C.O.s.

It was difficult for the men who made up the Camel Corps to have any genuine pride in it, since they all felt themselves to be very much in competition with men in other detachments. They were to ride on camels instead of on horses, had been put together into one artificial unit instead of being in their own regiments, and were dressed in uniforms that seemed to many of them to come out of the seventeenth rather than the nineteenth century. They wore red serge jumpers, later abandoned for the grey jumpers carried in their valises, ochre cord breeches, dark blue puttees (the officers wore long field boots instead), brown ankle boots and white pith helmets. They carried a rifle, a sword-bayonet, a bandolier holding fifty cartridges, pouch, frog and sling, haversack and water-bottle, and a variety of other things in their valises, including goggles and a veil as protection against desert sand. This seemed to many of them a slightly degrading sort of fancy dress, and it is likely that their appearance gave Wolseley some amusement, as he was certainly amused by the prospect of their introduction to camel riding. The essential difference between the Camel Corps and the rest of the expedition was that they were not to use the whalers, but to make their way from Wady Halfa to Dongola on camels. They reached Wady Halfa like the other troops, by train to Assiut and then down the Nile on barges towed by steamers. The steamer towing the Lights broke down, and there were delays because of the coal shortage. The first units reached Wady Halfa on October 26, the last did not arrive until nearly a month later.

One of the amenities of life at Wady Halfa, for the officers, was dinner with Buller. The Chief of Staff appreciated the pleasures of eating. Forty camels were needed to carry his baggage, and several among them must have been loaded with delicacies for the table, and with the champagne that was Buller's invariable accompaniment on a campaign. Lieutenant Marling of the King's Royal Rifles, who had been awarded the V.C. for his heroism in the Suakin campaign, dined with Buller and his A.D.C. Lord Frederick Fitzgerald, on Buller's dahabeah, and noted 'A 1 dinner with fizz'. On the same day Marling's Mounted Infantry had a taste of their camels:

> We had a mounted parade, at first at a walk, and did fours, right and left and wheeling, and only about six men fell off. Then Curly Hutton sounded the trot, and in two minutes the air was thick with Tommies flying about at every angle. Twenty-three camels got loose and went off with their tails in the air, towards the setting sun, and we never got back five of them. Curly Hutton came off on his head.[1]

The Mounted Infantry were a wild lot. Lieutenant Stewart, who was in charge of the Gordon Highlander detachment was, Marling said, the best looter he ever knew. At Wady Halfa he stole a leg of mutton out of the post boat for the mess, and hit a man who tried to stop him with the great joint. The man proved to be the new Commander of the Mounted Infantry, Major the Honourable George Gough, but it does not appear that Stewart, who was known as Bimbash, was reproved. Marling noted with approval that when Bimbash left Cairo he had only the kit he stood up in, but that by the time they reached Assuan he needed another kitbag to hold all the loot he had taken from his fellow officers. Bimbash survived to command in the South African War a unit called the Johannesburg Mounted Rifles, generally known as the Jews Mostly Russian.

The Mounted Infantry got the best of the camels and the saddles. Count Gleichen of the Guards' Camel Regiment, who wrote a lively account of his experiences during the campaign, was far from pleased with the equipment available for them, complaining that the knifeboard framework was of unseasoned wood which had to be lashed by wire, that the girth and straps were rotten and needed frequent greasing, and that the leather water skins and water-bottles often let out the liquid as soon as they were filled. 'We were told they would swell when wet and thus close up the pores, and in some cases they did, though in others they were holey. What would happen if we had to depend on them for our lives, we didn't know, but didn't trouble our heads about it.'[2] For a week the Guards, who had been frequently

[1] Marling, p. 124.
[2] Gleichen, pp. 25–6.

K

told that they would not fight on their camels or indeed as
cavalry at all, trotted and cantered, and then they set off on the
235-mile journey to Dongola. Gleichen's detachment took with
them a small train of baggage camels, a Field Hospital section,
and a few commissariat and transport men. Gleichen was rather
disappointed by the desert, which was not the waste of burning
sand he had expected, but simply scrub and gravel, which alter-
nated with rocky black hills over which the men had to dismount
and lead their camels. A typical day began at 5 or 6 o'clock in the
morning, with a walk of several miles. As the sun rose the men
mounted their camels, and rode on for another eight or nine
hours. The worst enemy was boredom, which arose from the
camels' refusal to vary their standard pace of something under
three miles an hour. Gleichen tried to read and write without
success, but found it possible to go to sleep for short periods. He
also developed some affection for his camel Potiphar, who
bellowed every time he came near, and made occasional playful
rushes at him. The men were disconcerted to find that the camels
were not the tough, endlessly enduring animals they had been
told of, who could keep going for many days without food or
drink, and could trot two hundred miles without a halt. In fact
they were delicate, and easily upset. They were susceptible to
colds if their saddles were taken off too soon after a halt, they
developed sore backs after four days' riding, and they could be
induced to trot only by a vigorous application of the kourbash.
The Guards' Regiment reached Dongola in a fortnight, an average of nearly twenty miles a day. The men knew nothing about
looking after camels, and many of the animals arrived with sore
backs and in need of rest.

They started almost immediately to practise camel drill.
Buller had issued a memorandum, 'Notes for the Use of Camel
Regiments', which emphasized once more that the Camel Corps
would fight on foot, and were mounted on camels only to
enable them to make long marches. In the event of sudden attack
they were to dismount, tie the legs of their camels, and fight
either in close order two deep surrounding the camels, or in two-
deep squares at the angles of the points where the camels were

collected. When there was no time to make preparation of this sort, the camels were to be placed close together with both legs securely tied, and guarded by some of the troops. There were also detailed instructions for making a bivouac with the camels. A great deal of drill was carried out with a view to rapidly forming varieties of square and column formation. The men did it, but for many of them it was unfamiliar and uncongenial work. Few felt so kindly towards their camels as Count Gleichen.

*

The Mudir of Dongola was busily playing both ends against the middle. He was a possible rival to the Mahdi as a religious leader, a fact which had escaped neither the Mahdi nor the British authorities. He was a Turkish slave boy, who after the death of his master had been sent to a military school, where companions knew him as the dervish. His reputation for piety and for military shrewdness had greatly increased since his appointment as Mudir in 1877. Kitchener had been at first greatly impressed by him, and Egerton wrote encouragingly to Granville of the Mudir's zeal in making preparations to help the expedition. The holy man assured Kitchener that a Circassian like himself could never make common cause with a black-skinned Mahdi. Early in September the Mudir's tribesmen defeated a group of the Mahdi's supporters at Korti and killed their leader, who had been appointed Emir of Dongola by the Mahdi. The victory placed the whole Nile area up to the foot of the Fourth Cataract in friendly hands, and naturally also gave the Mudir a high view of his own importance. Kitchener soon changed his mind and reported that the Mudir was not to be trusted, and his treatment of Stewart and Wilson made it plain that he was playing for high political stakes. Stewart was kept waiting for two days, and then given only vague promises about what supplies might possibly be available when troops were sent up. Yet it was important not to offend the Mudir. Stewart reported to Buller:

> I hold that he is a very powerful man in his own province, and, indeed, an autocrat, and that whether here or at Merowi, so long as he is in his province, it would be a hopeless task to try to work without him.

Wilson arrived a few days later, and was introduced to the Mudir by Stewart. He met with a reception even less cordial. No guard was turned out, and the sentry did not salute. When they reached the courtyard of the Mudir's residence,

> I saw that no preparation had been made for our reception, and the Mudir and his staff were all busy praying on one of the praying places. We had to wait a few minutes before a servant brought chairs, which were placed under a tree, and then we had a quarter of an hour until the Mudir had finished his prayers. According to all oriental etiquette this was a regular slight and insult, and you can imagine how my blood boiled within me.

When the two Englishmen were received at last, the Mudir placed them on his left hand, although the proper place for guests was on his right. There were rumours that Gordon's assistant, Colonel Stewart, had tried to get down the Nile in the steamer *Abbas*, and had been murdered. Wilson was told to urge on the Mudir that he should go with his native troops to Merowi where he would be well placed for avenging Colonel Stewart's death, but this request met with a positive refusal. During one of their later discussions, however, conducted in the presence of a cousin of the Mahdi, the Mudir proposed that this cousin should murder the Mahdi. The cousin was agreeable if the terms were right. 'They were much surprised when I told them that this was not the English way of doing business, and that I could not listen to any proposal of the kind.' Wilson had eventually to go to Merowi on his own, and although he could not obtain definite information about the wreck of the *Abbas*, he telegraphed back that he feared the worst. On the way he met Kitchener at Debbeh, which had been occupied by the Mudir's men. The two were disgusted by the savagery with which the Turkish troops had treated the Sudanese, and Wilson commented bitterly: 'No wonder that these wretched people hate the name of Turks, and the latter are the people whom we have come to help, and whom we are to treat as friends.'

The Mudir intended to ignore Wolseley's arrival, as he had done those of Stewart and Wilson, but was persuaded to come out to meet him. On the following day the Commander-in-

Chief went to the Mudir's residence. He had a disconcerting reception. The Mudir's followers pranced about, dancing and screaming, and then suddenly charged straight at their visitors, brandishing their lances. 'I imagined that I saw the slightest wince on the part of our General as a man raised his spear as though to thrust at him', said one observer.[1] The thrust was checked, however, and Wolseley pinned Buller's K.C.M.G. on to the Mudir's cloak.

Both Wilson and Wolseley have left descriptions of the holy man. 'He has an intelligent face, fined down by fasting and prayer, so that his large nose shows out prominently', Wilson wrote. 'He is rather short, wears a white cap of camel's hair felt, with a kufiyeh round it, and the usual cloak with white trousers.' Wolseley noticed his pale, drawn expression, and his crab-like movements. 'When he sits down his legs are twisted together, whilst his feet and toes turn inwards, as if they were deformed.' He wore a long black 'sort of paletot', shiny black alpaca trousers and elastic-sided patent leather boots. He never smoked or drank coffee, prayed five times a day and 'although a vain and designing fanatic', was a remarkable man.[2] John Mason Cook, who came later to Dongola, thought the Mudir 'one of the most powerful men from a brain point of view that I have ever been in presence of', and was astonished by his offer (which Cook wisely did not take up) to provide at any time a safe escort to Khartoum.[3] Wolseley's headquarters at Dongola were in a tumbledown mud-built house, which served both as office and mess room, with his staff in tents pitched around it. There were fewer flies, and no fleas or bugs, but they had been replaced by hordes of white ants, which could eat the soles of boots in a single night. Wolseley negotiated with local tribesmen about supplies and saw the Mudir frequently. It did not prove easy to pin him down to any positive action. He said that there would be plenty of supplies available, and that his tribesmen would support the British Army when it arrived—but when would that

[1] Prior.
[2] Wolseley Papers, R.U.S.I. Unpublished autobiography.
[3] Cook.

be? The only troops who had actually reached Dongola were the Royal Sussex who had been there since September, and a wing of the Mounted Infantry, less than fifteen hundred men in all. The Mudir's caution was understandable, and Wolseley's telegrams to Wady Halfa grew more impatient every day.

CHAPTER FIVE

GETTING THROUGH THE CATARACTS: NOVEMBER

The whalers that left Sarras with their crews of a dozen men, and the four tons of stores that rose high above the gunwale and half-hid the men at the oars, found themselves confronting within a few days conditions such as most of them had never imagined in their lives. The section of the Nile they entered was called the Batan el Hajar, 'the womb of rocks', and it extended for sixty-two miles. Throughout this distance the river rushed and swirled, changing its course every day as it fell, so that 'the little resting-place behind a rocky islet' thankfully noted one day had become 'the nucleus of a cascade on the morrow, and on the after-morrow a treacherous tooth of rock buried beneath a smooth swift current'.[1] In truth it was impossible to provide a guide to the rapids, and the great difference between the problems of the Red River and those of the Nile was now seen. The Nile rapids were almost continuous, and the marking of the Cataracts from one to six was utterly misleading. Between the 'Second Cataract' at Wady Halfa and the 'Third Cataract' at Hannek lay no fewer than seven major obstacles as well as innumerable minor ones, and each of these obstacles varied in nature and extent and presented different problems. The cataract of Semneh consisted first of ten miles of broken water, through which it was dangerous but possible to row or sail. At the end of this stretch came the Gate of Semneh, a narrow gorge between rocky cliffs through which the river rushed with the force of a sluice gate. Here all the stores had to be unloaded box by box and

[1] Colvile, *Official History*.

carried half a mile over the cliffs to the other side of the cataract, before the boats themselves were hauled up by main force. Sixteen miles farther on—and even in this and other comparatively clear stretches the tide was strong, and rocks lay just below the surface —came the cataract of Ambako, five miles long, where a tremendous number of rocks and islets made it necessary to row, sail or gently paddle in some places, using the track line at others. After another eight miles the cataract of Tanjur, two and a half miles long, presented a day's work to the crews going up it. Later came Akasheh, which resembled Semneh, and then the five-and-a-half-mile cataract of Dal, which was thought by many to be the most difficult of all. That was the end of the Batan el Hajar, a region made additionally oppressive to those passing through it by the great cliffs of black basalt that rose up on either side, so that often nothing was to be seen but the rushing water and the black rocks which were so hot that they burned hands and feet when the time came to tramp over them while portaging stores. Butler might express his appreciation of the 'serrated ridges and calcined peaks of a savage solitude' and admire the ruined temples standing on the summits of cliffs, but the men in the boats found the rocks gloomy and frightening and the heat almost unendurable. And still there were more cataracts ahead: Kajbar, a rocky causeway stretching right across the river, and then Hannek, which like some of the others was barely noticeable in the few weeks of high Nile, but by mid-November had become so shallow that not only the stores, but the boats as well, had to be portaged for more than three miles.

Most of the officers and men had made up their minds that the little native kyassas with their huge triangular sails were better suited to these conditions than the whalers, but the ever-sanguine Butler set himself to disprove this. At Semneh he ordered his whaler out into the stream when a kyassa was just abreast of it, and the two boats raced each other through the rapids:

> Before us lay a troubled mass of water, growing rapidly stiffer until at the head of the rapid a large rock stood full in the centre of the stream. Round this rock the current broke furiously, and between the two severed rushes lay the usual interval of seething and whirring, but comparatively

quiet water. The art of forcing up a rapid consists in running up this lane of easier water, clinging to it as long as possible, and leaving it only at the very edge of the rock. Then, with all the strength of oar and paddle, the effort is made to lift the boat over and through the neck of the rush. It is at this point that the art of steering tells.[1]

The soldiers in Butler's boat were Staffords, and his helmsman was Chief Prince, an Indian friend of Red River days. Prince was not yet accustomed to the Nile, and he turned so that he offered too wide an angle to the rushing stream. The rudder failed to operate, they were caught in the rapid, and at the same time a sudden breeze threw the boat over and knocked the men off the thwarts. For a moment it looked as if they would overturn, but the boat kept its balance until sheets were let go. Then it faced again head on to the rush of water, and this time the men got it over the rapid, 'walking clear away from the kyassa, whose utmost efforts were powerless to pass', and seeing at the next bend of the river dozens of wrecked kyassas and nuggers, which had struck rocks or turned over, and lay half-submerged in the water. Now these wrecks formed another obstacle, for it proved necessary to use the track lines for passing them. This was slow work because the river was running even here at eight or nine miles an hour, and the lines kept fouling the wrecks. By night time all the thirty-two boats in this convoy had been tracked through, and Butler, as he lay down that night, was able to recall with pleasure that 'not a soldier had been hurt, not a pound of the heavy freights had been damaged, not a boat had been lost or even injured. . . . Truly, there were false prophets in other lands besides the Sudan.'

The prophets were false, certainly. The whalers, as they proved now and later, were able to ascend the Nile rapids where native craft failed, and they did so with few losses in boats and men. The Red River men were right, and the naval experts were wrong. Yet it remained true that they had underestimated the difficulties of the Nile cataracts, so that men and supplies took far longer to go up the river than they had expected. The passage of the Batan el Hajar took the first boats about eighteen days. At some rapids all of the four tons of stores from every boat had to be taken out,

---

[1] Butler, *Campaign*, p. 152.

brought round by the crews, with the help of the West African
Kroomen who manned the whalers for convoy work, and then
reloaded. At other rapids it was possible to manage by taking out
only half the stores, and it was said that the boats pulled and sailed
better when loaded, but these portages and part-portages damaged the stores as well as taking up time. No calculation seems to
have been made about the time that it would take the whalers to
ascend the cataracts, but it is likely that these first boats took at
least twice as long as Wolseley had hoped.

Life was hard for the men in the boats. After the first groups had
left Sarras, only eight men and one voyageur embarked. Buller
had issued orders which emphasized that an officer or N.C.O.
must always be in charge, that nobody under any pretence was
to sit in the gunwale, that the sheets must always be held in the
hand when under sail and never allowed to run free, and that 'if
a boat should be upset, everyone must recollect that it is of the
greatest importance to strike out directly one is in the water'.[1]
Such orders were not calculated to cheer those unused to the
river, and very likely some of the voyageurs showed their contempt for the inefficiency of the soldiers. One of the officers reported to Denison that 'his men and mine do not agree but are
fighting all the time, and that if they go down together there
may be trouble'.[2] Reveille for the men was an hour before sun-
rise, and the boats made a start at dawn. They fought their way
up the river from dawn until sunset, with breaks only for breakfast and a midday meal. At some places the pull against them was
so strong that the men would row for half an hour without gain-
ing an inch, and Andy Wauchope, who commanded the Black
Watch, said that he felt ashamed of what he had to ask his men
to do for tenpence a day. The officers of that time were far more
considerate of the needs and safety of their men than those of the
1914–18 War, perhaps because they were in such close and continual contact with them. Buller showed an almost fanatical care
for the health and comfort of the troops, and Wolseley fought
continually for them to be less miserably paid, and on more than

[1] War Office Records.
[2] The Nile Voyageurs.

one occasion rebuked officers who forgot 'those gallant private soldiers who fight our battles for us with no prospect of C.B.s in the distance'.[1] The strain on the men can be clearly seen in an account of their work by Colonel Denison, the commander of the voyageurs:

> As a usual thing six men pulled. The voyageur took the rudder, sometimes the bow. When the boat came to a strong current, the men would pull their best, and with a good way on would get up; but if they failed and were carried back, I have seen them make the attempt a second time, straining every nerve, and then succeed. If it was impossible to row up, all the crew but the bowman and the man at the rudder would disembark, get out their tracking line, put it over their shoulders, and walk along the bank, tracking the boat, until they reached smooth water again. When they come to a bad rapid, instead of having one crew on the rope, 3, 4 or 5 crews, according to the rush of water, would be put on. This was avoided as much as possible, as it took 5 times as long.[2]

The soldiers were lice-ridden, exposed to the ferocious sun and the continual attack of mosquitoes, equipped with clothing totally unsuitable to the climate and doing work that they knew little about, and they were condemned to hard labour, day in and day out. It is not surprising that when Butler asked Hammill why he had been mistaken about the whalers' ability to ascend the rapids, the naval officer replied: 'I did not think the boats would not carry the expedition, but I did think the expedition would not carry the boats.' Skill was required as well as strength. Great care had to be taken to see that tracking ropes were not slack, for if they were the current would catch the boat and overturn it. This happened at Tanjur, when the slack of the rope was not pulled in quickly enough, and it got out into the current, filled, and turned over. Denison says: 'The two voyageurs climbed on to the bottom and I told them (soldiers) to let go the long rope, and got out a crew of Canadians in a boat in a moment, pulled out, took them off, and recovered boat and nearly all the stores.'[3] There were frequent time-consuming arguments about the best channel to take, for half a dozen often offered themselves. Wauchope lost

[1] Wolseley Papers, R.U.S.I., unpublished autobiography.
[2] *The Nile Voyageurs.*
[3] Ibid.

twelve hours one day because a sergeant in one of his boats took a river fork leading up a side channel, delaying the whole convoy. Wauchope threatened to have him shot, but reprieved him on the following day. At Ambigol Cataract Denison saw the chance of avoiding a bad portage by crossing to the opposite bank of the Nile. He told Colonel Alleyne, who said that he had been trying to get some crews to try it, but that both they and the voyageurs refused to take the risk. Denniston crossed the current safely, and several other boats followed him successfully, only one being damaged on a rock. Such incidents were common. Most of the voyageurs were wonderfully skilful, but there were exceptions, not all confined to the professional men from Manitoba. Butler saw boats wedged on rocks or aground because of the lumber-jacks' impatience or lack of skill. 'The attitude of one huge tree-cutter from the backwoods I well remember. He had got his boat fast aground at stem and stern. Recklessly and with unskilful strength he laboured at his pole, shouting to the men on the track line to haul away, while he relieved his over-burthened feelings by repeatedly kicking the ribs of his boat with heavy hob-nailed boots.'[1] What is remarkable is that so few whalers were seriously damaged, and that so few men were drowned. The voyageurs, who ran by far the greatest risks, since in bad rapids they alone remained in the boats, had six men drowned during the whole expedition, all of them between the Second and Third Cataracts.

When all praise has been given, the rate of progress was extremely slow. It took the rear wing of the Staffords eleven days to cover the thirty-eight miles from Sarras.

*

At Dongola Wolseley was fuming. The whalers were late, and the Nile boats used for carrying stores were continually breaking down or running aground. His letters to his wife in early November are full of complaints about the steamers, and the delay which meant that he would not be at Shendi 'for at least a month later than I had in a sanguine mood calculated upon'. He relieved his feelings by blaming the 'detested and contemptible Govern-

[1] Butler, *Campaign*, p. 178.

ment ... of course all that pack of curs who always grumble at my heels will now bark and say the delay is all my fault'.[1] He was delighted but embarrassed by the arrival of Colonel Burnaby. 'There will be the devil's own row if I give him anything to do, and yet I should like to do so, as he is clever and as brave as a lion.'[2] He resolved to ignore the interdict on Burnaby's employment, and made him an inspecting officer on a section of the Nile.

Suddenly he decided to return to Wady Halfa, and, telling nobody there of his intentions but Buller and Wood, he set out, accompanied only by two A.D.C.s and an Arab guide. He had travelled quickly before, but now his journey had a frantic urgency about it. He travelled day and night, and where before he had done a seven-day journey in six days, this time he did it in four. 'I never took my boots off coming here, and never washed at all.'[3] He came from Sarras by the train, which was now giving a much improved service, and arrived at two in the morning. Butler, with typical eagerness, had been waiting for the train, and now he saw in the carriages the two aides-de-camp lying prostrate, and 'a third figure, wakeful, watchful and erect'. Wolseley began to fire questions at him. 'What was the cause of the delay? Why were the troops not moving up yet? Why had not the Stafford battalion reached Dal?' Butler arranged to start up river on the following day, and try to hurry up the troops. The basic causes of the delay were the coal shortage and the frightful difficulties of the rapids. In practice there was little that he could do, although he may have been right in thinking that his return would have a good effect 'in brightening up any who may have gone asleep along the line in rear'. Wolseley was very dissatisfied with Evelyn Wood, saying that Wood was totally unmethodical and unenterprising, and never stirred from his desk. He was just the sort of man who would have put obstacles in the way of the expedition had he been left out of it. 'In order to *purchase* Evelyn Wood's goodwill, I was obliged to flatter him and tell him that as I considered he would make the very best Commandant of the

[1] Letters, 10.11.84.
[2] Ibid.
[3] Ibid., 17.11.84.

Line of Communications, I offered him that position. . . . He has done even worse than I expected.'[1] Whether or not Wood was as inefficient as Wolseley suggested in this burst of bad temper, he was certainly vain, quarrelsome, and like Buller a great eater and drinker. When he moved up to Korti later on, one of the voyageur officers noted: 'General Wood's baggage passed through today. Besides tents, camp furniture, etc. he had 96 cases with stores, about 40 being wine of different sorts. He evidently intends being comfortable.'[2]

Wolseley stayed only one day at Wady Halfa. He had, of course, been in constant telegraphic touch with Buller, and if he did not know the exact positions of all the troops, anything he learned now cannot have pleased him. His original plan had been to concentrate 5,000 or 6,000 troops at Shendi, but it was plain that if a desert march was necessary, the point of concentration must be farther down the Nile. Accordingly, he now planned to concentrate 8,000 men at Korti, ready to continue up river or to move across the desert. The situation on November 18 was that 1,400 men were at Dongola, and could easily move on to Korti, the Guards Camel Regiment and the Staffordshires (about 1,000 men) were between Dongola and the cataract of Dal, another 2,000 men were between Dal and Gemai, and a further 6,000 were spread out along the river as far back as Assiut, more than 700 miles from the point chosen for final assembly. Since the whalers were carrying both troops and supplies, they had to come up to Korti before further progress could be made, and a calculation was now made of the dates on which various units would reach Korti, and on which the concentration there would be complete. The calculation gives January 22 as the date on which the last unit, the Cameron Highlanders, would arrive at Korti, and it proved correct almost to a day. By the end of the year there would be 3,000 infantry, and most or all of the Camel Corps, at Korti. Would Gordon be able to hold out so long?

At Wady Halfa Wolseley received a long letter from Gordon, written on November 4, which gave a great deal of information.

[1] Letters, 11.11.84.
[2] The Nile Voyageurs.

He confirmed the loss of the *Abbas*, and that Colonel Stewart
had been with the steamer. He had received a letter from
Kitchener dated October 14, and one in cipher from Wolseley,
which he could not read because Stewart had taken the cipher
book. 'Warn Foreign Office when you are sure about loss of
steamer, about loss of cipher books . . . because it was looked
on as perfectly safe, I sent Stewart, Power and Herbin down,
telling them to give you all information. . . . The steamer
carried a gun, and had a good force on board her. It is very sad.'
He made clear the paucity of his own information, saying that
since March they had received only two despatches, of April 27
and May 5, before Kitchener's letter. 'Kitchener says he has sent
many letters, and got none in reply. I have sent out during last
month at least ten.' But he gave cheering news, saying that five
steamers, with nine guns on them, were at Metemmeh, on the
bank of the Nile opposite Shendi, awaiting Wolseley's orders.
'We can hold out 40 days with ease, after that it will be difficult.'
If this statement was to be taken literally, it means that Gordon
could hold out until December 14, and when a summary of the
letter was sent to Hartington, he asked whether it would mean
any change of plan. 'News from Gordon makes no change in my
plans,' Wolseley replied, and in fact it was now impossible to
speed up the forward movement. They were committed to getting up the Nile, and there would be no considerable force even
at Korti by the middle of December. A few days later another
letter from Gordon arrived. Written on September 18, it said that
Khartoum would be all right for four months, 'after which we
shall be embarrassed'. This meant that the town could hold out
until the middle of January.

'What a strange man Gordon is,' Wolseley commented, although the letters were for Gordon very coherent and rational.
'I hope I may not have any trouble with him.'[1] He replied with a
letter sent in clear, and worded with deliberate pomposity, in
which he said that he would have an army 'strong enough to wipe
Mohammed Ahmed and all his followers off the face of the earth',
which would be between Debbeh and Ambukol 'on a date which

[1] Letters, 24.11.84.

you can fix by counting 283 days on from this year's anniversary
of the date of your commission as Major-General', a circumlocu-
tion designed to tell Gordon that this date was January 7, while
leaving the Mahdi ignorant of it. He had a great liking for home-
made ciphers, and now he devised one made from a page of his
own *Soldiers' Pocket-Book*, to which the keys were the Christian
name of his mother's father, the amount of cash in a stated number
of taels, and the day of the month in which Gordon was born.
He also issued an order that the regiment which made the best
time to Dongola with least damage to boats, gear and cargo,
would have a front place in the further movement south, and
would also receive a price of £100. Such an order, issued when
he was a young man, would, he said, 'have made every nerve in
my body tingle, and have sent the blood pounding through my
veins, until I should have longed to have gone forth and fought
the Mahdi by myself'. This order had a different and unexpected
result, in the form of a sharp rebuke from the Queen, who thought
that the offer of a money reward was very much out of place, and
told him that British soldiers did not have to be bribed to do their
duty.

Wady Halfa. Thomas Cook's office

Wady Halfa: the Hospital, with a group of doctors outside

Wolseley (*centre*) with members of his staff. Beresford is also seated, wearing the sailor's cap

CHAPTER SIX

KHARTOUM: AUGUST–NOVEMBER

THE most intelligent of Gordon's native soldiers was Mohammed Ali, who had led the attack on Abu Girgeh in July. This was followed by another attack on August 12, when a force of 600 men in steamers went up the Blue Nile to Gereif. They opened fire on the Mahdi's fort, and a land force of similar size came out of the Messalamieh Gate and attacked Gereif in rear. The operation was highly successful. Abu Girgeh was wounded, the fort he had built was razed to the ground, and 1,000 rifles and a considerable store of dhurra was taken. A few days later Mohammed Ali took six steamers much farther up the Blue Nile, this time as far as Abu Haraz, the trading centre for the Eastern Sudan and Abyssinia. The dervishes were driven out, and quantities of coffee, sesame and dhurra were brought back to Khartoum. Two of the steamers went up as far as Sennar, which they found to be invested but still holding out. These victories restored confidence in Gordon. By the latter part of August many inhabitants had returned to neighbouring villages, cows, sheep, grain and butter were coming freely into Khartoum, and a market had even been opened at Halfiyeh.[1] It was possible for somebody of Gordon's temperament to believe that he would be able to drive off the Mahdi unaided, although even if he did so he was still left with the problem of creating a stable Government.

It was decided at a meeting of his principal officers that a force should be sent down river to retake Berber, but that before this operation they should destroy a dervish force that had gathered

[1] *Sudan Notes and Records*, 1930.

at El Eilafun, a village about six hours' distant from the town, on the banks of the Blue Nile. Mohammed Ali was again in command, and within two days he had captured the place, together with a good deal of oil, grain and coffee, which he sent back to Khartoum by one of the steamers. The dervishes had been driven inland, and he followed them, eager for glory or for plunder. Following the directions of a pretended deserter from the Mahdi, he formed up his men in square in the British fashion, and took them into a forest where they were surrounded and hopelessly trapped. In the ensuing fight Mohammed Ali and almost the whole of the force of 800 men he had taken with him were killed, and the remnant who escaped fled back into Khartoum, causing consternation among the inhabitants. Order was not restored until Gordon, who was himself in tears when he heard the news, issued an order that anybody found disturbing the peace would be driven beyond the defences and would lose his house and property.

The blow was heavy, and as it proved fatal. Gordon's position was such that he could not afford a reverse of any kind, and in this defeat he had lost most of his best soldiers, nearly 1,000 rifles, and 75,000 rounds of ammunition. Not until the last desperate days of the siege did he again undertake offensive action, and the effect on the people of Khartoum was profound. 'The natives who had lately given up Mahdiism now returned to the dervishes, the market at Halfiyeh was soon deserted, all trade ceased, and the town again fell under a state of siege.'[1] The Sheik El Obeid, who had won the victory, sent messages to neighbouring tribes to tell them of it, Abu Girgeh hurried back towards Khartoum reinforced by some Krupp and mountain guns as well as by soldiers, the Mahdi himself stirred and sent reinforcements. It was after this defeat that, on September 10, Gordon sent Stewart and his companions down the Nile in the *Abbas*.

Gordon himself never gave up hope. His attitude towards apparently hopeless situations had been well expressed years before, when he had entered a camp of 7,000 men knowing that he would be made prisoner: 'People may say, You tempt your

[1] *Sudan Notes and Records*, 1930.

God in putting yourself into positions like my present one, yet I do not care. I do *not* do it to *tempt* Him. I do so because I wish to trust in His promises.'[1] He could understand, however, that men less buoyantly sustained might be dismayed, and according to his Journal, Stewart, Power, and the French Consul Herbin, all felt that the position was now hopeless. 'These three men's ideas were that it would be shabby to leave me', but Gordon said that although he could not and would not go himself, they could do no possible good by being made prisoners. Stewart wanted Gordon to order him to go, but Gordon refused to do more than say in a letter that Stewart would perform a great service in going and could do no good by staying in Khartoum. So the last Englishmen steamed away, leaving Gordon alone by his own wish. With Stewart went his own Journal, which had been meticulously kept, and the cipher books, which were sent because Gordon looked upon the descent of the *Abbas* as safe and the fate of Khartoum as uncertain. The move was maladroit, because it left him with no means of deciphering any telegrams, like the one that arrived early in November from Wolseley.

Two of the other steamers, the *Mansurah* and the *Safieh*, went with the *Abbas* past the danger points of Shendi and Berber. They did not pass unmolested. At Shendi there was sporadic rifle fire, and a little later they successfully fought a small pitched battle. After the convoy had passed Berber, Stewart sent the other steamers back and continued north, towing four small boats. When he reached the country of the Monassir tribe he was pursued by a steamship under Mahdiist command. He had to leave or cut adrift the boats he was towing, the occupants of which were caught and killed, and at the Wadi el Homar cataract the *Abbas*, which was going at full speed because of the pursuit, struck a rock and could not be got off. Stewart, Power and Herbin, together with a number of Greek merchants who were aboard, accepted the offered hospitality of the Sheik of the district. They landed, went to his house, and there were all killed.[2]

[1] Barnes and Brown, p. 61.
[2] *Sudan Notes and Records*, 1930. Other versions differ in small details.

Gordon heard the first rumour of this tragedy on October 14, but did not believe it. He had begun his own Journal on the day that Stewart left, and at first simply noted a report of Stewart's capture with the remark that 'it *would be dismal*'. It was not until early November that he finally credited the news, and then his comments are characteristic. He was much concerned by the problem of whether or not he was to blame, '*If Abbas was captured by treachery, then I am not to blame; neither am I to blame if she struck a rock*, for she drew under two feet of water . . . *if they were attacked and overpowered, then I am to blame*, for I ought to have foreseen the chance, and prevented their going.' As for their actual deaths, 'it is very sad, but being ordained, we must not murmur.' Stewart was a man who never thought of danger, 'he was not a bit suspicious (while I am made up of it)'. And what did he feel about them? His obituaries were not sentimental. 'Stewart was a brave, just, upright gentleman. Can one say more? Power was a chivalrous, brave, honest gentleman. Can one say more?'

For events in Khartoum between September and December, Gordon's voluminous Journal must inevitably be our main source. It is an extraordinary document which reflects his rapid and rambling mind, his ingenuity, his humour, his impatience, his inclination to refer every abstract problem back to God. Small sketches and cartoons illustrate many of the pages. The impression that comes through from it most strongly is that such a place and such conditions brought out Gordon's most remarkable qualities, his endless energy and optimism, his continued interest in many aspects of life unconcerned with the siege. In September he was still busying himself with the two hundred children being taught in school:

> Each boy has a wooden board, on which his lesson is written, and on using it the object of each boy is to be called out to read his lesson, which they do with a swaying motion of body, and in a sing-song way, like the Jews do at their wailing place at Jerusalem. . . . Little black doves with no pretension to any nose, and not more than two feet high, push forward to say the first ten letters of the alphabet, which is all they know.

He visited the hospital and made a sketch of the heart of a man who had lived eleven days with a ball lodged in the wall of the ventricle. 'The doctor has this heart in spirits.' He noted the wonderful cleanliness of the Negro soldiers, compared with the fellaheen and Turks, and listed his order of preference among coloured peoples: 'I like the Chinese first, then the pig-faced blacks, then the chocolate Sudan people. I do not like the tallow-faced fellaheen, though I feel sorry for them.' The deserters who came in from the Mahdi—and in spite of the desperate position there were still a good many of them—all paid him a visit, at which they were given a dollar, shown their faces in a glass, and asked if they approved of what they saw. 'It stands to reason that in countries where there are no mirrors, every one must be a complete stranger to himself, and would need an introduction.'

On some days he wrote no more than a couple of lines in the Journal, on others he filled several pages. His views fluctuated wildly, even after the defeat of El Eilafun, but even when most gloomy he never lost the concern for practical details which helped to make the defence so successful. On September 10 he noted that the matches used for the mines were finished, and that they would have to go back to powder hose and link the mines in groups of ten. A few days later he devised an improvement on this. 'When self-acting mines are placed, it is as well to connect them with twine to facilitate taking them up.' He kept a close and careful eye on the ammunition. On September 23 he worked out the number of cartridges used during the siege—more than 3 million for Remingtons, nearly 10,000 mountain-gun cartridges, and 1,570 for Krupp guns. They still had left more than 2 million cartridges for Remingtons (and the arsenal was making more than 50,000 a week), more than 8,000 for mountain guns, and 660 for the Krupps. Things were far from desperate, and it was said that the Arabs outside had little food and were in a bad state. But these cheerful remarks succeeded a paper argument with himself about whether he would be justified in coming to an arrangement with the Mahdi by which all refugees went free while warlike stores were handed over (he decided that he would not give up the town), and another argument about whether he should blow up himself with the palace or be taken prisoner (he elected for being taken prisoner, because to blow himself up would have 'more or less the taint of suicide' and would be 'taking things out of God's hands'). To take things out of God's hands was for him almost the worst course a man could take, and he would have no dealings with apostates who had saved their lives by accepting Mohammedanism. So when Cuzzi, his agent in Berber, came to the lines Gordon refused to see him, because Cuzzi had become a Mohammedan and adopted dervish dress. So also when in October he received a letter from Slatin, who had surrendered to the Mahdi and was alternately said to be the Mahdi's confidant and to be living in chains, telling him of Stewart's death and protesting that he had fought twenty-seven times against the enemy and had 'done nothing dishonourable, nothing which should hinder your Excellency from writing me an answer', Gordon commented that he had nothing to say in response to the letters and could not understand why they were written. He rejected Slatin's idea of coming to Khartoum, because 'his doing so would be the breaking of his parole, which should be as sacred when given to the Mahdi as to any other power'. Gordon's curiosity about the Mahdi was mixed with contempt for him, and he eagerly absorbed the discreditable stories he heard. How could he surrender to a man who, it was said, put pepper under his nails so that in the presence of visitors he could touch his eyes and weep? And in any case, he assured himself in this continuous dialogue, he could make his own retreat at any moment if he wished. He observed as late as September 10 that he was as safe in Khartoum as in a London drawing-room, and that there was no need to send out an expedition to relieve *him*.

The insistence that he showed on this point, and the importance it assumed for him, shows the difficulty that any Government must have found in dealing with a man who was as great a word-chopper as Gladstone. When he understood, from letters and papers which came in, that the object of the expedition was to relieve him, he was furious:

> I altogether *decline* the imputation that the projected expedition has come to *relieve me*. It has *come to SAVE OUR NATIONAL HONOUR*. . . .

I was relief expedition No. 1. They are relief expedition No. 2. As for myself
I could make good my retreat at any moment if I wished . . . we the *first*
and *second* expeditions are equally engaged for the honour of England.
I am not the *rescued lamb*, and I will not be.

Much of the Journal for the next month is in the same vein,
and Wolseley was right to wonder whether he might have
trouble with Gordon. A secondary theme of the Journal during
September and October was indignation against Baring and
Egerton. The length of time that it took messages to reach
Khartoum meant that they often referred to an out-of-date
situation, and the way in which the messages were put also
caused misunderstanding. So when a letter arrived from Kitchener, sent from Debbeh on August 31 and received by Gordon
on September 22, in which he passed on a request from Egerton
'to be informed through Dongola exactly when he expects to be
in difficulties as to provision and ammunition', the phrasing
provoked Gordon to an ecstasy of irony:

> I am sure I should like that fellow Egerton. There is a light-hearted
> jocularity about his communications, and I should think the cares of life
> sat easily on him. . . . I really think if Egerton was to turn over the 'archives'
> (a delicious word) of his office, he would see we had been in difficulties for
> provisions for some months. It is as if a man on the bank, having seen his
> friend in the river already bobbed down two or three times, hails, 'I say,
> old fellow, let us know when we are to throw you the life buoy, I know
> you have bobbed down two or three times, but it is a pity to throw you
> the life buoy until you are really *in extremis.*'

Baring, Egerton, Kitchener, he attacked them all for their
caution, their feebleness, their failure to get messengers through
to him: unjustly, for Baring had urged his cause by all means
short of resignation, Egerton was no more than the Government's mouthpiece, and Kitchener had showed as much resource
in sending messages as Gordon himself.

The first parts of the Journal were addressed to Colonel
Stewart. After Gordon had become convinced of Stewart's
death they were addressed to the Chief of Staff of the Expeditionary Force. The occasional intemperance of phrase and feeling
to be found in it are less remarkable than the practical common

sense shining continually behind them. The lonely man who spent so much time on the roof of the palace with his telescope, and who sat down to dinner with a fat mouse occupying Stewart's place, never for a moment let his dreams, his fantasies, his hatred of English formality and officialdom ('I dwell on the joy of never seeing Great Britain again, with its horrid, wearisome *dinner* parties. . . . I would sooner live like a dervish with the Mahdi than go out to dinner every night in London'), distract him from maintaining the defences efficiently, and keeping up the spirit of the people. A salute of 101 guns heralded the arrival of the mail which brought news that an expedition was on the way, houses were hired and furnished to receive the English officers when they arrived, and three steamers were sent down to Shendi to await the English troops.[1] All this was done very prematurely, before the end of September, and the hopes raised in the Khartoumese by the preparations were rapidly dissipated. A new boiler was made for the little steamer *Husseinyeh*, a small lion was put on it as figurehead, and in mid-October it made a trip up the White Nile. As the net round the town was drawn closer and guns were brought up, the steamers became more vulnerable. On November 8 the Arabs crossed the White Nile. Gordon ordered up the two steamers left in the town, the *Ismailia* and the *Husseinyeh*, and said confidently that they would drive out the Arabs, but the *Ismailia* was struck by a shell and the *Husseinyeh* ran aground, was also struck, and then subjected to a merciless fire. Gordon paid a visit to the steamer himself and found that all the officers in charge at this point, close to the junction of the Blue and White Niles, had gone home to bed. He thought that it would be possible to get the boat off, but in fact did not try to do so, and on November 24 she sank.

In October Gordon learned that the Sheik El Obeid had been told to capture Halfiyeh, and decided to evacuate the village. The houses were pulled down and the wood brought back to Khartoum. The Arabs did not occupy the place immediately, but its abandonment meant a further restriction of the defence. Fortifications were built by the Arabs at Khojali, on the east

[1] *Sudan Notes and Records*, 1930.

bank of the Blue Nile, and one of the recently-arrived guns was put in position to fire at the town. Guns and rifles were also brought into play from Gereif, and for some days Khartoum was subjected to almost continuous fire. Its effect was slight. On November 8 Gordon reckoned that the Arabs had fired 30,000 rounds, killing one man and wounding three. A week later there were only fifty-four wounded men in hospital. At this time the arsenal was still turning out 40,000 cartridges a week, and although were now only 541 rounds of Krupp ammunition left (November 22), there was no sign of any attempt to storm the town. The Mahdi had set out from Rahad for Khartoum on August 8, after Ramadan, but his progress was leisurely. His followers moved in three columns by separate routes, not for any military reason but because the cattle-owning tribes used a route well supplied with water, while many of the rest walked the whole way through pathless districts. It was less an army than a religious pilgrimage, the men being accompanied by their families and baggage. Their total number was estimated by Father Ohrwalder, who went with them as a captive, at 200,000. On October 23 the Mahdi settled his camp near Omdurman, and wrote to Gordon telling him of Stewart's death and summoning him to submit. The papers and documents found on board the *Abbas* had been sent to the Mahdi, and from the Arabic letters and reports he obtained a clear idea of the shortage of supplies in the town. He sent some of these documents to Gordon with his letter, and they left no doubt that Stewart had in fact been killed and the *Abbas* captured. Gordon returned a defiant reply:

> Whether he has captured twenty thousand steamers like the *Abbas*, or twenty thousand like Stewart Pasha, it is all one to me. I am here, like iron, and hope to see the newly-arrived English. . . . It is impossible for me to have any more words with Mohammed Ahmed, only lead.

The Mahdi was no general, but his arrival gave fresh impetus to the siege, and led directly to the first determined offensive move by the besiegers, an attempt to capture the fort of Omdurman. On November 12 the Arabs tried to explode the fort's protecting mines by driving cows on to them, but this device was frustrated by the firing of rockets which frightened the cows. The *Ismailia*, now the sole river defender of the fort, was hit by three shells and lost one man killed and fifteen wounded. When at last the attack ceased, Gordon wrote: 'I have lived *years* in these last *hours*! Had I lost the *Ismailia*, I should have lost the *Husseinyeh* (aground), and then Omdurman and the North Fort. And then the Town!' The *Husseinyeh* was eventually lost, as has been said, but the attack on Omdurman was not renewed.

In late October the shortage of food became serious, and thereafter many people went hungry. On October 24 Gordon noted in the Journal, 'If they do not come before 30th November the game is up, and Rule Britannia.' Three days later a black Bashi-Bazouk complained of the inadequacy of his pay and rations. "Go to Sheik El Obeid', Gordon told him, and remarked that he 'did not care a bit now', because they must be relieved by the end of November. On November 11 he discovered with indignation that thirty of the merchants had been systematically robbing the stores. There was biscuit left only for a month or so in the town, and for about six weeks at Omdurman. Nor was this all. A few days later he learned that one of his most trusted clerks had been stealing. There was nobody, in fact, who could be trusted and even now, when those left in the town knew that if it fell they might be killed, several of his staff failed to report, saying that it was unreasonable to expect them to work on a Friday. What could be done with such people? He sold 90,000 lbs. of biscuit to the townspeople and gave 6,000 lbs. to the poor, resigning himself to the thought that probably half of it would be stolen.

Apart from his anxiety about Omdurman, the military situation seemed to him upon the whole a little less serious. He made a drawing showing five Arab camps within a few miles of Khartoum, numbering something like 20,000 soldiers with nearly twenty guns, but he thought optimistically that there were really no more than 4,000 fighting men and 800 horsemen among them. As happened with him very often, cheerfulness broke in upon despair. If the Expedition arrived with instructions for immediate evacuation, he decided to resign immediately. 'PERSONALLY, looking at the matter from a VERY SELFISH POINT OF VIEW, I should be much relieved at this denouement, for I should be in Brussels on 20th January.'

CHAPTER SEVEN

CONCENTRATING AT KORTI: DECEMBER

WOLSELEY left Dongola on December 13, and arrived at Korti three days later. Sir Herbert Stewart, who had been appointed Brigadier-General, reached there on the same day with the Guards and Mounted Infantry Camel Regiments. An outbreak of smallpox at Dongola had caused Stewart's removal from the camp, and he wrote to Wolseley from Shaba-dood, on the way to Korti, to say that they had their first case of smallpox. 'As the man belongs to a party of the Mounted Infantry that was in quarantine they think it is a remnant of Dongola—I am sending the man back in a small boat with two natives.' He said that they would go slowly to Korti because of Wolseley's anxiety not to overwork the camels. 'I am still thinking out the march (across the desert) you foreshadowed.'[1] The Royal Sussex were already at Korti, and on the 17th the South Staffords followed. They were the first troops, apart from half a company of Royal Engineers, to have come the whole way up from Gemai in whalers, and they had taken forty-one days to make the journey. The longest time, forty-nine days, was taken by two companies of the Duke of Cornwall's Light Infantry, and Wolseley's prize was won by the 1st Battalion of the Royal Irish, which left Sarras on December 17 after considerable experience of the river had been gained, and made the trip in thirty-seven days.

Korti was a pleasant place. The Headquarters camp had been laid out by Stewart in a grove of date and acacia trees against which the white tents showed up well. 'A narrow mall ran along the top of the river bank and was the common line of communica-

[1] Hove.

tion between the staff tents. From it several rough ramps were made to the water's edge, which was crowded with boats of various sizes.'[1] One of Wolseley's staff called it the nicest place they had pitched their tents in yet. The Commander-in-Chief planned to accompany the dash across the desert himself in the middle of January, 'If I see any chance of being able to do so with men on camels.'[2] In the meantime he urged the progress of the troops up the river, engaged in protracted and unsatisfactory negotiations with local chiefs about the supply of camels, and regularly entertained two guests to dinner each night in the wigwam of straw and reeds which had been constructed to serve as a mess hut. Often they were newly-arrived officers, and a sample menu was 'watery soup, chicken curry, roast mutton, some pumpkin as vegetable, sardines on toast, jam tart.'[3] Wolseley said that it described better than it ate. Like the men he had only two flannel shirts, and so did not wash them but hung them out to air in the desert. 'I have always found that after some time of living in a flannel shirt in a hot country there is a nasty bitter and sour *odour* about one's body unknown in a state of civilization', he remarked.[4]

During the last days of November and the first of December Butler was carrying out, with his invariable enthusiasm but without concern for the ruffled feelings of others, Wolseley's instructions to speed the whalers. With his old friend Prince at the helm, another Indian voyageur and six Kroomen in the boat, the full complement of which was made up by an Arab guide, a Syrian interpreter and his English servant, he sped up the river. He carried a store of supplies and tools for boats in trouble, and an endless stock of advice and criticism for their crews. He was far from satisfied by what he saw. He had been convinced all along that the Egyptian Army officers were deliberately delaying the whalers, and now he came to believe, perhaps as a result of his brush with Beresford at the Second Cataract, that the naval officers along

---

[1] Unpublished autobiography.
[2] Letters, 10.12.84.
[3] Ibid., 19.12.84.
[4] Ibid., 6.12.84.

the river were also not working as hard as they might have done. Butler knew himself to be an Irish outsider, and noted caustically that 'all the swells are passing up to Korti by camel, too precious to trust themselves in boats apparently'. Even the officers and men in the boats seemed to him late sleepers and starters. The breed of soldiers was falling off, he thought, their work was mechanically done.

> In its normal state it was lethargic; at its worst it was unwilling, careless, and even worse. Heart there was none in it. There was neither insolence nor refusal, no positive insubordination; simply a clogged, lethargic 'hands-down' attitude that was even more hopeless than the most insubordinate refusal.[1]

The skill of Butler's crews, the force of his example, and of course the fact that his boat was not loaded with tons of provisions, took his whaler, Number 387, past every boat on the river, including the leading party of Engineers. He reached the head of the Third Cataract, after which there were 230 miles of clear water, and it seemed to him that he must go on to Dongola, see Wolseley again, and explain to him the reason for the delays. The prime one, which seemed to him even more important than the slackness shown by officers and men, was the fact that the boats had been overloaded. To their agreed load of 100 days' rations had been added the same quantity of rations for the mounted troops, those swells going on camel back to Korti, making 120 days' rations in all. He thought, probably with justification, that the extra load had a major effect in slowing the boats, and that if it were taken off 'that long line of slow-moving hard-labouring little vessels will fly forward over this great stretch of rock-encumbered river'. He had sent telegrams forward to Dongola and back to Wady Halfa, and no doubt they were phrased in his usual picturesque language. At the head of the Third Cataract he was halted by a message to say that he should wait for a telegram from Wolseley. He waited for several hours and then set sail along the great open waterway in the direction of Dongola. After a few hours he saw at the end of a long river reach a white dot with a puff of smoke above it. The dot became a small steamer. It carried an

[1] Butler, *Autobiography*.

order, severely phrased, telling him to go back. 'It was decreed that I was not to pass beyond the head of the Third Cataract! I was not to see the commander-in-chief! I was to go back to Dal!'

Butler said afterwards that 'the telegraph had been at work from Wady Halfa to Dongola', and no doubt it had. He is not likely to have been sparing in criticism of either Buller or Wood, and he had ended by infuriating everybody, even his worshipped Wolseley. It was in vain that his pencil 'flew over the blank backs of some nine or ten large Egyptian telegraph forms', and that he handed this message to be given to Wolseley 'with the heaviest heart and saddest brain I had ever known in my life'.[1] Wolseley told his wife that he had sent Butler a letter ordering him to go back again down river where he could be of use in hurrying forward the boats, and, never slow to discern the conceit of others, he added that Butler was 'a vain man, extremely clever at finding fault, and pointing out how much better he would have done or managed any particular duty'.[2] The load on the boats was, however, reduced by 500 lbs.

For the next month Butler went up and down the cataracts, bustling lagging boats, leading them through rapids, and 'often taking a hand on the tug-line to shame some loitering boat's crew into better work'.[3] He composed a song to cheer them forward:

> Row, my boys, row away,
> Cowards behind may stay,
>   Bend to the strain, man!
> Miles, as they rise and sink,
> Knock off another link
>   From Gordon's chain, man!
>
> Rough though the rapids be,
> Wild as a winter's sea,
>   Row on again, man!
> Ours is a greater strength
> E'en than this river's length,
>   Row on again, man![4]

[1] Butler, Ibid.
[2] Letters, 1.12.84.
[3] Butler, *Autobiography*.
[4] Hove.

He may have been partly responsible for the improved system adopted in handling the voyageurs, by which instead of working the eighty-five miles of river between Gemai and Sarkamatto, a number of them were established at fixed points where the water was worst, and remained at them permanently. Under this new arrangement they got to know individual cataracts much better, and the time that had been lost when they came down river back to Gemai was cut out. In the second half of December movement of the boats was greatly speeded up. On December 22 Butler observed that they had passed forty-six boats over a cataract, and that the Gordon Highlanders had taken only seventeen days between the Second and Third Cataracts. 'That is what should be!' Probably he was more useful on this stretch of river than he could have been anywhere else, but he felt that he was 'the Moses of the expedition, not to enter the promised land'. He was disappointed when Stewart was made a Brigadier-General, commenting later to his wife that his own position on the staff was lower in Egypt than in Devonport. 'So much for what you thought "my sincere friends" would do for me in the way of "local rank".' It was not until Christmas Day that he received a telegram from Buller asking him to come 'as soon as can', and that he joyfully set off for Korti, which he reached on January 4, having typically made the quickest passage of any boat between Sarras and Korti, eighteen days. He would have been less cheerful had he known what was being written of him at about this time by Wolseley to his wife: 'He is becoming an impossible man for me. He has great natural ability, but no business habits. I like him, but I shall have to drop him off my list.'[1]

*

Slowly everything came to Korti, the whalers and Camel Corps, arms and stores and generals, Buller and Earle. Above Wolseley's quarters were those of the Intelligence, Transport and other departments, then in upward succession the camps of the Mounted Infantry, Camel Regiments, 19th Hussars, artillery, infantry regiments, hospitals, Sussex Regiment, and Commis-

[1] Letters, 24.12.84.

Staff officer in full
Sudan uniform

(*Graphic*)

we have to work.

Melton Prior,
Illustrated London News
correspondent,
under his fly net

(*Illustrated London News*)

Troops arriving at Jakdul wells (seen in foreground)

(Graphic)

sariat and Ordnance departments. The whalers were moved along the shore of the broad river, much clearer here than it had been farther north, so that at a pinch it could be drunk without previous filtering. At the rear of the camp camels and horses were picketed, watered at intervals by natives operating the wheels which groaningly sent streams through into aqueducts which served as troughs for the animals.

The swells of the Camel Corps spent their time in field days on camel back. The Mounted Infantry Camel Regiment had been inspected by Wolseley on their arrival, and ten men had fallen off when they passed him at a trot. He had not been pleased, and had issued new instructions about training, as well as causing indignation by saying that spurs must be removed. The Corps got their camel drill to a fair state of perfection. ('Regiments will form up mounted one camel's length from front to rear rank. Men fall in with advanced arms. ... The movements executed by Infantry in fours will be done by sections.') The manœuvres also included the exposure of the camels to noise, in the form of a charge made by the 19th Hussars and some firing done at them with blank cartridge and over them with ball. They did not flinch, and 'the general opinion was that they would stand charging niggers or anything else in creation'.[1] The exercises were carried out in the desert, about a mile from the river, where the ground was covered with variously-coloured pebbles, including agates, garnets, rubies, and even some small inferior diamonds. The Corps carried out stable duties three times a day, grooming the camels like horses, to the disgust of many who thought you might as well groom an Irish pig. 'The natives understand this, and, instead of cleaning him, and making him thus more susceptible to the heat of the sun, plaster him over with mud during the hot months, which keeps the sun and flies off during the day, and, maybe, protects him somewhat from the cold at night.'[2]

Many found life at Korti monotonous. Major Adye, one of the aides-de-camp, complained that he had little to do. Lord Airlie, of the 10th Hussars, used to spar with Captain Maxwell on most

[1] Gleichen, pp. 57–8
[1] Ibid., p. 60.

M

evenings, in front of Wolseley's tent.[2] Wolseley went on giving
his little dinner parties every night, and the newly-arrived Guards
officers came to them. Colonel McCalmont, still chafing under
his deprivation of authority over the Light Camel Corps, found
the Commander-in-Chief sympathetic, but he said that the
appointment had been made and could not be undone. Buller
also came to dinner in the mess. He had been complaining, before
he reached Korti on Christmas Eve, that he had not seen Wolseley
for two months except during his short visit to Wady Halfa, and
that he was 'absolutely ignorant of his information and his plans'.
He said that the proposed dash across the desert came as a surprise
to him, and that Wolseley 'has not here either the men, the camels,
or the food I should have liked to have had for the operation he
proposes'. He added that Wolseley seemed to have forgotten 'that
I was not in touch with his mind during the last two months, and
consequently that it was out of my power to follow his line of
thought'. These remarks are strange enough when it is remembered that the whole idea of a Camel Corps envisaged their use
in such circumstances, stranger still in view of the fact that Buller
himself had put forward a similar plan early in November. It is
likely that at this time Wolseley was far from satisfied with his
Chief of Staff, and in fact he wrote to his wife that next time he
held a field command he would appoint Brackenbury to that
position. 'He has far the longest head of any man out here, and
although he is not liked personally, I cannot help that.'[2] Buller
himself gave very much grander dinner parties than Wolseley's,
with seven courses and, of course, 'fizz ad lib'.

On Christmas Day there were no turkeys, but Christmas puddings were made, stuffed with dates and dosed with whisky, and
there was 'a ripping stump speech' from a trooper in the Blues.
There was also a concert with the usual comic and sentimental
songs, 'Oh, George, Don't Take a Liberty', 'The Lost Chord'
and 'Killarney' among them. The last item seems an odd choice.
It was 'Khartoum's Falling', sung by Surgeon Pratt of the Army
Medical Department. The cards sent home by the men were more

[1] Wolseley, Unpublished autobiography.
[2] Letters, 22.12.84.

cheerful. 'The Triumphal Return' showed Gordon and Wolseley, arm in arm, riding on a crocodile which pulled the Mahdi in a cage. In 'The Siege of Khartoum' oil, labelled, 'Bilin' 'Ot', was poured by Negroes inside the walls of the town on Negroes outside, while Gordon hooked up the Mahdi's clothes as he tried to escape on a penny-farthing bicycle.[1]

The collection of men and supplies increased every day, and on December 27 Wolseley issued movement instructions. These were on the lines that had for some time been foreseeable. The force was to be divided into a River Column and a Desert Column. The River Column was to be under the command of Earle who, in spite or perhaps because of Wood's view that he was fit only to be a sergeant major, had won Wolseley's good opinion. Brackenbury was to be his second in command, and the force was to consist of the Staffords, the Gordons, the Royal Highlanders, and the Duke of Cornwall's Light Infantry, together with one and a half squadrons of the 19th Hussars, a battery of Egyptian artillery, the Egyptian Camel Corps and 400 transport camels. The Hussars were later reduced to a single squadron, and Butler on his arrival at Korti was given command of them. This column was to work its way up the remaining cataracts, the problems of which had not been dealt with in Hammill's survey and were almost completely unknown, to punish the murderers of Colonel Stewart, capture Berber, and go on as far as Shendi, which it was reckoned to reach by March 10. There it would meet the Desert Column.

This was to be under the command of Herbert Stewart, and included the Camel Regiments, one and a half (later two) squadrons of the 19th Hussars, an artillery battery and part of the Royal Sussex. 'All the transport camels, not detailed for the water force, will accompany this force.' They would march across the desert, forming a post about eighty miles from Korti at Jakdul Wells, where the water supply was known to be adequate. The Sussex would garrison the wells and form a depot there with sixty days' supplies. The Camel Corps would then ride on to attack Metemmeh, and after that either go on up the river to Khartoum if

[1] Hove.

Gordon's boats were waiting for them, or bring more supplies and men from Jakdul Wells to Metemmeh or Shendi, thus leap-frogging forward the advanced post. A Naval Brigade under Beresford was to march with the Desert Column, and man the conjectural steamers at Metemmeh. Wolseley was stirred by the prospect of this romantic dash across the desert, and intended to go with the force. 'I hope to start myself with all the mounted troops on 7th January for Khartoum,' he told his wife. 'My spirits rise at the prospect and all the fighting instinct that is in me comes bubbling up, until at last I feel inclined to draw my sword and try its temper on the tent pole.'[1]

On December 30 there arrived a messenger from Gordon. He had passed examination by the Mahdi's troops successfully, bringing with him a letter no bigger than a postage stamp which the man had sewn into the hem of his clothing. This letter said simply, 'Khartoum all right. 14.12.84. C. G. Gordon.' Gordon's seal was on the back. He carried another letter which had escaped detection, concealed in the strands of the rope which formed the headstall of his camel.[2] This was for Wolseley himself, and its tone was ominous. It spoke of lack of grain and biscuit, no butter, no dates, little meat. 'We want you to come quickly. You should come by Metemmeh or Berber. Make by these two roads. Do not leave Berber in your rear. Keep enemy on your front, and when you take Berber, send me word from Berber. Do this without let-ing rumours of your approach spread abroad.' The messenger also said that fighting went on day and night, that the Mahdi was outside Khartoum, and that Wolseley should bring plenty of troops if he could.

Wolseley's reaction to these messages, with their evident urgency, seems at first only comprehensible on the assumption that, like the authorities in Cairo and London, he had come to believe that Gordon could hold out forever. He told Baring that since Gordon warned him not to leave Berber in his rear 'I must move by water and take it before I march upon Khartoum'. He

---

[1] Letters, 29.12.84.
[2] Hove, letter to Frances Wolseley, 12.1.85. Other accounts say that this was a verbal message, but Wolseley is quite specific that it was a letter.

would feel most confident of success if Khartoum could hold out until the River Column came up, which by his own reckoning would be the latter part of March. This extreme caution was to a certain extent contradicted by his intention to push forward the Desert Column quickly across to Metemmeh. From there 'I shall be able to communicate with Gordon by steamer, learn exact position, and, if he is *in extremis* before infantry arrive by river, to push forward by camel corps to help him at all hazards.' There is another possible explanation. The Government had consented to offensive operations with great relectance, and Wolseley may well have thought that, even at this last hour, they might flinch at the prospect of an operation that carried the risk of failure. Since he must have known that there was now no question of the River Column arriving in time to be of immediate help, and that pushing forward the Camel Corps 'at all hazards' must be a necessity his telegram would, on this second reading, have been designed to break the news of the impending dash across the desert and then up to Khartoum as gently as possible.

Whether excessive confidence in Gordon or a mild duplicity was responsible for this telegram, there was no hesitation about Wolseley's actions. On December 30, the day that Gordon's message arrived, Stewart left for Jakdul Wells.

PART THREE

THE FIGHTING

CHAPTER ONE

THE MARCHES TO JAKDUL WELLS

THE convoy that set out at 3 o'clock on the afternoon of December 30 was not the complete force that Wolseley had hoped to send across the desert, nor was it able to make the spectacular dash that he had originally in mind. It was not a complete force because some of the Heavy and Light Camel Regiments had not yet reached Korti, and it was not able to move directly across the whole 180 miles to Metemmeh because of the shortage of camels. To see how this shortage had arisen, it is necessary to look in more detail at the story of how the camels were bought and used.

At the time that the original order for 1,200 camels had been increased to 4,000, there seems to have been no idea that they would be difficult to buy, or that they would be anything but reliable. When the Camel Regiments reached Assuan, however, ready to begin their march along the bank of the Nile, it was realized that some of these heavy men would need exceptionally good and sturdy beasts to bear them for hundreds of miles and the purchasing officers, under the direction of General Grenfell, who was in command of the Egyptian troops on the Nile, offered £16 each for a hundred superior riding camels, compared with the £10 to £12 they were paying for ordinary animals. They were immediately flooded with offers of undersized and under-aged camels, which when rejected were hopefully brought forward again a few days later. Some of those originally turned down were eventually bought, either because there was nothing else available or because the purchasing officers were deceived. Many of the camels had already been

overmarched when they were bought, and needed rest before
they could work again. A hundred and fifty of them already
used in Graham's Suakin campaign arrived at the Remount
Department established at Assuan. These animals, who had then
been marched all the way from Cairo to Assuan, were found to
be in a hopeless state so far as any further marching was concerned, and some were sold while others were used locally.
Purchasing was not made easier by the contradictory orders
given by Buller to the Director of Transport, Colonel Furse.
Buller hought, sensibly enough, that it was foolish to buy
camels in or near Cairo for use in Lower Egypt and the Sudan,
since they would have to undertake long marches before being
used in action. At the end of September Furse was told not to
buy any more camels north of Assiut, a week later that he should
stop buying riding camels but continue to buy those used for
baggage, and early in November Buller told Furse that when
the last of the Camel Corps had left Assuan he should stop buying altogether north of that point, and that Sir Herbert Stewart
was making purchases in Dongola.[1]

Buller had ignored a warning in September from Kitchener
that riding camels were scarce in Debbeh. Now it was found
that they were scarce throughout Lower Egypt, and that an insufficient number of baggage animals had been bought. There
were many reasons for this. One was that the baggage camels
were asked to do much more than had been expected in carrying
supplies. At Sarras on December 6, for instance, there were 210
sets of whaler supplies which could not be taken in the already
heavily loaded whalers. Each set needed sixteen camels to carry
it. They were also often loaded with things that they were
totally unsuited to carry, planks of timber ten feet long, great
iron rods, rolls of matting ten feet long by three feet wide,
hospital stretchers, bundles of oars. They developed bad sores and
severe galls, but when Buller was told this he replied that while
they must do the best they could for the baggage animals, 'we
shall have to work them with sore backs or not'. He answered
in a similar spirit a protest made by Stewart in October about

[1] War Office Records.

overloading the riding camels. Stewart thought that anything more than 200 lbs.—that is, the weight of a heavy man—would be overloading them, and proposed that spare camels should be provided to carry equipment, like the tent and filled water skins, which brought the load up to double that. Buller agreed to strike out a few items, including the tent, but he insisted that the animals should be able to carry a weight of 400 lbs. thirty miles a day. He pointed out also that there were no spare drivers or saddles available. It was true that there was a great lack of camel drivers. Nearly 600 good men had been brought from Aden, but the demands of the expedition soon called for many times that number, and the local substitutes almost all turned out badly. Either, as Furse said, they did not know the front of a saddle from the back, or they refused to go south of Wady Halfa. Men were brought from Cairo and paid the high rate of three shillings a day, with the result that local drivers stopped work because they were receiving less than this. Many drivers were imperturbably inefficient. To quote Furse again:

> No amount of punishment could make them comply with an order. How many hundreds of times were they told that riding on a loaded camel was interdicted; that the camels were to be tied in batches of 3, not in lines of 10 or 20. It was no good.[1]

When these men refused to go on from Wady Halfa their places had to be taken by natives who had been engaged in portage and hauling. Many of them professed to be camel drivers by occupation, but they proved to be nothing of the kind. There were many old men and boys among them, and when complaint was made of this it was said that naturally the robust men were at home with their wives.

There was another reason for Buller's refusal to buy many camels north of Wady Halfa. He had become convinced that the Arabs would sell only their worst animals, and that the best prospect of getting an efficient transport column was to hire camels, together with drivers. In this he proved only partly right. The Arabs were prepared to hire camels and to provide drivers,

---

[1] War Office Records.

but only at an exorbitant cost. They asked for and obtained £2 10s. for the convoy journey from Korti to Jakdul Wells, so that if three or four journeys had to be made the purchase price of a camel would be quickly earned. The drivers loaded their own camels with a speed and skill which reinforced Furse's observation that there was an immense difference between the time taken by good and bad drivers in loading, and in the subsequent number of readjustments needed. These owner-drivers did their best to find bags to put on their animals, rather than the tin boxes in which many of the supplies were carried, which were likely to cause sores. 'The craftiest Arabs have seized the bags, and there has been a terrible hullaballoo going on all the time, and a free fight for the pleasantest loads', Buller remarked. Even hiring at this high price did not provide anything like enough camels, and a great many had to be taken from the line of communications and sent to Korti. By an unhappy error on Furse's part, they were accompanied by the 3rd Company of the Transport Corps which had been recently formed, had particularly bad drivers, and was officered by men who knew nothing about transport work.

Wolseley tried hard but unsuccessfully to induce the sheiks of neighbouring tribes to sell him camels after he arrived in Korti. He said years afterwards that he had been led to expect that the Kababish and other tribes would furnish 'many thousands of camels',[1] but this was special pleading after the event. However the responsibility is distributed (and Buller must certainly bear the greatest part of it) the Desert Column was short of camels right from the start. This first convoy numbered 1,100 soldiers, with more than 200 natives, and they had just over 2,200 camels. Of this number 600 were taken up by the Commissariat and Transport, and another 200 by the Artillery and Engineers. 'They have taken away every spare camel we have, and there is only just one per man', said Marling. 'We take seven days' ration for men and five days for the camels, all of which we carry on our own camels.'[2] Each man's luggage was limited to 40 lbs., which

[1] Unpublished autobiography.
[2] Marling, p. 128.

included a change of tunic, spare boots and shirt, a sponge, towel, soap and pair of socks. The few spare camels carried odds and ends like cooking-pots and mess cans. This lack of camels played a large part in dictating Wolseley's orders to Stewart. He was to march the ninety-odd miles to Jakdul Wells, form a post there, and then return with the camels to Korti, to take back more men and supplies. The force would not start on the further journey to Metemmeh until the second convoy had arrived at Jakdul. This time-wasting procedure was made necessary by the need to bring the camels back to Korti.

Stewart was a cool man, able to absent himself at will from his general preoccupation with the march. One of his interests was in redesigning and modernizing houses (some of which he was buying on Wolseley's behalf), and after the home mail had come in to Korti one of the war correspondents was astonished to find him occupied with plans which had just reached him for installing new-fangled electric light in some houses in Sloane Street. His preparations for the march, however, were meticulous. Commanding officers were told to make sure that water skins and bottles did not leak, and to insist that no water must be drunk without a brigade order. All the camels were to be watered two hours before the march began, and loading was done with particular care in the attempt to avoid stops for readjustment. Watches were synchronized. After marching past Wolseley the column set off, led by an advance guard of the 19th Hussars, the only men mounted on horses. A distance of about thirty yards was kept between the various units. Stewart rode in the midst of them, his tall figure topped by a shining Guards' helmet with a distinctive puggaree of orange silk. Although no enemy attack was expected, the men were told to be ready for it. 'I don't like unnecessary slaughter, but I'm afraid we shall have to kill five hundred or so of the poor devils before we can establish ourselves in Metemmeh,' Stewart said. Half a dozen local men had been forced to act as guides, by the threat that if they did not come willingly they would be taken lashed to camels. They trotted in front, accompanied by some of the Hussars, who had orders to shoot them if they tried to bolt.

The track was easy, the weather fine, and Stewart knew the urgency of his mission. His devotion to Wolseley was complete, and he intended to act on the Commander-in-Chief's general advice that desert marches should be carried out by night if there was a moon. They halted at 5 o'clock for tea, started again two hours later, and marched until the following morning. The moon cast a beautiful white light on the scene. Gleichen, who was ahead of the column charged with making a road report and sketches, at first found it pleasant to march through the moonlit desert, but as the hours passed and the laughter of the men faded to silence, he became desperately sleepy and 'beastly cold, altogether not in a fit state for surveying'. Occasional bugle notes from the rear announced that baggage camels were falling behind, and then the column stopped until they came up. Sometimes the halt lasted a quarter of an hour, and at these points Gleichen noted the time, slipped off his camel, and slept until the advance sounded. He reckoned the rate of march as $2\frac{3}{4}$ miles an hour, and found that this measurement proved to be wonderfully accurate. A halt was called in the early morning, breakfast was eaten, a pint of water served out to each man, sentries were posted, and the column slept. They were wakened by the heat of the sun and by the insects, which were plentiful, but mercifully excluded mosquitoes and flies. At 3 o'clock in the afternoon they started to march again. They had covered 34 miles.

This was the pattern of the march. It was uneventful, but tiring. Stewart enforced a strict water ration of two pints a day, one at breakfast and the other at dinner. The wells of Hambok and El Howeiya, reached on the way, were found to be little more than funnel-shaped holes in the grass, filled with a little muddy fluid. When a few bucketfuls had been taken for the horses, the wells were dry. The only sign of the enemy was when a party of Mounted Infantry, scouting round the track leading to Abu Halfa wells, found some men in the Mahdiist 'uniform' of long white dress covered with scraps of red and blue cloth and coloured straw skull-cap. They took several prisoners, some of whom took off their uniforms and spat on them. The column reached Jakdul early in the morning of January 2, after a three-days' march. The approach to the wells was strewn with large round stones, on which the camels slithered about dangerously. Many men dismounted, and led their camels through the narrow rock pass into a tiny plain with a great wall of rock beyond it. Within this rock were three great wells, one below the other. The thirsty men marvelled at their depth and beauty:

> Eighty feet above my head towered an overhanging precipice of black rock; behind me rose another of the same height; at the foot of the one in front lay a beautiful, large ice-green pool, deepening into black as I looked into its transparent depths. Scarlet dragon-flies flitted about in the shade; rocks covered with dark-green weed looked out of the water; the air was cool almost to coldness. . . . I drank as much of the water as I could conveniently hold, filled my water-bottle as a specimen for the thirsty souls below, and went to the lower end of this beautiful pool, where a similar channel connected it with the lowest of all. I climbed into it, and found myself overlooking the large pool about twelve feet below, where rows of horses and camels were drinking at the far end.[1]

The water in the lowest pool was fit only for animals, but pumps and hose had been brought, which pumped drinking water out of the middle pool into biscuit tins for the men, and out of the lower pool into canvas troughs for the camels. Watering them, and unloading the stores, took most of the day, and in the evening Stewart began the march back to Korti. He left at Jakdul the whole of the Guards Camel Regiment and two dozen engineers, rather more than a third of the force. A few sick camels, and a few horses, were also left with the garrison. The Guards reckoned that it would be ten days before Stewart returned with the rest of the column, and although he had said that the position was practically impregnable, they improved it. They constructed two forts, built from the loose stones lying around and from others levered out of the rock with pickaxes and crowbars, made paths, laid out ground among the rocks for a camping place, and put up signboards. Kitchener, who had come out to represent the Intelligence Department, went out riding with the horses, scattered a caravan taking dates and stores

---

[1] Gleichen, p. 88.

to the Mahdi, and took a few prisoners. He could get no information about any Arab force lying between Jakdul and Metemmeh, or Shendi on the opposite bank where it was said that Gordon's steamers were waiting.

For Stewart's returning force the march back was not quite a repetition of the one they had already made. The baggage camels, of course, were now unladen, so that this was an easier journey for them. For the men it was more difficult, because there were now many more camels than men, so that they had to ride their own camels and lead two or three others. They got back as quickly as they had gone, making brief stops for rest and sleep. 'We lie out every night, just like animals, in the open. The only preparation we made was to scratch a hole in the sand to fit one's hip and thigh into.'[1] On the afternoon of January 5 they reached Korti again, to be welcomed by Wolseley with the words that they were the finest men he had ever seen, and that they could march from one end of Africa to the other. They had eaten almost all their rations, and the camels had nothing left at all. Marling was invited to dine with Buller, had 'a good tub and such a feed', and after the feed 'such a sleep, the first for seven days'.

Wolseley's hope of going into the desert himself had been frustrated by a telegram from Hartington deprecating his exposing himself in the field and expressing a wish to keep in touch with him at Korti, but his disappointment was lessened by the fact that any serious fighting now seemed unlikely. Part of the force was now more than half-way to the Nile. Surely they would have little difficulty in going the last seventy-odd miles? He asked his wife to buy for him 'wholesale in the City', 6,000 wooden pipes for the men who relieved Khartoum. 'They are all badly off for pipes, and I don't think I could give them from myself a more acceptable present.'[2] With success apparently near at hand he took a kinder view of a suggestion made by Hartington, after the arrival on December 30 of Gordon's 'Khartoum all right' message, that a considerable force should be sent to Suakin, to co-operate with him and to prevent any attack by

[1] Marling, p. 129.
[2] Letters, 4.1.85.

Osman Digna on the River Column. He had at first dismissed the suggestion out of hand, but now, although he called it an unnecessary and expensive luxury, he added that 'if you could afford it, the result would be of advantage from a political point of view, provided the force at once attacked and crushed Osman Digna'. He ended his telegram with a characteristic flourish: 'Please send me 2,000 strong, thick, white umbrellas at once, packed in strong bales bound with iron, each bale to weigh about 70 lb. I shall want them going to Suakin.' He wrote to his wife delightedly that he had said, 'Don't want 2,000 troops but would like 2,000 umbrellas.' Men were still reaching Korti every day for either the River or the Desert Columns, the long-term and short-term projects. On January 7 a convoy of 1,000 camels accompanied by three sections of the Light Camel Regiment left for Jakdul under the command of Colonel Stanley Clarke, and on the following day Stewart started out again with the rest of his force, some 1,500 men and over 2,000 camels. These camels, of course, included those who had already made the journey to and from the Wells. The condition of many of the transport camels, Veterinary-Surgeon Bennett said, was painful to behold. Twelve had been shot and forty-three abandoned in the desert, and of the rest 'many showed frightful wounds, not simply sores, but open raw places bigger than the palm of the hand'.[1]

Clarke was an inefficient officer. 'He is useless and a failure', Wolseley said, adding that 'he came to get a medal'.[2] He left two hours late, formed up his column in a hollow instead of on the plateau, and allowed the camels to straggle. He made no attempt to ration his men's water supply, nor to take care of the large iron tanks which were designed for a spare supply in case of emergencies. When his force reached El Howeiyat it was found that many of the water tanks were empty through careless hand-ling, and that the men had drunk all that was in their water skins. After they left El Howeiyat the situation worsened, with the Egyptian camel drivers stealing water and selling it for a dollar

[1] War Office Records.
[2] Letters, 15.1.85.

N

a bottle, and before reaching Jakdul Clarke had actually to ask the garrison to send out some water to him. Some two dozen of his camels had died on the way, and the rest of them arrived in wretched condition and badly in need of rest.

Stewart reached Jakdul very soon after Clarke, although he had started a day later. The journey had not been a comfortable one, and had to be taken more easily than the previous marches, for there was little dhurra left for the camels and stops had to be made to allow them to graze, or for the men to cut grass with which to feed them. Even so, their condition was alarming. On the day that they set out some of them had 'holes you can put your fist into', and three days later they were 'breaking down in all directions, and the native drivers falling down and shriek-ing for water'.[1] There was confusion and anger when the wells at El Howeiyat were found to have been left completely dry by Clarke, and they had to make another full day's march to Abu Halfa and open new holes to get water. Stewart, however, kept firm order. Officers and men were marched up and received a pint of water each, and later drew more for cooking. A stream of men going down to get water was kept up the whole night. Sir Charles Wilson, who accompanied Stewart, was critical both of the night marches and the treatment of camels, saying that much longer halts were necessary to keep the column together in the dark, that damage was done to the camels by marching them in close order on rough ground, and that they should have been allowed to graze on the plentiful savas grass in the desert and should not have been tightly tied together at night. (The arguments against him were that night marches were far less tiring, and that an immense amount of time would have been lost by permitting the camels to graze freely.) 'It would be heresy to say the camelry is a mistake, but if Tommy Atkins cannot march in such a climate as this, we had better give up fighting.'[2] The remark was made by a man who had not pre-viously seen active service.

The chief cause of the heavy losses in camels, Bennett said

---

[1] Marling, p. 130.
[2] Wilson, p. 11.

afterwards, was that marches of moderate length and slow progress, with plenty of rests after some days' marching, were indispensable for them. Next to this was the ignorance and, at times, callousness, with which they were treated. Nobody knew very much about such diseases as mange in camels and treatment with sheep dip, perhaps not surprisingly, proved ineffective. In some cases camels regarded as incurably sick were given treatment by natives and in a few days were miraculously restored to health. The men's attitude towards them was sometimes barbarous:

> One day I was talking to Charlie Beresford during a halt on the march. His bosun came up and reported to him, 'I've caulked all them sick camel seams, sir.' I said, 'What on earth does he mean?' 'Oh,' he said, 'he's been stuffing oakum and tar into the camels' sore backs.'[1]

Beresford was in command of the Naval Brigade. He had not reached Korti until January 5 because a telegram sent to him had been delayed in transmission. He found many of his men covered with black pustules caused by fly bites, but otherwise 'fit and well and all a-taunto', and began with his usual enthusiasm to gather such spares for the steamers as boiler-plates and rivets. Buller at first refused to let him have these stores, but was finally persuaded to do so after making a peculiarly Bullerian joke. 'What do you want boiler-plates for?' he asked. 'Are you going to mend the camels with them?'[2]

A couple of days after Stewart had left, a supply of dhurra reached Korti, and Burnaby was sent on with it to join the column. Wolseley had not forgotten the man who represented one of the kinds of soldier he most admired. On January 13 Burnaby rode into Jakdul with his 125 camels, asking at once: 'Am I in time for the fighting?' The detachment of the Blues cheered as they saw his huge figure approach the lines. The whole of the 13th had been spent in watering the camels, filling spare water tanks, and organizing the convoy for the march to Metemmeh. Clarke was to return with nearly 500 camels to Korti, and the shortage of them was becoming acute. Stewart

[1] Marling, p. 131.
[2] Beresford, i. 252.

had just under 3,000, of which more than a thousand were baggage animals, to accompany a force of about 1,800 soldiers and
300 natives.

Wolseley had given explicit orders to Stewart, Wilson and
Beresford. Stewart was to leave a small garrison at Jakdul, and
move on to Metemmeh, establishing a post on the way at Abu
Klea. He was to take Metemmeh, leave there about 700 men
including the whole of the Guards' Camel Regiment and the
Naval Brigade, return with a convoy to Jakdul and move forward more stores to Metemmeh. The return of the convoy was
made necessary, again, by the shortage of camels. He was to take
25,000 rations for the post at Metemmeh and 3,000 for that at
Abu Klea. A line of communications would thus be established
from Korti to Metemmeh, with Mounted Infantry posted at all
stations as despatch riders. The instructions to Wilson and Beresford were equally detailed. Wilson was to try to enter into
friendly relations with the desert tribes, 'and to induce them, if
possible, to carry supplies for us across the desert, and to sell us
sheep, cattle, etc.' He would go with Beresford to Khartoum on
Gordon's steamers, taking a small detachment of infantry. 'If
you like, you can, upon arriving there, march these men through
the city to show the people that British troops are near at hand.
If there is any epidemic in town you will not do this. I do not
wish you to sleep in the city.' He would confer with Gordon and
then return to Metemmeh, leaving three officers who would
assist Gordon 'until I am able to relieve that place'. Beresford's
orders were to take over and man any steamers at Metemmeh or
Shendi, taking instructions from 'the senior military officer at
the post'. The only qualification of these orders was the decision
to make Burnaby commandant of Metemmeh, on the ground
that he was a good fighting man. 'We Britishers are curious
people,' Burnaby said to a correspondent. 'Do you know, I've
been made commandant of Metemmeh, and we haven't got
there yet.' He added that he thought the odds against saving
Gordon were twenty to one.[1] Nothing was lacking in these
instructions (which included the provision of twenty-nine red

[1] Villiers, *Pictures of Many Wars*, p. 144.

coats, specially brought up by Burnaby, to be worn by the soldiers going up to Khartoum with Wilson) except allowance for error. They made the assumptions that Stewart would not face serious fighting in the desert, that the steamers would be there and would be usable, that the position in Khartoum was such that Wilson would be able to take his redcoats into the town and bring them out again, and also that their mere appearance would have such great effect that the Mahdi might raise the siege at their approach. All this was sadly over-optimistic, but the most surprising thing is that in the day of the field telegraph such orders should have been issued at all. No attempt had been made to lay a telegraph line across the desert.

The working of the telegraph system had throughout been hampered by the necessity of working with the Egyptian administration. An arrangement had been made by which they were to carry out all the telegraph work at a price of one piastre a word, but it soon became apparent that the local staff was quite unequal to the work, and a fresh agreement was reached by which the wire was lent to the British army, although its maintenance from Cairo to Wady Halfa remained in Egyptian hands. The Director of Army Telegraphs, Colonel Webber, received no co-operation at all from the Egyptian officers, and complained also that 'a state of tension existed between the army and the Inspector-General, whose telegrams to Cairo at the time remain as evidence of the impossibility of working telegrams during times of urgency when cordial co-operation with mutual confidence and self-sacrificing work for the common good are totally absent'.[1] The section of line maintained by the Egyptians broke down frequently, and inconvenience also arose from the fact that the telegraph line was on the left bank of the river and all the army stations on the right, so that the river had to be crossed by cable that might be a mile in length, or communications sent over by boat. A good deal of line had to be repaired or newly laid, and the problem of finding transport arose again and again, because telegraph stores came low down on the long list of priorities. Yet this does not explain, and nothing can

[1] War Office Records.

excuse, the failure to arrange any sort of communication between Korti and the Desert Column. As early as November 21
Webber wrote to Buller about the possibility of establishing
heliograph signal stations across the desert, but his letter was
ignored. By Christmas Eve the line had been brought to Korti,
and a temporary line had soon been laid thirty miles beyond—
not, however, across the desert but farther up the Nile to
Merowi. On January 4 Webber asked that he should be sent with
Stewart's column, but this request was denied, and it was not
until three days later that Buller asked whether he could establish
a telegraph line from Korti to Jakdul, and if so how quickly it
could be done. To this Webber had to reply that too much
material had been left behind at Wady Halfa for this to be
possible. He suggested that a system of part telegraph line and
part heliograph might be established, but received no instruction
to do the work.[1] Wolseley was thus cut off from all direct contact with the force in the desert, and had to rely on messengers,
who might well be caught by the Arabs.

This failure of communication did not weigh heavily on
Stewart, but his concern about the camels is shown in the letter
he wrote to Wolseley just before setting out for Metemmeh:

> . . . I write one line privately to tell you that everything is going on
> swimmingly except as to time. In the absence of dhurra, I am sure you
> would not have wished the camels to be tried beyond what they ought to
> be called upon to bear, and this, coupled with the operation of watering
> the number of camels and horses now here, has consumed time which I
> could wish had been employed marching. . . . The more I see of this road
> and its work, the more convinced I am that you will have largely to supple-
> ment the supply of camels.[2]

He added some suggestions about improving the water supply
between Korti and Jakdul by using planks for rough shafting,
said that a good many of the Nile stores brought up in the
whalers were useless because of poor packing ('the tea has only
been fastened up with canvas, and so has easily got wet') and
ended: 'I won't bother you with any more, but hope to write
to you from Metemmeh and send off Sunday afternoon.'

[1] War Office Records.
[2] Colvile, ii. p. 11.

CHAPTER TWO

THE ROAD TO ABU KLEA

THE little force that moved out of Jakdul Wells at two
o'clock on the afternoon of January 14 presented an odd
appearance. The Hussars led the way, mounted on wiry
pony-sized Egyptian stallions, which seemed to thrive on desert
air and crumbly grass. After them came a hotch-potch of forty
regiments, welded into the Heavy and Guards' Camel Regiments,
the Royal Artillery and the Naval Brigade, with the Mounted
Infantry at the rear. In the centre, between the Guards and the
Artillery, were the baggage camels and their native drivers, a
drove of horned cattle, and the medical staff. The camels moved
across the desert forty abreast, in close order, and all except a few
eccentrics were mounted on them. One exception was Burnaby,
who rode a polo pony lent him by Marling, and another was
Beresford, who rode on a white donkey. 'No wonder Charlie
rides a moke. He knows a thing or two, does Beresford,' remarked
one of the sailors. Several war correspondents accompanied the
column. By way of artillery there were three 7-pound screw guns
with 100 rounds of ammunition for each of them, and a Gardner
gun brought by the Naval Brigade, with 1,000 rounds. Three
powerful camels carried one 7-pounder and its ammunition, and
the Gardner was carried by four camels, one of which took the
barrels, the second the training and elevating gear and wheels,
the third the trail, and the last four boxes of feed hoppers. The
Gardner, named after its American inventor, was at this time
being used in preference to the Gatling and in competition with
the Nordenfeldt. In 1884 Hiram Maxim had demonstrated, to
Wolseley among others, his quick-firing gun which was mounted

on a tripod instead of on wheels, was fed by a belt instead of a tray, and which since it had only one instead of several barrels was far lighter than the Gardner or the Nordenfeldt. In due time it made them obsolete, but this was not yet the Maxim's day, and the Desert Column was cursed with the Gardner which fired over 100 rounds a minute, but as Wolseley was to say afterwards, jammed on every occasion when it was urgently needed. It had, in any case, enough ammunition to fire for only ten minutes—but then, in spite of the discovery of a Remington rifle near Jakdul and the recent tracks of horses in the desert, there was still no expectation of serious resistance from the Arabs. A native of Metemmeh had reported that there were about 3,000 Arabs at Metemmeh, but such a number would not present a serious threat.

On this day the column marched four hours and covered ten miles, then halted for the night. Reveille on the 15th was at 3 a.m., and they marched again as soon as it was light. In some places drift sand covered the track, but Stewart had an extremely accurate map showing local landmarks, and they did not lose their way. One of the war correspondents drew off to the right and watched the column as it approached. The Guards and the Heavy Camel Regiment were marching in open column at the front, with the red flag of Stewart and his staff waving over the left-front face. 'The men seemed as if they had been accustomed all their lives to the steeds they now bestrode. The height of the camels, their red saddles, and stalwart riders clad in light grey and wearing white helmets, produced an almost indescribably grand effect.'[1] The Camel Corps were always distinguishable by their saddles, which were covered with crimson sheepskin, and in some cases were fitted with cushions. Beside these imposing figures ran a small dog, a cross between a King Charles's spaniel and a Dandie Dinmont, which had come with the Grenadier Guards all the way from Assuan, and was to survive the march.

The men looked impressive, but their progress was slow. The baggage camels were showing signs of the overwork they had endured. They were tied in strings of three, so that every time a load fell off one of them, or a camel dropped down sick, the

[1] Macdonald, *Too Late for Gordon*, p. 211.

other two camels on the same lead became tangled together and all their loads needed readjustment. At other times the camels would lose their footings in the soft hills of drifting sand, go head over heels down the slopes and lie with their legs in the air unable to get up. Beresford had a short way with camels who fell. He had them lifted with a gun pole and then loaded them with men. It is difficult to believe that the animals flourished under such treatment, although Beresford said that he got good results by doing this, and at the same time giving them food in handfuls. It was his opinion that the camels were malingerers who rarely marched as long as they could, but this was not a general view:

> The way the poor brutes toiled on was something marvellous; you would see one go slower and slower, till the tail of the animal he was tied to in front seemed nearly coming off; then he would stop for a second, give a mighty shiver, and drop down stone-dead.[1]

When this happened the camel's load was put on to another animal, and the column moved on. It was impossible to free them for grazing even when they came, as they did on the afternoon of this second day, into a grass-covered valley, for now the advance scouts saw many marks of horses and recently-made fires. To have freed the camels would have been to invite attack, besides halting the whole column. That night, when a halt was called near the mountain of Gebel es Sergain, the camels were knee-lashed and other preparations made to receive an attack, but the hours of darkness passed peacefully. They were now almost halfway to Metemmeh from Jakdul, and a day's march from the wells of Abu Klea.

Stewart ordered the Hussars to scout well ahead on the following morning, in the belief that there were small groups of Arabs about. The march started before daylight, with some confusion. Part of the column went away to the left and did not regain their proper place for half an hour. They moved across a large flat plain, and halted at the far side of it. The track ahead led up an incline, and then through a pass commanded on either side by rocky hills. The wells lay about three miles the other side of this pass, and the Hussars went ahead to water their horses. Within a

[1] Gleichen, p. 113.

few minutes some of them returned. 'Like a flash the report spread
from mouth to mouth that the enemy were in sight on the hills
commanding the pass, and were evidently prepared to make a
fight of it.'¹ The time was about midday on January 16. Stewart,
Wilson, and other members of the staff advanced to reconnoitre.
They saw a long line of banners floating in the breeze, barring the
road to the wells. With the help of glasses, hundreds of white-
robed Arabs could be seen on the surrounding rocks. Tom-toms
were beating, and puffs of smoke rose from rifles, although the
shooting was too distant to do any damage. 'Well, gentlemen,
the enemy is ahead of us,' Stewart said to the war correspondents.
'I am going to attack him at once.' He sketched in the sand with
his swagger stick the formation in which he intended to advance.
Within an hour, however, he had changed his mind. Only three
hours of daylight remained, and he had decided to sit tight until
the morning.

    There was a standard procedure for such a situation, and
Stewart followed it. The men set to work to form a zereba, that
is, an enclosure made of stones and thorns to resist attack.² There
were not many loose stones lying about, and before the wall was
two feet high the sun had already gone down. This breastwork
faced the direction in which the Arabs had been seen, and there
was no time to make it higher. On the right face of the camp a
breastwork was made out of camel saddles and boxes, with wire
stretched in front, and elsewhere the baggage and stores were
protected by thorn and mimosa bushes, with wire hastily dragged
across them. The whole formed a rough rectangle, within which
the camels were tied together in groups. The men lay down beside
them, shifting stones to make themselves as comfortable as possible. A biscuit box fort was constructed to serve as a hospital at
the right rear, and similar forts were made at the right front as a
gun emplacement, in the middle of the left flank and at the left
rear. Outside the zereba, the naval detachment had dragged the
Gardner up a nearby hill and placed it behind a breastwork of

¹ Gleichen, p. 117.
² Rather confusingly, the word was also sometimes used at this time to
describe the formation of a square.

stones to guard the left flank. Lime juice and water was served out to each man, and they settled down to sleep.

This did not prove easy. Stewart had occupied the hill on his left flank, but there was another some three-quarters of a mile away on the right which he had left alone to avoid splitting his force. The Arabs had occupied it and put up their own stone breastwork, and now they proceeded to pepper the camp with rifle fire, which was answered during daylight by one of the 7-pounders. The Arabs went on firing after dark whenever any sort of light was shown, and although the shooting did little damage it became too uncomfortable for the Hussar sentries on the right. After one man had been hit they retired into the zereba. The whistling of the bullets was accompanied by continuous noise from the tom-toms, and this was kept up all night. It was very cold. The men with the Gardner stood to arms several times during the night, but they were not attacked and had no casualties. Within the zereba things were no more comfortable for the men, particularly if they were near the camels. 'The particular spot I I had stumbled upon was well protected from the fire of the enemy by three large camels. Its sanitary condition was not, however, all that could have been desired, for the camels around me reeked of the carbolic oil with which their sore backs had been treated, combined with the sickly odour of over-perspiration. There also seemed to be a prevailing epidemic of flatulence amongst them.'[1] Inside the zereba too there were false alarms during the night, one from a soldier who had a bad dream, others when the sentry outposts thought that an attack was being made and hurried back to the lines. In the early morning the Arabs on the hills lighted fires and began a war dance.

Stewart later estimated the number of the Arabs at between 8,000 and 14,000, and probably something near the higher figure is correct. The force was a composite one, partly of local tribesmen, partly of men from Metemmeh, and partly of soldiers sent by the Mahdi from Khartoum when he heard news of the relief column crossing the desert. Had Stewart been able to push straight on from Jakdul, it is almost certain that he would have reached

[1] Macdonald, p. 222.

Metemmeh unopposed, but the necessary shuttling between Korti and Jakdul meant that news of his approach had spread throughout the region. Although they outnumbered the British by some five to one, the Arabs behaved with intelligent discretion. Stewart had hoped that they would attack soon after daylight, giving him full chance to use his superior weapons and fire power. Instead, the fire from the stone breastwork grew hotter and hotter, while some of the more daring Arabs began to creep up towards the zereba. Skirmishers were sent out to push them back, and succeeded in doing so, but this had no effect on the rifle fire, which was becoming disturbingly accurate. It was concentrated on the right flank, and several horses and camels were hit. So were some of the soldiers. Major Dickson of the Intelligence Department, one of the three officers deputed to go up to Khartoum with Wilson, was shot through the knee. A bullet grazed the temple of Major Gough, and knocked him senseless. Lieutenant Lyall, an artilleryman, was shot in the back. The officers persisted in exposing themselves with a courage indifferent to rifle bullets. Both Stewart and Burnaby rode about on high ground within the zereba although Beresford, who had brought the Gardner back into the enclosure, implored them to dismount. At last this was forcibly accomplished, when Burnaby's horse was hit. As Beresford helped him to his feet, Burnaby said: 'I'm not in luck today, Charlie.' Bully beef and biscuits were eaten out of haversacks, and still Stewart waited for the Arabs to launch an attack which did not come. Casualties continued to increase until the improvised hospital was full of wounded, and fourteen dead were lying in a row outside.[1] It was plain to Stewart that if he stayed where he was, his men would be picked off by handfuls, and he knew also how vital it was for both men and animals to reach the wells of Abu Klea. Circumstances imposed the congenial decision to attack. At nine o'clock in the morning he gave the order to form a square in preparation for an advance.

[1] Macdonald, p. 227.

CHAPTER THREE

ABU KLEA AND AFTER, JANUARY 17-18

MISLEADING things have been written about the square
formation frequently adopted by British infantry during the nineteenth century. The poems of Kipling and
Newbolt about the gallant fuzzy-wuzzy and the square that
broke, so famous in their own day, are comic in ours, and there
is a natural tendency to find the square comic too, an emblem of
the outdated character of British military tactics. This is far from
being true. For the kind of little wars that the British were often
fighting in the latter half of the nineteenth century, in which they
were greatly inferior in numbers but very much superior in discipline and fire power, the square was an excellent formation.
Irregular troops almost always tried to move round the rear of
an opposing force, partly because they thought that this would be
its weakest point, partly because they hoped to be able to loot
stores and baggage. A formation which presented a front on all
four sides had obvious advantages—always provided that the
enemy had no artillery and were prepared to charge the square
in mass. Against effective gun or rifle fire the square, in which
men were drawn up shoulder to shoulder, would of course have
been a suicidal formation.

The use of a square for defence was comparatively easy.
Stewart was forced into the much more difficult operation of
using his square for attack. A square moving forward had to keep
exactly the same pace on all its sides if great gaps were not to
appear making one side straggle or bulge, and the normal method
of keeping in square was to check the speed of the front face frequently, so that the others would catch up with it. The operation

was never easy, and at Abu Klea it was made more difficult by the need to take some camels in the centre of the square to carry the guns and bring back the wounded. About a hundred camels were taken, half for carrying cacolets and litters, the rest for stores and ammunition. Their presence made the square bulge ominously this way and that, but particularly at the rear. With the camels were their terrified native drivers. The Mounted Infantry were at the front and went halfway down the right flank, the rest of the left flank and the left rear being occupied by the Heavy Camel Regiment, the rest of the right flank by the Royal Sussex, and the centre and right rear by the Naval Brigade and the rest of the Heavy Camel Regiment. The Royal Artillery had a place in the centre front of the square, where the three 7-pounders were positioned, and the Naval Brigade had the Gardner. Altogether there were 1,200 troops in the square. Stewart left behind in the zereba the rest of the baggage camels and the stores, with a detachment of the Royal Sussex to guard them. This separation of the stores from the main body was a decision that had been forced on him. They were obviously likely prey for Arab marauders and the Hussars, with some of the Mounted Infantry, were detailed to skirmish around the zereba and keep Arab horsemen away from it. The use of skirmishers was essential, but it might have been better if they had been told simply to protect the zereba. Many of them skirmished around the square, and in the end nearly wrecked it.

At about ten o'clock the square began to move forward, away from the zereba. One of the war correspondents, who had refused the chance of going out with the square because he thought poorly of its prospects, felt that its appearance 'at first sight suggested a moving fortress, but with walls of such material as to bid defiance to the assaults of any ordinary foe'.[1] Movement was very slow, for the ground was not level but made up of rocky hillocks intersected by deep ruts, ground difficult to march over at any time, but for a formation in square almost impossible. The men could go no faster, in any case, than the guns and camels. The camels kept slipping and falling, pressing always upon the rear face where

[1] Macdonald, p. 230.

the Naval Brigade and the Heavies found themselves tangled up
with a grunting and squealing mass of struggling animals. In the
midst of this confusion the sailors were dragging forward the
Gardner. The Arabs kept pace with the square as it moved, pour-
ing into it a steady rifle fire. The Adjutant of the Heavies, Lord
St. Vincent, was hit, and it proved necessary to halt several times,
so that the wounded could be placed on to the cacolets for attention by the doctors. The fire was returned by the soldiers and the
7-pounders. Mounted Infantry skirmishers came round beside
the left front and drove back the Arabs by the accuracy of their
shooting. The fire that had been so severe died away almost completely on this left flank.

It is difficult not to speculate on what might have happened if
the Arabs had simply kept their distance and maintained a harass-
ing fire, as the Boers were to do so often fifteen years later. Could
Stewart's force, stuck in a desert and with a steadily worsening
transport problem, possibly have survived? However, it would
have been against nature for the Arabs permanently to exercise
such caution, and their attack was not long delayed. The column
was marching along, leaving a deep wadi on the left when there
became visible, partly hidden by the wadi, the tops of a line of
green and white flags planted on long poles. Were they enemy
flags? An officer who had been in the Suakin campaign said
knowingly that it was merely a burial ground, and that nobody
was there. Stewart spoke to Burnaby, who by one account was
'in immediate command of the square',[1] and said: 'Move a little
more to the left. I want that green flag.' Most of the officers now
thought that the Arabs had fled from this side and that any serious
attack would come on the right flank, and although Stewart said
afterwards that the main Arab position (which was here on the
left) was soon apparent, his light-hearted words about the flag
belie this assurance.

Captain Campbell, who was leading the Mounted Infantry
skirmishers on this side, thought that the Arabs had bolted and
left their flags, and advanced to get one for himself. When he and

[1] Dawson.

his men were within two hundred yards of the flags a great host of Arabs sprang out of the ground. The sight was wonderful and striking. There were three phalanxes joined together, with a sheik or Emir at the head of each. After them came the fighting men, armed with javelins and hatchets, knobkerries and knives. These were not the sharpshooters who had been firing Remingtons, but warriors chosen to exterminate the infidel, as Hicks and his men had been slaughtered a year before. They advanced yelling, but the British were impressed more than anything else by the perfect order in which they moved, as quick and even as if on parade. Gleichen was amazed by the co-ordination with which they moved together, made for the left flank of the square, disappeared behind rocks and grass, reappeared, left wheeled into line, and charged.

They had chosen one of the many moments when the square was in a state of confusion. The right front corner was on a slight rise, and a halt had been made to let the rear face close up. Several tired camels carrying wounded men had laid down at the foot of the slope and refused to move. As soon as the Arabs appeared the camel drivers fled into the square, and several men of the Heavies rushed out and began to drag the camels and the wounded into the square. At the left-hand rear corner of the square a gap was yawning, and it was towards this gap that the Arabs charged, either because they knew that the rear corners were always the weakest part of a square or because the attack on the left front had been so sternly resisted. As they charged, Wilson, with remarkable impartiality, thought with admiration and pity that they would be shot down within a few minutes without reaching the square. But this reckoned without the skirmishers, who had previously been so useful, but were now in the way. The wadi where the Mahdiists had been concealed was 800 yards away from the British, but only a quarter of that distance from the adventurous Campbell and his men, and as they now raced back the men in the square held their fire. 'We shouted to the skirmishers to lie down and we would fire over them, as if anyone would lie down with 4,000 — Fuzzy-wuzzies prancing behind them with 6-foot spears. Old Johnny Campbell shouted "No, no, run like hell", and he was

Abu Klea. The attempt to break the square

(Illustrated London News)

Gordon's boats reach the British forces near Metemmeh

quite right too.'[1] All the skirmishers got back, with the exception of an officer's servant who was caught and speared, but the consequence was that the Mahdiists were allowed to come comparatively close before the Martini-Henrys spoke. The Arabs were massed together, and the shots could hardly miss. In a few seconds piles of bodies lay on the ground. It was now that they veered to their right and towards the rear of the square.

Here the position was further weakened through the actions of those two individualists, Beresford and Burnaby. 'It does not pay to pick a Cavalry man to do Infantry work,' Buller said after Abu Klea, and many of the Camel Corps were cavalry men who had no idea of the strict discipline necessitated by the square formation. Had Stewart been an infantry officer rather than a Hussar, it is not likely that he would have hampered himself with skirmishers who had to retire into the square. Had the men at the left rear been infantry soldiers instead of Guards they might not have broken ranks to bring in the camels and wounded. And certainly no infantry officers would have done what was done now by Beresford and Burnaby.

Beresford had been longing to use the Gardner, and had been given permission to use his own judgment in placing it. He said that when he saw the gaps opening at the left rear he forced his way through to the front of the square to tell Stewart what was happening, and that Stewart said, 'Quite right'. Whatever Stewart meant by this, Beresford took it as giving him a free hand, and he proceeded to order the Gardner to be run outside the square, so extending its left flank. At the same time Burnaby, on his own initiative, wheeled round Number 3 Company of the Heavies, the 4th and 5th Dragoon Guards, so that the left flank was further lengthened. Number 4 Company, the Scots Greys and the Royals, had already moved round behind Beresford and the Gardner. The action violated the elementary principle behind use of the square formation, that the soldiers must never on any account break ranks. The gap yawned further as some of the Heavies on the right flank made a movement to support their comrades who were being attacked, and the Royal Sussex on

---

[1] Marling, p. 132.

O

this side tried to patch the holes. The spearmen poured towards this thin and irregular line.

In the meantime Beresford was enjoying his moment of glory. He laid and fired the Gardner himself. The firing mechanism was operated by turning a lever, and again it was impossible to miss. 'As I fired, I saw the enemy mowed down in rows, dropping like ninepins,' but after firing about forty rounds he lowered the elevation to aim at the front ranks. He fired another thirty rounds and then the gun jammed because of an empty cylinder not ejected from one barrel. To clear it the feed-plate had to be unscrewed, and Beresford and a chief boatswain's mate named Rhodes began to do this. Within moments the enemy were on top of them. Rhodes was speared and killed instantly, and so was the naval armourer beside the gun. Beresford was luckier. He was saved momentarily by the feed-plate dropping on his head and knocking him under the gun, and was then hit by the handle of an axe, the blade of which missed him. He caught a spear blade that was being thrust at him, got to his feet, and was then borne backwards by the rush into the front rank of Number 4 Company.

> I can compare the press to nothing but the crush of a theatre crowd alarmed by a cry of fire. Immediately facing me was an Arab holding a spear over his head, the staff of the weapon being jammed against his back by the pressure behind him. I could draw neither sword nor pistol. The front ranks of our men could not use rifle or bayonet for a few moments. But the pressure, forcing our men backwards up the hill, presently enabled the rear rank, now occupying a position a few inches higher than the enemy, to fire over the heads of the front rank right into the mass of the Arabs. The bullets whizzed close by my head; and one passed through my helmet. The Arabs fell in heaps.[1]

Now that they had a little space the front rank fired, and used their bayonets, but less effectively than might have been expected. Some of the rifles jammed, and many of the bayonets bent and twisted when the men thrust with them. Beresford says that they were blunt because nobody had thought of sharpening them, and they bent because they were made from inferior metal. Nevertheless, in this furious hand to hand fighting, the dragoons in front

[1] Beresford, i. p. 264.

did great execution. Captain Piggot, who was next to Burnaby, used a shot gun loaded with buckshot, and the sailors kept calling to him, 'Here's another joker, sir.' When he fired at the bald head of one Arab Beresford 'saw the bald crown riddled like the rose of a water-pot'. Burnaby had quickly realized his mistake in taking his men out of the square. He ordered them back, but too late to prevent its penetration by the Arabs, who surged into its centre. Wilson saw a sheik on horseback ride in, holding a banner in one hand and a book of prayer in the other. He planted the banner in the centre of the square, chanting prayers as he did so. The sheik was shot down, but a great mass of men pressed behind him, stabbing the camels and getting among the wounded. Burnaby himself seems to have made no attempt to get back. He stood his ground outside the square, parrying the spear of one tribesman with his cavalry sabre, being speared through the shoulder by another, who was immediately run through with a bayonet, and then receiving a fatal spear wound in the throat. His immense strength did not immediately fail him. He got to his feet again and laid about him with the sabre for a few moments, before collapsing.

The square was saved by the presence of the camels. Had the centre been hollow the tribesmen must have gone straight through, and created such chaos that the square would have been completely broken. Instead, the defenders at the rear and left flanks fell back upon the wall of the camels. Those on the front and right sides, who had not been attacked, could see nothing of what was happening on the fighting flanks, but they felt suddenly a terrific shock as the Scots Greys, the Royals and the Sussex were forced back against the camels. Lieutenant Dawson, on the right, rushed across to his brother and shook his hand in farewell, thinking that the end was near. For a couple of minutes a desperate hand to hand mêlée went on between the attackers and the thin defence line, with the Arabs 'hacking, hewing, hamstringing, and yelling, like a crowd of black devils on a ground literally piled up with dead and dying'.[1] But now some of the rear rank at the front of the square turned and began to fire into the mêlée. They caused

[1] Gleichen, p. 132.

casualties to their own force, as was inevitable when the crush was so great. Two British officers and several men were killed, and Stewart had his horse shot from under him. As the horse fell three Arabs rushed at the General, but one was shot by Wilson and the others by Mounted Infantry officers nearby. This burst of organized firing at point-blank range had, however, a devastating effect upon the Arabs. They had faced withering fire to reach the square, had broken into it, and now they were faced by organized volleys again. It was too much for them. They wavered, turned, and retreated, not in total flight but slowly and sullenly, so that the riflemen picked many of them off before they disappeared behind the hills.

The charge, the penetration of the square and the Arabs' retreat, had taken no more than ten minutes. Not a man who entered the square remained alive in it. When Stewart gave the word his men, wild with excitement, began to cheer. Orders were given to close up, in expectation of a second attack, this time upon the right face. This did not come, although a few Arabs turned and attacked again in groups. Some of them reached the square before being bayoneted. A few deliberately exposed themselves to British bullets, and one horseman charged at the right face on his own, and got quite close to it before being shot down. Occasionally marksmen would creep over the broken ground and take potshots at the square. Their courage was extraordinary. 'I saw a boy of some twelve years of age, who had been shot through the stomach, walk slowly up through a storm of bullets and thrust his spear at one of our men. I saw an Arab, who was wounded in the leg, sit up and hurl his spear at a passing soldier. As the soldier stopped to load his rifle, the Arab tried to reach another spear, and failing caught up stones and cast them at his foe; and then, when the soldier presented his rifle and took a deliberate aim, the Arab sat perfectly still looking down the barrel, till the bullet killed him.'[1] Immense courage had also been shown by the British. When the square was penetrated any wavering would have meant that they must be overwhelmed by sheer weight of numbers, but the precise drill technique by which the rear rank of the

[1] Beresford, i. pp. 265–6.

front face turned and fired into the square helped as much as any other single factor to decide the engagement. The superiority of the trained infantry over the cavalry taken off their horses was marked. 'A cavalry man is taught never to be still, and that a square can be broken. How can you expect him in a moment to forget all his training, stand like a rock, and believe no one can get inside a square?'[1]

The Hussars, whose horses were too weak to be of much use in pursuing the retiring Arabs, set out for the wells, and in the meantime the square moved on fifty yards and men set to work to collect the dead and bring back the wounded. Overshadowing all else was the death of Burnaby. Lord Binning, a Lieutenant in the Blues, reached him where he lay, thirty yards outside the square, before he died.

> I was not the first to find him. A young private in the Bays, a mere lad, was already beside him, endeavouring to support his head on his knee; the lad's genuine grief was touching, as were his simple words: 'Oh! sir, here is the bravest man in England, dying, and no one to help him.'[2]

Binning took his hand, but Burnaby was indeed beyond help. In a few moments he was dead, upon his face 'the composed and placid smile of one who had been suddenly called away in the midst of a congenial and favourite occupation.' The death of a man who, by his courage and gigantic size, had seemed almost immortal, deeply affected his comrades, particularly the men in the Blues, some of whom sat down and cried. The losses suffered had been heavy for such a tiny force. Nine officers and sixty-five men had been killed, another nine officers and eighty-five men wounded, many of them severely. The Heavies, who had borne the full weight of the attack, had lost most men, but eight of the Naval Brigade had been killed and seven wounded, of the forty who went into action. Every man handling the Gardner outside the square had been killed, except Beresford. The wounded had suffered greatly when the square was penetrated. Their cacolets had been knocked on to the ground with the spearing of the camels. Lord St. Vincent was in one of a pair of cacolets, with a

---

[1] Wilson, p. 33.
[2] Alexander, *The True Blue*, p. 203.

soldier on the other side. The camel was killed and fell on him, temporarily saving his life, although he later died of his wounds. The soldier in the other cacolet was speared to death immediately. Some of the wounded were put back on to the camels, and the rest were carried on litters by men of the Grenadier Guards, who had been hardly involved in the fighting.

Fatigue parties collected the arms and ammunition lying about, broke up spears and burned damaged rifles. Several boxes of ammunition had to be burned, because there were no camels to carry them. The men were suffering terribly from thirst. Several fainted, and many more found their tongues swelling and their lips turning black. There was little water left, and almost all of it was kept for the wounded. At last the reorganized force began to limp slowly towards the wells, moving at the pace of the wounded, and of those men in the Naval Brigade who were still dragging the Gardner. The Hussars had had some trouble in finding the wells on the large featureless plain, but at last they discovered them, and the square reached them at five in the afternoon. The wells were a series of pits in the sand of the valley bed, with little basins at the bottom into which the water trickled. It resembled yellow mud, but as one man who drank it said, tasted like the very best cream. Gleichen called it 'cool, milky-tea-coloured water, of the consistency of thin mud', and added that it was delicious. Detachments formed up in perfect order, with no break in discipline, until their turn came to drink. A party of volunteers was sent back to the zereba to bring up the baggage in the early morning, and the force bivouacked for the coldest night many of them had ever spent. They had no blankets or greatcoats, no covering more than shirt, trousers and serge jacket. Some tried to shelter between two camels, which often lurched over on top of them. Wilson, with two other officers, tried to sleep under a prayer rug looted by one of them. Lieutenant Dawson shared his six cigarettes with Beresford. They agreed that it would be hard to die without knowing who had won the Derby.

The zereba had been subjected only to sporadic attacks, which were easily beaten off. After the men sent by Stewart had arrived, most of the night was spent in loading up the stores, and by seven-thirty in the morning the whole force was together again. At last, too, they were able to eat a proper meal, the first for nearly two days. Afterwards, a burial party returned to the scene of battle and buried the dead. A Union Jack was placed over Burnaby's body, and he was buried twenty yards from where he fell. One or two of the other officers were buried separately, but most of the dead were interred together in one long trench. The Arab dead were counted, and found to number 1,100. A difficult decision now confronted Stewart, as a result of information gleaned from four Negroes who had surrendered themselves. All of them had been with Hicks's force and had, they said, subsequently been forced to fight against the British. They said that the Arab force contained men from Berber, including some Egyptian soldiers from the garrison there, local levies from Metemmeh, a great many natives of Kordofan, and about 1,000 riflemen sent by the Mahdi, some of whom had also been with Hicks. This force of about 10,000 men was, they said, only the advanced guard of a large army which was on its way to Metemmeh. Would Stewart's column be able to survive another attack like the one at Abu Klea? When he held an informal council of war, one of his commanding officers was in favour of falling back again on Jakdul. Stewart rejected the idea decisively. To return would mean eating up more of their valuable rations and giving the camels another long day's march. They were only twenty-five miles from Metemmeh and the river, and he hoped that if he made a night march he would avoid any serious attack. He decided to go on, leaving the wounded at Abu Klea wells guarded by a detachment of the Sussex Regiment. It is not likely that he would have received any other advice had he been in telegraphic touch with Wolseley, but he could at least have made clear his almost desperate transport situation. To one of his aides-de-camp Stewart said, 'Tomorrow I intend taking Metemmeh, and if Gordon's steamers are there I will the day after send them up to Khartoum with Wilson.' A hundred men of the Sussex were left with the wounded, who could be given little in the way of medical attention. A despatch describing the battle was written and sent to Korti, accompanied by many messages sent by officers and several accounts by war correspondents, and an order was issued asking the men for one more effort to get to Metemmeh. Most of the war correspondents went on with the column. Parade was ordered at 4 o'clock and half an hour later the ragged and untidy column set off. The transport was at the rear, a thousand camels which marched in columns of sections tied together in a string. Some fifty spare camels followed them. The whole column covered about 600 yards. The wounded, and the Sussex left to guard them, watched the column move off and wondered if they would ever see their comrades again.

CHAPTER FOUR

BEFORE METEMMEH: WILSON IN COMMAND

EVEN Beresford, who was not a cautious man, thought that this further march was a desperate venture which might impose an intolerable strain on men who 'had had no sleep for two nights, had fought a battle in between, had suffered agonies of thirst and the exhaustion of hunger'. It went wrong almost from the start. Stewart had apparently not revealed to his officers his intention of marching all night, and they were under the impression that they would halt at dusk. As they moved across the plain, Gleichen had spotted exactly the place where they would stop, a point where trees and low scrub were visible in the distance. They reached the place and passed it. There was no order to halt. The column was shortened and broadened, no lights were allowed, orders were given in whispers. Slowly realization came that Stewart meant to reach the Nile by daybreak.

On Stewart's other night marches there had been a bright moon, but this night was utterly dark. On other marches the columns had been halted by bugle, but on this night no bugle was permitted for fear of giving information to the enemy. The words 'Halt in front' were to be passed on by word of mouth. As the men became sleepy, however, 'it was found impossible to communicate with the front, unless a responsible officer himself carried the communication'.[1] Yet officers, however responsible, are as subject to tiredness as their men. Marling, for one, kept falling asleep on his camel, and twice lost both himself and his company. Gleichen, who had been told off in charge of his regimental stores and baggage, found that the 'mongrel niggers' who were driving the baggage camels fell asleep and let the

[1] Colvile, ii. p. 22.

animals drift. At one moment he determined to keep his eye on a driver with a string of water camels, then 'somebody got between me and him, and in another moment he had vanished into the blurry outline of the column'. The column had for guide a local robber named Ali Loda, and Captain Verner of the Intelligence Department was checking the direction frequently with his compass. Their guidance seems to have been as accurate as could be expected, and it was not their fault that by midnight the column was sprawled about all over the place with transport, medical stores, regimental baggage and commissariat all hopelessly mixed up. At 1 a.m. the leading company of the Guards, commanded by Colonel Gordon-Cumming (later the principal figure in the Baccarat Case) reached a mimosa thicket. They pushed their way through, and so did some of those who followed them, but the track had narrowed, and the baggage camels with their sleepy drivers began to wander about aimlessly rather than going forward. Frequent halts were called, or rather whispered, but these instructions did not reach many of the drivers. The advance guard went round in a circle, and suddenly found itself following the rearguard. The insistence on silence had by this time become absurd, because the swearing of the men and the squealing of the camels were audible for some distance, and it occurred to many of the men that if the column was attacked they would be utterly unable to defend themselves.

At last they got through the mimosa, and the advance continued, with dozens of men now falling asleep and straying from the column. Stores fell off the camels and had to be haphazardly replaced. When daylight came at last they looked eagerly for the river, but saw no sign of it. They had been marching for 14½ hours, and had covered about eighteen miles. The men near the head of the column had snatched some sleep during the series of halts, but those at or near the back had halted for a much shorter time and had hardly rested at all. The number of camels lost during the night has been put as high as 100, although this is almost certainly an overestimate. All of Gleichen's lost animals drifted together again, although 'one of my niggers, a hoary-headed old chimpanzee, was reported to me as having cut his two rear camels adrift in order to go to sleep more comfortably; so he got the kourbash, and was condemned to walk all the rest of the way, whilst the others rode'.[1] The men's spirits might have been expected to be low after what Beresford described as the longest and most exhausting nightmare of his life, but the coming of daylight found them remarkably cheerful. They marched on readily enough up a great gravelly slope, and when they reached the top they saw below them a wide valley with the yellow river flowing through it. On their side of the river were the roofs of villages and the walled town of Metemmeh, on the other side the huts of Shendi. To the surprise of the commanders Metemmeh, which was shown as less important on the maps, was much the larger of the two places.

Their approach had not gone unobserved. In Metemmeh the tom-toms were beating, and the Hussar scouts brought word that crowds of Arabs scattered about in the bush had opened fire on them. Perhaps Stewart's gamble had been worth taking, but now that it had failed his position could hardly have been worse. He was still four miles from the river, his men, camels and horses were all in urgent need of rest, and in no condition for another Abu Klea. Some of the men were heard to say that they wanted to go straight on to the Nile, but Stewart saw that they would have to fight their way to the river. 'We ought to have been here two hours ago, and should have been but for those unfortunate camels,' he said. He ordered the construction of a zereba, so that the men should have something to eat before they fought. There were few stones on the bare gravelly ground where they had halted, but a parapet about two and a half feet high was hastily made out of biscuit boxes and camel saddles. Within this the camels were once again knee-lashed, a hospital was rigged up in the middle, and food was given to some of the men. Only to some, for as they ate the Arab riflemen crawled nearer, using the cover of scrub, and breakfast was eaten in a rain of bullets. The position was on open ground with excellent views in every direction, and had presumably been chosen to prevent any risk of surprise attack, but it was much exposed to rifle fire.

[1] Gleichen, p. 148.

'We had beyond the open ground, 200 or 300 yards wide, miles of scrub, thin, but sufficient for cover. Thus the marksmen could fire at us in the open, themselves concealed.'[1] The zereba was also slightly below the level of the ground on the right, so that the hospital was exposed to fire and many camels were hit. The British persistently underestimated the Arabs' skill as marksmen. Both here and at Abu Klea they made, as one participant put it, wonderfully good shooting. A company was extended along a low ridge outside the zereba to try to keep down the fire, but they had little to aim at except puffs of smoke in the scrub several hundred yards away. No doubt Stewart had hoped that the Arabs would charge the zereba immediately, but they showed every intention of keeping up this damaging rifle fire. The Gardner also was placed just outside the zereba, but it was of little use without a body of men to aim at, and a spoke was knocked out of one of its wheels. It was obviously necessary to occupy some ground above the scrub, and thirty volunteers from the Guards ran out across the bullet-swept ground with boxes, and occupied a ridge about sixty yards away. Several of the men were wounded. Gleichen was hit, and his account of the incident shows the risks taken by officers. 'Every one of my men was extended flat on his stomach, potting everything in the shape of niggers or smoke. I prudently assumed the same position at first, but found I couldn't bring my field-glasses to bear comfortably. Accordingly I sat up, and was prospecting round satisfactorily, when suddenly I received a violent blow in the pit of the stomach. A couple of my men immediately rushed up, caught hold of me, and at a sepulchral "Take him away" from C——, bore me off between them at a fast "double" for the hospital.'[2] The bullet had hit a brass button on his uniform, and he was only winded. Some time between 9 o'clock and 10.15, however, Stewart was hit. He was walking round telling the men to get something to eat before fighting, when the bullet struck him. The wound was in the groin, and he was immediately taken to the hospital.

[1] Dawson.
[2] Gleichen, p. 152.

With Stewart wounded, the command fell upon Wilson. It may be said that during this march Stewart hardly fulfilled Wolseley's description of him as one of the best soldiers he had ever known. The last night march had unfortunate results, and the spot he chose for the zereba outside Metemmeh was little short of disastrous, but it must be remembered that he had too little time and too few camels, and that he was fighting against an enemy much more skilled, persistent and numerous than anybody had expected. Stewart may have been rash, but there was no doubt of his enthusiasm and energy. His replacement by Wilson made speedy and decisive action much less likely. Wilson was a surveyor and a gatherer of intelligence, not a fighting soldier. The references to him by those who were with the column are almost openly contemptuous. Gleichen calls him a diplomatic messenger, Marling 'an old woman who doesn't know anything about drill and funks responsibility'. It had never been Wolseley's intention that Wilson should assume command, and it was partly to avoid this possibility that Burnaby had been appointed commandant of Metemmeh. It was out of the question to make him officially second in command of the column, partly because of the disfavour with which he was regarded at home, and partly because Wilson was the senior officer (he was a Colonel of 1883 and Burnaby one of 1884). A positive appointment would have been too great a slight to Wilson, but it was understood that if anything happened to Stewart, Burnaby would take command. No provision had been made for a successor to both of them. In any case, the officers next in seniority were Colonels in the Foot Guards, who had little more experience of fighting than Wilson himself.

News of Stewart's wound was successfully kept from the men for an hour or two, and in the meantime Wilson consulted with the next senior officer, Colonel the Honourable Edward Boscawen (later Lord Falmouth) of the Coldstreams, the commander of the Guards Camel Regiment. They then went to see Stewart and found him certain that his wound was fatal, but still perfectly cool and collected. Wilson asked what Stewart had meant to do and Stewart told him what was obvious, that they must advance

either to take Metemmeh or to establish themselves on the Nile.
While they advanced they must, as at Abu Klea, leave stores and
wounded in the zereba. Wilson said that he would go out and
fight as soon as he could, and went off to make the necessary
arrangements. The fortlet on the knoll was strengthened and so
was the hospital, and then the organization of the square was
settled. All this took what seems a very long time, some three
and a half hours. The work of constructing the redoubts was
difficult and dangerous, for it involved in one case carrying boxes
sixty yards under fire, and in the other dodging about among the
camels and bringing in boxes from the outer parapet to strengthen
the hospital defences. Among those killed during this time were
Cameron, correspondent of the *Standard*, who was shot as he
rose to take a box of sardines from his servant, and St. Leger
Herbert, who doubled the roles of war correspondent for the
Morning Post and secretary to Stewart. Lieutenant Crutchley,
adjutant of the Guards, was badly hit in the leg as he talked to
an Engineers officer who was asking for a receipt for some en-
trenching tools. Many more camels received wounds, which
they endured with extraordinary patience. 'One heard a heavy
thud, and looking round, saw a stream of blood oozing out of
the wound, but the camel went on chewing his cud as if nothing
at all had happened, not even giving a slight wince to show that
he was in pain.'[1] Another cause of delay was the utter tiredness
of the men. Many were so worn out that they could not eat, and
some fell asleep even under the intense rifle fire. When they were
wakened, it was to learn that the situation had worsened. The
sun overhead was hotter than ever, the rattle of rifles sounded
continuously, every minute there was the thud of bullets hitting
camels, and less frequently the cries and groans of wounded men.
The interregnum began to cause impatience and anger. Beresford
sent a message to Wilson to say that if they did not march they
would be done for. The messenger was killed and Lieutenant
Munro, who carried a second message, was wounded.

At last Wilson was ready to move. The zereba was in such
obvious danger that a considerable part of the little force had to

[1] Wilson, p. 70.

be left to protect it. Half of the Heavies, the Naval Brigade, the Royal Artillery and the Hussars were left behind under the command of Beresford and Colonel Barrow, the senior military officer apart from those marching with the square. The guns were also left to guard the zereba. The rest of the column, no more than 900 men, lined up behind the zereba. Wilson had given executive command to Boscawen, who had been present at Tel-el-Kebir. While the square was forming several more men were hit, and according to one account some civilians with the force tried to start back for Abu Klea, but were deterred by the Arab horsemen. At three o'clock the square moved off. Many of those in it, and in the zereba, thought it unlikely that they would get through the great cloud of Arabs who could be seen ahead, gathering behind a line of green and white banners.

The progress of the square was slow, and was attended by continuous Arab rifle fire, to which the men replied by making occasional halts during which they fired volleys at the still mostly invisible enemy. At one halting point seven men were shot dead within a minute or two, and the stretchers and cacolets were filled. Wilson was walking just behind the Marines, and one man fell dead almost into his arms. At last, however, large bodies of Arabs began to collect in front of the square, and it was plain that they were about to charge. The zereba was not attacked at all, and its guns—two of the 7-pounders and the Gardner—made good target practice on the three groups of Arabs, two of them hovering in front of the square and the third threatening the zereba. 'Now, men! No single firing! Give them volleys,' Colonel Barrow said, and the volley firing was so effective that the third group never approached nearer than half a mile to the zereba. In the square the men waited, perfectly steady, with set, determined faces, for the Arabs to come on. And on they came, the horsemen ahead with the flags, and the shrieking spearmen running after them. Their charge must have looked magnificent, but it was precisely the kind of attack which the square formation and volley firing were perfectly suited to meet. The attack had come this time on the front face, although it extended round both sides. The Guards' Camel Regiment—the Grenadiers and

Coldstreams—the Marines and the Mounted Infantry met the
brunt of it, and stayed as calm as though on parade. At first their
fire had little effect because the distance was too great, and on the
'Cease fire' sounding, they stopped immediately. When the
shrieking enemy had got to within 400 yards the call 'Commence
firing' was given, and they began again. This time there were no
impeding skirmishers. They fired in volleys at the order, one
rank after another, never faltering and in perfect time, at the
perfect targets presented to them. The Arabs went down in rows,
in heaps. The living stumbled over the dead and then were shot
down themselves. It is said that there were more Arabs on the
field (although not in the attack) here than at Abu Klea, but the
slaughter was so great that those at the rear of the charge turned
and fled. The real fighting at Abu Klea had been over in ten
minutes, and here it was finished in five. Not a single Arab got
within fifty yards of the square, all the leading horsemen were
killed, and nobody in the square was wounded during the attack.
Nevertheless, the losses during the day had been heavy. One
officer and twenty-two men had been killed, eight officers and
ninety men wounded, and again most of the wounds were
serious. The officers hurt, besides Stewart and Crutchley, whose
leg was amputated on the following day, included Lord Arthur
Somerset of the Blues. The Arabs left about 300 dead piled in
heaps all around, but removed most of their wounded.

They were still three miles from the Nile, and another council
of war was held by Wilson and Boscawen, with the participation
of several other officers who were within earshot. Boscawen
suggested that he should march the front face of the square to the
Nile on its own, but a protest was made in such forcible language
by Major Gough, who commanded the Mounted Infantry, that
the idea was given up after the front face had gone a hundred
yards. 'The joke of the whole thing is that everyone gives their
opinion and advice in the freest manner, from the junior subaltern upwards, and the man who gets Wilson's or Boscawen's
ear last, his advice is followed.'[1] At last it was settled that the
whole square would move on to the Nile. An hour later, in the

[1] Marling, p. 137.

(*Illustrated London News*)

One side of the square firing on the Arabs at Gubat. An interesting, if idealized, view of the effect of volley firing at short range

(Graphic

Christmas at Korti. Making Christmas puddings

(Graphic

Wilson's attempt to reach Khartoum, which is seen in the background. The island of Tuti is on the left. The boats are the *Bordein* and the *Telahawieth*

growing dusk, they reached the top of a ridge and saw silver streaks below them in a belt of green vegetation. They descended a shallow ravine, at the end of which grew peas and some dhurra, and there at last was the Nile. By now it was dark, and they saw the river only by the light of a crescent moon.

This was the night of January 19. For three full days the men had been marching, or under fire, or fighting, without any chance of a decent rest or a proper meal. The camels had gone for five days without water and four without food. Their bodies were covered with sores, their ribs showed through their skins, and they were hardly able to walk. Yet there was no breakdown of discipline or of spirit. The wounded were held up so that they could see the river, and then taken down beside the bank. The front face of the square went down to the river, and when the men had drunk their fill they marched round to relieve the rear face, so that in case of attack no flank would be undefended. Bush was cut for a zereba, and pickets were posted on either side of the ravine. The camels were watered and given dhurra. Few of the men had burdened themselves with rations, to add to the 150 rounds of rifle ammunition they carried, and in any case they were too tired to eat. Officers and men dropped down and slept where they lay. Only the doctors worked on through the night, dressing wounds and giving laudanum. One doctor fainted from exhaustion, but the work continued until all the wounded men had been treated.

They had reached the Nile, but they had almost at once to leave it, so that the stores and men left behind could be brought up. Before daylight on the morning of the 20th they were on the move, filling up water skins and tanks, and then scouting for a strong natural position in which to camp when the column's two parts were rejoined. A number of mud hut villages lay along the river bank, and scouting parties in extended order passed through them. They were all completely deserted, and cleared of everything movable, food, utensils and forage. They halted eventually at one of these groups of mud huts, known locally as Abu Kru but called by the British Gubat. It was in construction a rather superior village, with several houses made of mud which

P

had set as hard as concrete, some of them containing two or three rooms, and topped by conical or horizontal roofs of straw and dhurra stalk. From here they could see Metemmeh, which looked as deserted as the country through which they had passed, and another discussion took place about whether it should be attacked at once. In the end a decision was taken against doing so, chiefly because of the lack of guns, and with a small garrison left at Gubat to look after the wounded, some 600 men marched back to the zereba, which could also be seen in the distance. Crowds of Arabs were visible near it, and two camels with the distinctive red saddles of the Camel Corps were being led towards Metemmeh. They feared the worst, but after a march back of some two and a half hours, with much sporadic shooting at Arabs on the way, they were greeted with rousing cheers.

The men who reached the Nile had had water but no food, those left behind had plenty of stores but no water. They had not been attacked during the night and so were able to sleep, but they suffered wholesale plunder by the Aden drivers and other natives, including some of those among the bearer companies. All of Stewart's private stores had been stolen, brandy and other medical stores had gone, the wounded Crutchley had lost his revolver, and Wilson's private supply of cocoa, milk and compressed tea was missing. Corporal punishment in the Army had been finally abolished, at the urging of Wolseley and other reformers, in 1881, but when Wilson found one of the medical staff blind drunk he 'longed for a return of the days when a man could be triced up and given four dozen lashes'.[1] In default of this he had the culprit tied to a tree in the sun, he does not say for how long. Neither Beresford nor Barrow had worried about overseeing the stores and they were in utter confusion, with many boxes broken open and the contents scattered around.

Now the dead were buried, and Beresford read the service over them. Buller had refused to allow a chaplain to go with the column, and some of the men were distressed by the thought that they were dying without the consolation of religion. No less than 100 camels had to be shot, because they were obviously

[1] Wilson, p. 89.

dying, and the rest were so feeble that there were not sufficient animals to carry all the stores, some of which were left behind with a small detachment of Hussars. They rejoined the main force on the following day. Apart from these few men, the whole force marched back to Gubat, unbothered by Arabs. The Hussars went first to give their horses a drink—many of them had been for three days without water. The camels followed, and Gleichen says that his camel Potiphar drank for nearly a quarter of an hour, and then began to eat the cotton plant all round as if he would never stop. One baggage camel began to drink, and dropped dead while doing so.

The men were heartened by the news that Stewart had borne the journey to Gubat well, after his doctors had said that he would not last the night, and they were pleased by Wilson's announcement that on the following day he would attack and take Metemmeh.

CHAPTER FIVE

THE STEAMERS ARRIVE: THE DELAY

IN the story of the relief expedition the attempt on January 21 to take Metemmeh is a piece of almost pure comic relief. Just after dawn the troops paraded, some 750 of them, and began the two-mile march towards the small walled town. Some of the fittest of the ammunition and hospital camels went with them. Two of the 7-pounder guns were taken, but not the Gardner, possibly because Beresford was incapacitated by a painful boil on his bottom, and was unable to walk without help. One has at times the impression that Beresford regarded the Gardner as his personal property. The force was preceded by Colonel Barrow and his Hussars, who took with them a prisoner who carried a letter calling on the people of the town to surrender without fighting. He was to be sent into the town, and if no satisfactory response to the letter was received, Wilson intended to attack the government house, which he knew was on the desert side of Metemmeh. He does not seem to have thought that the operation would present any difficulty.

Wilson therefore marched his men, in double column, into the desert. The obvious line of approach was from the southern side of the town, with the right resting on the river. By approaching from the north Wilson left his right flank open, and also exposed his base at Gubat. At a point about 1,000 yards from the town Wilson went forward to talk to Barrow, who had taken his Hussars still farther to the north. In the meantime Boscawen had seen some Arab flags between the town and the river. He at once deduced that an attack on Gubat was developing, and ignoring his nominal commander formed a square and advanced towards

the flags. Crowds of Arabs were running about outside Metemmeh, and Boscawen called out a few picked marksmen and told
them to fire five volleys at a distance which Gleichen gives as
2,000 yards. Two or three of the Arabs dropped, and the rest fled
back within the walls. There was obviously no question of surprise, or likelihood of immediate surrender. The flags, when
reached, proved to be stuck over the graves of fallen chiefs.
There was no sign of any impending attack.

In the meantime the astonished Wilson had left Barrow and
galloped back to Boscawen. He did not insist on carrying out his
original plan, nor suggest that the men be reformed in column,
but simply accompanied Boscawen on a leisurely perambulation
in square round the walled town, from the loopholes of which
scattered rifle fire was now directed. The two 7-pounders were
brought into play, but although the common shell they fired
went through the mud walls as though they were made of paper,
they did nothing more. What was to be done? Both Wilson and
Boscawen seem to have been thoroughly foxed, and they continued the slow march between the town and the river, out of
sight as they supposed of enemy fire. They received a shock when
a loud report from Metemmeh was followed by the whizzing
through the air of what proved to be a large round stone shot.
This was followed by others, one of which wounded a man and
killed a camel, while another blew off a camel's lower jaw. They
hastily moved farther away from the town, and orders were at
last given to deploy again in column.

The need to take positive action must have been pressing hard
on Wilson and Boscawen, when four small steamers were seen
coming down the river, flying the Khedive's flag. They were
Gordon's steamers, the *Bordein*, *Telahawieh*, *Safieh* and *Tewfikieh*,
commanded by one of Gordon's most reliable lieutenants,
Khashm-el-Mus. The men in them quickly brought ashore two
of the small brass guns that had been in the turrets. They were,
Gleichen observed, splendid fellows, mostly coal black Negroes
(as distinct from the 'niggers' fighting on the Arab side), and they
were eager for action. They linked up with Wilson's men beside
the river, and another meaningless attack was set up by the guns,

which 'were allowed to pepper away for an hour or so to try to effect some damage somewhere',[1] while the infantry retired in the direction of Gubat, firing occasionally. Major Poe of the Marines, who had insisted on wearing a red jacket because his grey one was not fit to be seen, was hit while standing in the open talking to his men, who were lying down. 'I fear this made him too conspicuous,' says Wilson, with his gift for understatement. His leg had later to be amputated, high up on the thigh. Now at last Wilson decided to retire. He had belatedly realized that his force was wasting the artillery ammunition of which they had none too much, Khashm-el-Mus told him that he had passed a large Mahdiist force on its way down the river, there were a hundred wounded men at Gubat, and altogether he had lost 10 per cent of his effective strength. These were all cogent arguments, but most of them existed before the attack. Wilson thought that Boscawen managed the withdrawal very cleverly, giving the Arabs a chance to attack if they wished. They did not wish, and soon after midday his force, with one man killed and two wounded, was back at Gubat, having burned two or three mud villages on the way. Some of the war correspondents commented upon the operation unfavourably, and one jokingly used the phrase 'reconnaissance in force', which was eagerly seized on by the staff. Marling in his diary was scathing even about Boscawen's clever withdrawal:

> Nothing could have been more disgraceful than the dispositions made for the attack. We were actually marched up in square to within 800 yards of a loopholed town with guns, and kept paraded in front of it without advancing for over three hours, and when we were retired we did so two-deep from the flank, presenting to the enemy the largest target possible.

He added a thought that was in the minds of many officers and men: 'I wish to goodness Buller was here.'

After Wilson returned to Gubat there were further discussions about what move should be made to counter the advance of Mahdiist reinforcements. If they remained where they were, they might be cut off from the river, if they went down to the river they could be fired on from the high ground on which Gubat

[1] Gleichen, p. 173.

stood. It was decided to split the force again. The Guards and Marines were left to hold Gubat, and the rest of the column, with the wounded, were established on sloping and rather damp ground beside the Nile. A rough defence of camel saddles and biscuit tins was constructed in both positions. There were not enough tents for the wounded, and some had blankets hung over them as protection from the sun. The war correspondents were down by the river, and made houses for themselves from stakes covered with canvas sacks and blankets. While the new camp was being organized Wilson settled down to read the correspondence that had come with the steamers.

There was, first of all, Gordon's Journal, written up to December 14. Wilson does not say that he read any of it at the time, but he may have looked at the end, with its despairing plea:

> NOW MARK THIS, if the Expeditionary Force, and I ask for no more than two hundred men, does not come in ten days, *the town may fall*; and I have done my best for the honour of our country.

In any case, he certainly read the short letter to Gordon's friend Colonel Watson, also dated December 14, which began, 'I think the game is up' and said that a catastrophe might be expected in or after ten days. There were several letters written earlier, among them two to Wolseley and two to 'The Officer Commanding H.M. Troops'. One of these, written on October 20, asked that all Egyptian soldiers and officers should be taken out of the steamers. 'I make you a present of these *hens*, and request you will not let one come back here to me.' There was, finally, a little scribbled note in Gordon's hand and with his seal, dated December 29, which said: 'Kartoum all right, could hold out for years.' Gordon had put out several of these notes to deceive the Mahdi, and Wilson seems to have understood that his note was to be read in this light. He told both Boscawen and Stewart that he was going to Khartoum with the steamers.

This was on the afternoon of January 21, but he convinced himself that a delay of a couple of days would not make much difference.[1] He says that he came to this conclusion after question-

---

[1] Wilson, p. 114.

ing the commanders of the steamers, but at least one of them, Khashm-el-Mus, was anxious to set off for Khartoum immediately. Certainly there were urgent problems to be dealt with, but they could have been delegated to Boscawen and others. The position of the column grew more difficult every day. They had started from Jakdul with three weeks' provision per man, some of which had been stolen or spoiled. Occasionally a sheep or a goat was caught, but there was no prospect of maintaining themselves off the surrounding country, and Gleichen reckoned that after February 2 they would have to eat the camels. Had any signalling system existed, it would have been possible to use it to ask for provisions. As it was, a convoy had to be sent seventy miles back to Jakdul, and it had to be strong enough to resist possible attack on the way. This was carrying out Wolseley's instructions that Metemmeh should be used as a concentration depot for the advance on Khartoum, but those instructions had not taken into account the possibility of such heavy losses in camels and men. A despatch had to be written, and Wilson considered it his duty 'to see that the small force which had been so roughly handled on its march to the Nile was safe from immediate attack'.[1] These were all laudable objects, although the last was really beyond Wilson's power.

No preparation for the departure to Khartoum was made on January 21. On the 22nd several of the mud houses at Gubat were blown up, and the debris was used in the construction of a fort. Two of the screw guns were placed on it, and presented a menacing appearance, although there were now only eighty-three rounds of ammunition left for them to fire. Entrenchments were made by fatigue parties to protect the troops by the river. But what about the steamers? In the afternoon the Hussars did as much scouting as their enfeebled horses could manage, and then Wilson set off up the river in the *Telahawieh*, accompanied by the *Bordein* and the *Safieh*. Everything about the steamers was filthy and neglected except the engines, which were in reasonably good order. The foreholds were crammed with ammunition, dhurra, wool and fuel, and in the main holds there were women with babies,

[1] Wilson, p. 114.

refugees, more ammunition and dhurra and bedding, along with
goats and swarms of rats. Slave girls were cooking dhurra cakes
throughout the day. According to Beresford there were on the
Telahawieh a commandant for the ship and a separate commander
for the black Sudanese soldiers. The commandant had under him
several petty officers, called by such names as chief of the sailors
and chief of the carpenters. Then there were Turkish, Kurdish
and Circassian officers for the Bashi-Bazouks—that general name
given to half-castes, Turks and Egyptians indifferently. The
successes achieved on the river by this medley of races seems to
show that they were more efficient than the British officers
thought. A notice was hung up in the *Telahawieh*, signed by
Gordon, saying that the men had done good service, and asking
that any Englishmen who came on board should be considerate
to them.

A company of Mounted Infantry went with Wilson, and he
also took with him Beresford, whose boil was now so painful that
he had to be helped on board, and there lay down in the cabin.
Gordon had expressed disapproval of Nusri Pasha, the previous
commandant of the steamers, and Khashm-el-Mus was confirmed as commander in his place. The Hussars had scouted to the
south, in the direction of Khartoum, but Wilson went down river
to the north, because he was still worried about the large force
said to be coming from Berber. The voyage was uneventful.
Shots were fired from Metemmeh and Shendi, and were answered
by ten rounds from each of the brass guns. One of Khashm-el-
Mus's men was picked up and reported that the party from Berber
had been deterred from advancing by meeting fugitives from
Abu Klea. The boats then steamed back to Gubat and the river
camp, returning at sunset. January 22 had gone by. Beresford was
now in such pain that he had to go into hospital. All the other
naval officers were either killed or seriously wounded, and one of
the war correspondents, Ingram of the *Illustrated London News*,
was appointed Naval Lieutenant, in preference to any of the
regular sailors.

On the 22nd Wilson said that he hoped to start by midday on
the 23rd, but this proved impossible. His reconnaissance had

wasted fuel as well as time, and men were set to chopping up the
water-wheels along the banks, a procedure unlikely to endear
them to the natives. Cutting parties were sent out which needed
other armed parties to cover them in case of attack. An engine
room artificer from the Naval Brigade repaired defects in the
engines. The 'hens' were separated from the Sudanese and taken
out of the boats, a task which had to be carried out through inter-
preters, and so took some time. It was nearly sunset when everything was ready, and Wilson decided that there was no point in
setting out before daybreak. He had decided to go up in the *Bordein*, accompanied by the *Telahawieh*, which towed a nugger
carrying a cargo of grain. Divided between the two boats were
twenty men of the Sussex Regiment, nearly 250 Sudanese soldiers,
and two of the naval artificers. Gascoigne and Stuart-Wortley,
two of the three officers originally designated to be left at Khartoum, also accompanied the expedition. The red coats on which
both Wolseley and Gordon had set so much store had been lost
or looted, and red serge jumpers belonging to the Guards and the
Heavies had to be used instead. Many of them were too big for
the Sussex men, who spent the night wrapped up in them, just
outside the steamers. On this evening the convoy set out for
Jakdul. It consisted of 1,000 camels escorted by 300 men, and with
it went letters and despatches. The camels were in a deplorable
condition, but even so they were better than those left behind.
There remained at Gubat after the convoy's departure less than
900 fit men, together with just over 400 camels and 100 horses.
The force was pinned by this lack of transport and by its wounded
men to the by no means impregnable position it occupied. It
says much for the courage of Victorian soldiers in the face of odds
that there was no panic, nor even any apparent thought of defeat.
Nobody in this little band of ragged men, short of food and
ammunition, hampered by wounded and threatened by sickness
(many of those on the ill-chosen river site went down with fever)
seems to have thought of any possibility but that success would
be theirs. How else can one account for the letter written by
Stewart to Wolseley on the 23rd, to accompany the convoy? The
General had been moved on to the smallest of the steamers, the

Tewfikieh, and although the bullet had not been removed he seemed better, or at least no worse. He wrote to Wolseley:

My dear General,
    I am too much ashamed of myself. Here am I instead of being of use to you a horrible encumbrance on your hands. Never was such bad luck—I was walking round entreating the men to get something into their stomachs before advancing when I was rolled over. I hope and believe we have all but carried out your orders. We have not taken Metemmeh but we are established on the Nile in a better position than Metemmeh itself. . . . Wilson goes on to Khartoum, which is much the best thing as he is a politician not a soldier. I have told Beresford to remain here to command sea forces and Boscawen commands on land. They come and talk things over with me and everything I am sure will be right. You only want the troops you proposed and some groceries by the Jakdul line and Earle at Berber to finish the whole thing to perfection. . . . The doctors all said I was a dead one and I was so knocked out of tune by the shock which paralysed my side for a bit that I was disposed to agree with them, but I am beginning to hope that I may yet again have the honour of once again working with you. . . .[1]

In the morning Wilson at last got away, although not until 8 o'clock. With twenty-odd British soldiers in ill-fitting red jerseys, some of the Sudanese who had come down the river, and a cargo of grain, he was going to steam through country either openly or covertly hostile. Afterwards he wrote himself of the heavy odds facing the two penny steamers, and says that although he tried not to show anxiety he could not help feeling it, but nobody else in the camp seems to have worried unduly about the journey. As the little boats rounded the green point above the camp there was speculation instead about the likely date of their return.

[1] Hove.

CHAPTER SIX

THE LAST WEEKS AT KHARTOUM:
DECEMBER–JANUARY

SEVERAL weeks before all this, on November 25, the inhabitants of Khartoum were greatly excited when they saw the smoke of a steamer. Surely the advance guard of the expedition had arrived? The Arabs at Halfiyeh were firing on it, and Gordon sent down the *Ismailia* to cover the incoming boat. 'If any officer of the Expedition is on board, he will know what it is to be in a penny boat under cannon fire,' he reflected. But the boat was the *Bordein*, back from a journey to Metemmeh, and it brought no news except that the relieving force was apparently no farther than Ambukol, next to Korti. ('Which is LIVELY!', Gordon commented.) Otherwise there were only a few private letters, and two telegrams. One of these was a July communication from Granville, and since it enquired whether danger had arisen or was likely to arise, it was perhaps as well that Gordon lacked the cipher to decode it. The other was from Tewfik, and had been sent in September at the instance of Granville to cover any possible refusal on Gordon's part to leave Khartoum. It directed Gordon to place himself under the orders of Wolseley and Baring, and it also deprived him of the office of Governor-General, on the pretext that British troops would soon occupy Dongola, and 'it becomes necessary, under these circumstances, to modify the Firman which we had granted you, so that your authority will now be confined to being Governor of the Sudan'. This telegram was in Arabic, and Gordon's clerk either did not fully understand it, or hesitated to pass on its contents. In any case, Gordon understood from it that Baring was with the Expeditionary Force, and was coming up with Wolseley.

So one more hope of early relief had vanished, but he did not allow this to become publicly apparent. On the contrary, grandiloquent notices were hung up in the streets saying that the English force was coming in 800 ironclad steamers, each holding ten men. 'They have been hitherto delayed, as they were obliged to exterminate the dervishes *en route*. Therefore cast aside anxiety.' As an additional incentive to the casting aside of anxiety, an issue of biscuit was made to the poorer people, the employees at the arsenal, and the soldiers. But when he had taken these practical measures the little Englishman was left alone with his dreams and speculations, in a town which every day came nearer to the point of starvation. His schoolboy sense of humour remained with him, and he took pleasure in the thought of the great administrator Baring bumping his way up to Khartoum on a camel. He imagined Baring writing to Egerton after reaching Metemmeh and reading Gordon's Journal:

> At last, after the most fearful sufferings, every bone in my body dislocated with those beastly camels. Found here his journal, from which it appears that that duffer, the Mahdi, has at last roused himself, but I fear it is too late. As to the tone of the journal, it is *simply deplorable*.

But still, Baring deserved something for coming all this way on camel back. Perhaps, Gordon thought (for his misunderstanding of Tewfik's telegram increased with the passing of time, so that he eventually persuaded himself that his Firman was superior to any appointment given to Baring or Wolseley), he would appoint Baring Governor-General and then bolt. 'He, on his part, may name someone else, but that is his look out.' Or perhaps it would be better to appoint Kitchener, who had been characterized by Valentine Baker in a letter as one of the few really superior British officers with a good head and a hard constitution. Or perhaps, after all, the best thing of all would be to appoint Zobeir. Supposing Gordon himself, and not the British Government, made the appointment, might not that be a good way out for everybody? It would be at least, he thought, 'a splendid dodge; it first clears Her Majesty's Government of any blame, it puts the blame on me, and in the storm that is caused, I shall have been so effec-

tually blackened that everyone will forget the—well! we will
not say it in direct words (count the months), we will call it the
DELAY'. Perhaps, perhaps! In any case his own intention was
simply to get out as soon as he could honourably do so, and take
service with King Leopold. So far these pipe dreams took him but
then again, with a shift to a different kind of unreality, he would
think: what does it all matter?

> In ten or twelve years' time Baring, Lord Wolseley, myself, Evelyn
> Wood, &c, will have no teeth, and will be deaf; some of us will be quite
> passé; no one will come and court us; new Barings, new Lord Wolseleys
> will have arisen, who will call us 'bloaks' and 'twaddlers'. . . . This is very
> humiliating, for we, each one, think we are immortal.

The last weeks of the Journal make no reflections on religion,
and this was partly because Gordon was always ready to meet his
God, but partly too because his trust was so great that he always
expected a successful issue to his troubles. It was true that he
could not remember a time when, thinking of the spiritual joys
ahead in the life to come, he had done anything but long for
death, but then it was true too that he placed himself in positions
of danger because 'I wish to trust in His promises'. So, sitting at
night in the Palace, he wrote about the problem of ruling Khartoum and the absurdities of politicians, and not about the future
life of which he was assured. His faith was so complete that he was
prepared not to mention it, but to concern himself purely with
practical things.

There were enough of these to occupy him. A new small
steamer was launched, and he insisted that it should be called
Zobeir, although the people had asked for it to be given his own
name. It was launched on November 27, and brought the number
of his steamers up to four, of which one, the *Chabeen*, was in dock.
The launching of the *Zobeir* was a small gesture of defiance on the
part of the hungry town. On the same day he noted in the Journal
that 'about forty females congregated under my window, yelling
for food', and a couple of days later he learned that the officers had
been robbing the men of their rations, and that the storekeeper
had been giving them short weight. He had the offenders
punished, but what could you do with such people? Each week he

noted the dwindling stores, on November 28, 174,400 okes of biscuit and 1,165 ardebs of dhurra, a week later 121,300 okes and 737 ardebs, on December 14, 83,525 okes and 546 ardebs. Were the figures correct? There was such trickery and venality among those in charge of the stores that he could not be sure. The food situation still caused him more concern than the storming of the town by an attack, for after the assault on Omdurman the Mahdi had lapsed into comparative lethargy. The Arabs had a good deal of artillery, including Krupp and Nordenfelt guns, but they made inadequate use of it. When they set up a battery embrasure to bombard the Palace from over 2,000 yards, Gordon remarked that 'as *we* never hit anything we fire at, at that distance, I think I shall be safe in the Palace'. This did not prove to be quite right, for a few days later he had to bob before shells which would have taken off his head if he had not moved. In general, however, although his Journal mentions 'terrific fights' with the Arabs, these were only contests of gun or rifle fire, in which the men sent up to snipe from the Palace roof claimed many victories. Gordon himself almost lost his sight when the base of a brass cartridge blew out and sent the fire back into his face. The Arabs paid chief attention to the Palace, but fired also at the two forts established on the Blue Nile, Mukran and Buri. The defenders answered with a Gatling, but the reply was limited by the need to conserve ammunition. On Thursday nights a band of small boys went on to the roof of the Palace to play. When fired at they retorted with rifles, and then played 'Come to us, come to us', on their bugles. Desertions, however, which had at one time been from the Mahdiists to the town, were now in the other direction, a steady trickle of soldiers disappearing every week. Often Gordon felt that if he had fifty reliable men he would go out with them and 'give the Arabs a dose they would not forget', but he added, 'it is no use, we are not up to it.' On December 14 the three steamers went down and engaged the Arabs outside Omdurman. 'Consequently I am on *tenterhooks.*' When they returned he decided, because the Nile was so low, to send down the *Bordein* with his Journal and letters, and on the following day it started.

The key to Khartoum, if it was not to be taken by direct

assault, was certainly the fort of Omdurman. Once the Arabs had captured it they would control also the river island of Tuti, and the fall of the town could not be long delayed. Gordon's anxiety is reflected in the Journal's repetitions of the phrase 'Omdurman all right', 'Omdurman fort all right', and in his unsuccessful attempt on December 6 to land reinforcements. When this failed he gave promotions wholesale to the officers at Omdurman, and to Faragallah Bey, who commanded the defence. The promotions may appear idle, but there is evidence that they had an effect in maintaining morale. The fort was reasonably well supplied with food and ammunition. On November 13 Gordon noted that they had six weeks' supply of food and water, and a quarter of a million Remington cartridges, which they had a tendency to squander. The fort was defended by more than 400 men, and although the telegraph line had been cut in November, communication was possible by flags.

Little is accurately known of events in Khartoum after December 14, the day on which Gordon ended his sixth Journal. There is a good deal of evidence, given in the later accounts of merchants and others in the town, but each of them tended to grind his own axe of faithfulness to the British cause, and there is a marked tendency towards hyperbole and heroics. There seems no doubt, however, that in the first days of January one final attempt was made to relieve Omdurman, which had become very short of supplies. The plan was to draw away the dervishes surrounding the fort by launching an attack from the Messalamieh and Buri Gates, and then to send the *Ismailia* and *Zobeir* across with supplies. Two separate attacks were made from Khartoum, and it seems that the soldiers fought courageously, but the attempt failed, by one account because a deserter from Omdurman told the Mahdiists what was intended, so that they were ready to meet the attack. The Khartoumese story is that only twelve men among the defenders of the town were killed or wounded, while the dervishes lost more than 600. Faragallah then led half his force out in a sortie designed to break the blockade and evacuate the fort, while Gordon sent a steamer, presumably the *Ismailia*, to the east bank of the Nile to cover the evacuation. Arab shelling of the steamer was so intense that it had to return to Khartoum, and Faragallah was compelled to return to the fort.

> The next day, Faragallah, having nothing left in the stores, and seeing that no assistance could be given him, in despair signalled to Gordon Pasha that if no steamer could be sent to relieve him, he must either surrender or fight till they were all killed. The General answered that he had better surrender.[1]

Faragallah surrendered. He and his men were given dervish dress and accepted the Mahdiist creed, and Faragallah was made an Emir. It is said that Gordon saw them leave the fort, and as they disappeared from view wept bitterly. The date of the surrender has been put as early as January 5 and as late as the 15th.

From the beginning of the year the town was in a state of famine. There were no stores left. The crops on Tuti Island were reaped under gunfire, but they were very small. According to Bordeini Bey, the most vocal of the merchants, he was asked by Gordon to search the town for hidden food. He did so, in company with the Greek consul and forty soldiers, and they found a little corn in merchants' stores and more buried underground. Most of this was given to the soldiers, and when the few feeble cattle had been killed, this meat too was given to them. Even so, this was enough only to provide a meat ration every three days. Gordon called together a committee to find and distribute food. Gum was collected, palm trees were cut and their core was worked into bread with the little dhurra that was left, but these supplies were not sufficient to keep the people alive. People died of hunger every day, and the guards appointed in each of four sectors in the town were not able to bury them all. Money now meant very little, but Gordon tried to maintain it as a medium of exchange, no doubt feeling that once money had lost its power, mass desertion and revolt were inevitable. Receipts were given for all the cattle and corn collected, a reward of two dollars was promised to anybody who buried a corpse and the soldiers were given two weeks' pay, but the meaninglessness of money was more apparent every day, and although women would offer gold and silver ornaments for a little dhurra, they could often buy

[1] *Sudan Notes and Records*, 1930.

Q

nothing. There is an unconfirmed story that Gordon sent 5,000 civilians out of the town to seek food and make their peace with the Mahdi, and certainly there were desertions on an ever-increasing scale. In the second week of January donkeys and mules were eaten, and dogs were hunted in the streets. Many of the soldiers were so weak that they could hardly carry their rifles. Each day more people died, and each day Gordon would say that the English were certain to come tomorrow. On January 20 the Mahdiists fired a salute of 101 guns as the mark of a great victory over the expeditionary force, but Gordon sensed that this was a stratagem, and the starving people seem to have been unaffected by it.

During these days the Mahdiists were in a state of great indecision. The fights at Abu Klea and Gubat appear to us, who know the small size of the Desert Column and its transport weakness as expensively-won victories, but to the Arabs they were crushing and astonishing defeats. The Mahdi had sent many of his best fighting men, and had given them an assurance of victory. How was it possible that they could be defeated, if he were the true Mahdi? On the evening of January 20 the Mahdi called a meeting of Khalifas and Emirs and told them that he had had a vision in which the prophet said that he should make a journey to El Obeid. 'For, he argued, if one Englishman, Gordon, has been able to command the Sudanese and Egyptian soldiers and keep us at bay for almost a year, how much more will these thousands of English who have defeated our bravest men at Abu Klea be able to crush us and drive us away?'[1] Only one Emir resisted the idea of retirement, but it was decided to wait a day or two for news of the arrival of the English force. When it did not come the Arabs regained confidence. On the 25th a messenger came in to say that the boats had started up the river from Metemmeh on the previous day, and it was decided to attack Khartoum before they arrived. The Mahdi now publicly communicated an entirely different vision, saying that 'the Prophet had assured him that God had put the lives of all the garrison of Khartoum into his hands, that they should attack on the following morning, and should fear nothing, for no harm could happen to

[1] Wingate, *Mahdiism*, p. 192.

them.' Wilson's delay in starting may have been crucial. The Arabs' fear of British military might was very real, and perhaps it is not absurd to think that the appearance of a few soldiers in red coats would have made them retreat.

Gordon knew nothing of this fluctuation of feeling in the enemy camp. On the 25th, looking out from the roof of the Palace, he saw the dervishes leaving their positions and loading up their camels. He immediately sent word to the fortifications that an attack might be expected, and ordered that any man or boy in the town who could bear arms should go to the lines and help the soldiers. It would be only for a few hours, he said, since he had no doubt that the English would arrive by eight o'clock on the following morning.

CHAPTER SEVEN

GORDON DEAD, WILSON WRECKED
AND RESCUED

KHASHM-EL-MUS, the commandant of the *Bordein*, was much trusted by Gordon. He was a man in his early fifties with a greyish beard, 'rather short, not very beautiful, but with a certain amount of dignity', according to Wilson. He sat in the saloon with Wilson and Captain Gascoigne, gave his orders, and conversed with the Englishmen through an interpreter. Ten men of the Sussex were placed together on top of the deckhouse in a little citadel which commanded the ship, in case the Sudanese showed signs of mutiny, although this seemed unlikely, since many of them wore with pride Gordon's Khartoum medal. There was a similar arrangement in the *Telahawieh*, except that here there was no interpreter, so that orders had to be given by Stuart-Wortley in pidgin Arabic.

They steamed up the river until past midday, coming to a concealed and fortunately deserted battery, picking up one or two friendly natives, and receiving scattered fire from horse and camel riders on the banks. When they halted at a deserted village to take in a store of wood the Sudanese at once began to fire their rifles and to look for loot. One of them asked Wilson if he wanted a camel, and after replying in the negative he saw the camel's bones lying on the ground. 'He had been killed, stripped of his flesh, and fires lighted to roast him. It was a horrible sight: the blacks wild with excitement, covered with blood, and running about with huge pieces of flesh, which they tore like wild beasts.'[1] Wilson ordered that some of them should be given the

[1] Wilson, p. 149.

kourbash, and they returned to the boats, which steamed on until sunset. Then Stuart-Wortley and Captain Trafford, who commanded the *Telahawieh*, came to dine with Khashm-el-Mus, and they all ate from a huge dish on the floor. Rats ran races round Wilson's cabin all night, and some of them landed on his head.

The second day was for a time a repetition of the first, steam up and away at daylight, stopping for wood which was obtained by destroying houses or water wheels, rounding up the soldiers, starting again. There was little sign of the Mahdi's men. On the contrary, enemy guns were found deserted at more than one place. An hour and a half before sunset they approached the Sixth Cataract. The captains of the steamers wanted to tie up for the night, but at Wilson's insistence they went on, with the *Bordein* on this occasion following the other boat. At the head of a rapid, just before reaching open water, the *Bordein* struck heavily on a rock. Six hours' work failed to get the little steamer off, and anchors were laid for the night. The men slept in the middle of the rapid, with the water running round them like a mill race. In the morning all the stores and ammunition were taken off, the soldiers were landed on a sandbank, there was much pulling on hawsers and anchors, and at last the *Bordein* was free. She was undamaged, but the operation had taken several hours, and within a short time it had to be repeated, when the boat stuck on a sandbank a little farther up the Cataract. Again it took several hours to get her refloated, and by sunset they had made only three miles. It was, as Wilson says, a most unlucky day, its only alleviation being the absence of enemy snipers.

Another day. At last they were past the Sixth Cataract, and entered a narrow and mountainous gorge where a few good shots on the hills could have picked off everybody on deck. There were no marksmen on the hills, not a shot was fired. Were they to reach Khartoum without meeting resistance? During the afternoon a man on the river bank called out that the town had been taken and Gordon killed, but Khashm-el-Mus said that such reports had been current for months, and nobody believed it. There was a certain amount of rifle fire, but nobody was hit.

Now they were all eager to speak to Gordon, and to see how he had kept his people together for a year under siege. On the morning of the 28th they set out in high spirits, expecting to meet Gordon that day. They knew that to reach Khartoum they had to run through the Mahdiist blockade, and Wilson ordered the Sussex to fire volleys at the embrasures of the batteries, which would also be engaged by the steamers' guns. Stuart-Wortley and his signaller had a heliostat with which he would try to attract Gordon's attention, in the hope that a diversion might be made from the town. Before midday they had a sight of Khartoum, still in the distance, and another native shouted that the city had been taken, but they steamed on. Now, as they got nearer, a tattoo of rifle fire was opened on them. Wilson went to the midship turret where he stood on a stool so that he could see all round. Khashm-el-Mus came with him and doubled himself up in a corner, where he stayed throughout the firing. When they reached Halfiyeh, which Gordon had once occupied in the palmy days of July, several large boats could be seen lying by the bank. Khashm said that they must be Gordon's, but within minutes they had proof that this was not so, for fire was opened on them from some guns and many rifles. The bullets tapped the boat's plated sides like hails, the shells mercifully screeched wide, and the Sudanese shrieked with delight when the *Bordein* passed unscathed through the barrage. Wilson, looking anxiously back, saw that the other penny steamer had also passed through unharmed, its red Egyptian flag flying. They could see the Palace, but what was the flag on it? And where was Gordon, who had stood so often on its roof?

They steamed on, fired at by two guns on the right bank, until they reached Tuti Island and came within range of the guns at Omdurman, which they knew to be in the Mahdi's hands. For a few minutes Wilson hoped that Gordon still held Tuti, as the shots fired from the edge of the island struck spurts of sands among the Mahdi's riflemen on the opposite bank of the Nile, but when he approached the shore of Tuti and stepped outside the turret, some better-directed fire drove him in again. They went on until they came under the fire of guns from Omdurman and from Khartoum itself. On the sandspit close to the town hundreds of dervishes stood ranged under their banners. There was no flag flying. Khartoum was lost.

Wilson gave the order to turn and run full speed down river. The *Telahawieh* had run aground, but was got off quickly and without damage. It was four in the afternoon when the steamers got clear of Halfiyeh again and out of the range of guns. The *Bordein* was undamaged, the *Telahawieh* had been hit by a shell. The Sudanese soldiers were in a state of utter despair, not because of Gordon's death, but because their wives and families had been in Khartoum. When they made fast that night none of the Arabs would eat. For Wilson also it was a crushing blow. ' "Khartoum fallen and Gordon dead"—such was the ending of all our labours and of his perilous enterprise.'

*

The attack on Khartoum came on the morning of the 26th, two or three hours after midnight. The Mahdi himself had crossed the river from Omdurman to bless the troops, and to assure them that all who fell would go at once to Paradise. The attack was made from the south, on the semicircle of fortifications, and it had two prongs, one directed at the lines between the White Nile and the Messalamieh Gate, and the other near the Blue Nile towards Buri. The falling Nile had left a space of about 1,500 yards devoid of fortifications, and although the defenders had extended the line for a part of this distance they were too feeble to do more. It was therefore possible for the Arabs to approach the parapets without fear of mines. Riflemen from Kordofan and Darfur led the way over the marshy ground, followed by spearmen, and then by more men with rifles. The attackers got quite near to the parapet before opening fire and the defenders, some of whom were too weak to stand, often realized what was happening only just before the dervishes were upon them.

The attack on the Buri side was successfully resisted for a time, but in the weakest part of the line, near the White Nile, the Arabs broke through almost immediately. Shouting 'There is no God but God, Mohammed is the Prophet of God', they speared and stabbed their way through. The defenders were formed into square here, but they were in no condition to resist for long. Some escaped into the desert, some swam across the Nile, but most of them were killed. Farag Pasha, the overall commandant of the defence line, fled by the Messalamieh Gate when he saw that the position was hopeless. He surrendered to the Mahdi, but was later put to death. Within an hour resistance had collapsed and the Arabs were in the town, killing, looting and raping. When the commander of Fort Mukran raised the white flag the Arabs killed him and everybody in the fort. The Austrian Consul, Hansall, was killed in his house, and few Europeans escaped. The killing lasted about six hours, and several thousand people died.

Gordon was on the top of the Palace with a few men, and he opened fire on the Arabs when he saw them advancing. The accounts of his death differ in small points, but agree in most things. While the Arabs crowded round the Palace, afraid to enter for fear of mines, Gordon went to his room and put on his uniform and sword. Then, carrying his revolver, he went to the head of the stairs. Many of the dervishes rushed up to the roof, where they found and killed the guards and servants, but others made for Gordon. The Mahdi had given strict instructions that his life should be spared, but these were ignored or unknown by the attackers, four of whom stabbed him to death. He did not draw his sword, fire his revolver, or attempt to resist them in any way. Perhaps he recalled his own words, written a year earlier, that 'we have nothing further to do, when the scroll of events is unrolled, than to accept them as being for the best'. His head was immediately cut off and taken to the Mahdi at Omdurman. There it was hung on a tree for three days. His body was dragged down the stairs and left in the garden, where many Arabs plunged their spears into it. At the time of his death Wilson and his crew were struggling to get the *Bordein* off the rock on which it had struck.

So died this courageous, perverse, God-intoxicated Victorian hero, whose fate was to cause national sorrow and indignation, together with the clouding of his complicated character expressed in Tennyson's embalming lines:

> 'Warrier of God, man's friend, not here below,
> But somewhere dead far in the waste Sudan,
> Thou livest in all hearts, for all men know
> This earth has borne no simpler, nobler man.'

*

In the early morning of February 1, in the faint light of dawn, Lieutenant Dawson was wakened by somebody outside his hut calling for Boscawen. It was Stuart-Wortley and he brought not only the news that Gordon was dead, but that the *Telahawieh* and the *Bordein* had both been wrecked, and that the unhappy Wilson and his men were stranded on Mernat Island, about forty miles up the river from Gubat. These disasters had been brought about by the complete collapse of Khashm-el-Mus and the demoralization of the captains and reises. Wilson says that the *Telahawieh* struck because as the boat approached a sandbank the captain held up his hand in one direction, the reis in the other, and the helmsman steered straight ahead. The steamer at once began to sink and was left as a wreck after arms, rations and some ammunition had been got off it. Two days later the *Bordein* was running down towards the enemy batteries at Wad Habashi when she struck on a sunken rock with a crash. She came off the rock at once, but was so badly holed below the water line that pumping had little effect. Again they managed to get most of the stores off on to a small wooded islet, and from there to the island of Mernat, which lay in mid-stream. Wilson at first wanted to make a forced march back to Gubat, but had to give up this idea when the Sudanese officers and men refused to move. He then sent back Stuart-Wortley in a small boat, with a crew of four English soldiers and eight natives, to ask for help.

Surgery had excised Beresford's boil, and he had been busy issuing a proclamation which he signed as Sirdar of the Advanced Guard of the English Army, shelling Metemmeh with the *Safieh*, and collecting forage and food from the country nearby. The convoy had returned from Jakdul, bringing quantities of supplies, two mountain guns, and eight boxes of Martini-Henry ammunition picked up on the battlefield of Abu Klea. It had then gone back again, with 400 soldiers and all the sick and wounded who were fit to be moved. Beresford was spoiling for naval action, and must have been delighted by the chance offered here. Pausing no longer than was necessary to cut and store wood, he set off in the *Safieh* early in the afternoon, taking with him men from the Naval Brigade, some of whom had come from Jakdul with the convoy, and officers who had also just arrived from Jakdul. He took also twenty picked marksmen from the Mounted Infantry. The *Safieh's* armament was two 4-pounder mountain guns, housed in the fore and aft turrets made from railway sleepers and boiler-plate, and two Gardners, the second of which must presumably have come up with the convoy. It was wrongly believed at this time that the boats had been wrecked through treachery, and Beresford had the reis who was guiding his naval helmsman handcuffed to a stanchion. A quartermaster with a loaded revolver stayed at his side, and he was told that he would be shot if there was any indication of treachery, but rewarded if he took the boat up and down the river safely.

It took Beresford almost a day and a half to get up the low and dangerous river, and then he had to crawl past the Arab batteries in a boat which he called a penny steamer in a packing-case. 'Where the packing-case was deficient, bullets went through her as through paper, and a shell would pierce her wooden jacket.' Since the armouring was so defective he felt that the best chance of getting through was to overwhelm the land batteries by gunfire. This was successfully done. One man on the crew of the Gardner was killed, and an officer was hit in the leg, but the *Safieh* was able to stifle the shore guns and run past the battery. They were congratulating themselves on having got through successfully, when a great cloud of steam rose from the after hatchway. The boiler had been hit. Two of the engine-room artificers were brought up on deck badly scalded, with 'the flesh of their hands, forearms and faces hanging in strips, like the flesh of a boiled chicken', and one black stoker died from burns. The chief engineer, Henry Benbow, drew the fires, pumped out the boiler, and then set to work to make a new plate to fill the hole in the boiler. The plate, made from those stores which Buller had thought might be used to mend camels, was too thin to take the steam pressure, and an iron bar had to be fitted across it. The work took six hours, and when the plate and bolts were ready the boiler was still too hot for anybody to get inside to fix them, even though Benbow had twice pumped cold water into and out of it. A Negro boy was smeared with tallow, and agreed to enter the boiler when promised money. At first he found the heat unbearable, but on a second attempt he was able to pass the bolts through while Benbow caulked them and screwed them home. By seven in the evening the work was done, and according to Beresford the boy was 'none the worse in body and richer in possessions than ever in his life'. It was not, however, until ten o'clock at night that the fires were laid, ready for lighting. During the whole of this time—that is, for something like ten hours—fire had been exchanged between the *Safieh* and the Arab batteries, at a range of about 300 yards. The direction of the *Safieh's* guns had to be changed, and one of the Gardners was placed aft, where it worked all day, firing over 5,000 rounds without jamming. One of the brass guns was also used, and this fired 150 rounds during the day. Beresford claimed that this fire was so accurate that the Arabs never had a chance to get their guns to bear, but the gunnery of those manning the batteries must have been wretched. It is remarkable also that no attempt was made to attack the boat from the shore, by running up one of the battery guns to a point at which it could hardly have missed.

The place where the *Safieh* anchored was near enough to Mernat for the boat to be visible to Wilson. He had not been attacked, although he had suffered several desertions, and now he sent Gascoigne across to the *Safieh* in a small boat. It was arranged that Wilson's force would try to get down below the batteries, and there wait for the *Safieh*, and during the night Wilson managed to do this, although the nugger that was bringing his supplies ran aground on a rock from which it could not be moved. At dawn Beresford employed the time-honoured device of trying to make the Arabs believe that the *Safieh* had been abandoned by stopping all firing, and hauling boats alongside as if to take off the boat's company. Like many another simple device this one succeeded, and when at five in the morning Benbow lighted the boiler fires, Beresford was able to take the *Safieh* upstream, turn, run down at full speed and get past the batteries without damage or casualties. He was even able to send half a dozen sailors to help the nugger, which after some sacks of dhurra had been thrown out was floated again and picked up by the little steamer. Wilson and his men were taken on board lower down the river, and the whole party was back in Gubat by the evening.

So the inglorious attempt to relieve Gordon from Metemmeh ended in a passage in the best tradition of heroic British improvisation. Beresford did not recommend Benbow for the V.C. because he had not realized that he would be eligible. He was, however, promoted to the rank of chief inspector of machinery, and was later knighted. Sub-Lieutenant Keppel, who commanded the naval party that went to the help of the nugger, in time became a Rear-Admiral. Wilson on his return was surprised to learn that there was no news from Korti, and after a day's rest set out to go there and report to Wolseley. He did not see Stewart before leaving, fearing that 'the excitement of talking about Khartoum and Gordon with me would do him harm'.

CHAPTER EIGHT

THE NEWS REACHES LONDON

FOR Wolseley at Korti the days went wearily. His belief that Stewart would meet no serious resistance was reinforced when on January 8 a Reuters correspondent came in from Jakdul, having left it four days earlier accompanied only by a native guide. 'You can draw your own inference from this fact as to the truth of absurd rumours that desert is occupied by large hostile armies,' he told Hartington, and a week later he wrote to his wife that he expected Wilson 'with two steamers and about 100 soldiers and 50 of the Royal Navy to reach Khartoum next Tuesday the 20th'. He felt no real doubt that they would be in time.

In the meantime he was occupied in making arrangements to speed supplies along the line of communications. District Commandants were appointed, whose job was to oversee the Station Commandants and to co-ordinate the movement of boats. The new arrangements worked fairly efficiently, but with so many stations to be served along the way, and such an excellent reason for delay as the falling Nile provided, there were inevitably points at which supplies were blocked. Although fifteen tons of stores were now being forwarded daily from Wady Halfa to Korti, one station or another was always running short. The opportunities for theft were immense, and to losses by theft were added those caused by faulty packing. It was reckoned that half of the tea in the whalers went bad because damp got to it through the shellacked linen covering, and that a quarter of the sugar was stolen or spoiled because it was not properly protected from the wet. An estimated half of the hospital supplies were stolen, and thirty per cent of the biscuits proved uneatable because the tins and cases were too weakly soldered to stand the rough handling they received. The Assistant Commisary-General complained that they carried 'a large quantity of liquor up the river and across the desert when transport was very scarce', presumably the officers' supplies, since this was officially almost a teetotal expedition, except for the champagne taken for medicinal purposes. There was another complaint about this. 'The champagne was of very indifferent quality, and calculated to depress rather than to exhilarate the system.' The problems extended right back to Cairo where Ardagh had continual arguments with Cook's about the liability for repairs of boats, and about such trivialities as the return to them of dirty linen, which they thought should have been washed by the Army.[1]

The biggest problem remained that of the camels. The tremendous losses sustained in the desert were not yet known, but the shortage was evident from the time the Column set out. 'Sir Redvers Buller did not, however, consider that the time had arrived for purchasing camels,' says Colonel Furse, referring to the middle of January. This is not quite fair to Buller, for the shortage was of grain as well as camels. 'If only I was well off for camel food now I should be quite happy, but it becomes more and more difficult to feed our camels every day, and we are now quite unable to send away a convoy for want of food,' Buller wrote on January 24.[2] He ordered large quantities of grain to be bought in Egypt, but this was of no immediate help. It was now almost impossible to buy camels, because the Arabs found it so much more profitable to hire them. An arrangement was made with a local sheik, who agreed to take charge of sick camels, give them grazing and treatment, and either return them in good condition or produce a piece of their skin bearing the Government brand as proof that they had died. Yet there remains an impression that the lack of transport was treated with extreme complacency. Wolseley's letters home hardly mention it, and Buller never seems to have realized that if sufficient camels were lost the whole expedition might be wrecked.

[1] Cook Archives.
[2] Melville, *Buller*, i. p. 217.

Apart from dealing with these administrative problems, there was nothing to do but wait. Wolseley rode out into the desert every day and looked out through his glasses from a commanding knoll, in the direction of Jakdul. He entertained each night, insisting still that every member of the staff should wear a red serge coat at dinner. On January 11 Evelyn Wood came up to Korti, and appeared in the evening with a great many ribbons on his red coat, each framed in a black border. Wolseley, who never attempted to resist his inclination to tease Wood, expressed surprise at their number and asked if some had come from the Mahdi, a question to which Wood turned his deaf ear. Those who talked to the Commander-in-Chief during these days found him as equable as usual, but he wrote to his wife on the 27th: 'My very heart is being consumed with anxiety about Stewart's column.' He had taken to playing patience in the evening, and that night read by candle light until three o'clock in the morning. An hour later he was wakened by Captain Piggott, who brought Wilson's despatch giving the news that they were outside Metemmeh and that Stewart was wounded. 'Thank God, my suspense is at an end,' he wrote. 'It is a great disappointment to me that we have not occupied Metemmeh, which I think we should have done if Stewart had not been wounded. Sir Charles Wilson, very useful for the political work, is no soldier.'[1] But he thought the news good on the whole, and his despatch to Hartington stressed that communication with Gordon by steamer was now possible. When the news of Abu Klea became known in England the Queen had greatly annoyed Hartington by telegraphing her congratulations direct to Wolseley. She was herself annoyed by Hartington's protest to Sir Henry Ponsonby, and wrote to Ponsonby herself:

> The Queen always *has* telegraphed direct to her Generals, and *always will* do so, as they value *that* and *don't* care near so much for a mere official message. . . . She thinks Lord Hartington's letter *very officious* and *impertinent* in *tone*. The Queen *has* the *right* to telegraph congratulations and enquiries *to any* one, and won't stand dictation.[2]

[1] Letters, 27.1.85.
[2] *Queen Victoria's Letters*, 2nd Series, Vol. 3., pp. 594-5.

Ponsonby conveyed the sense, but not the words, of this message to Hartington, and now the Queen through Hartington expressed satisfaction, warm thanks and deep concern, and promoted Stewart Major-General. Hartington added his own 'congratulations on the successful issue of this operation, so admirably designed and so brilliantly executed'. This telegram, with others from the Duke of Cambridge and the Lord Mayor of London, were posted up on trees outside Headquarters.

As soon as he received the news about Stewart, Wolseley decided that Wilson must be replaced as fighting commander, and on the following day Buller left Korti to take command of the Desert Column, handing over the post of Chief of Staff to Evelyn Wood. He was accompanied by his A.D.C., Lord Frederick Fitzgerald and by Kitchener, and followed a couple of days later by a battalion of the Royal Irish Regiment. McCalmont had already gone forward to Jakdul with sixty of the Light Camel Regiment, seventy men of the Naval Brigade, some Egyptian soldiers, a field hospital, and 400 hired camels. Wolseley's instructions to Buller began: 'Above all things, don't get wounded. I can't afford to lose you,' and went on to discuss in detail the possible moves open in clearing the dervishes out of the Metemmeh area, collecting dhurra, and co-operating with Earle in an attack on Berber. Gordon was not mentioned in these instructions because Wolseley knew from the despatch that Wilson had gone up to Khartoum. He asked that Wilson should return to Korti to report, and ended: 'Keep me constantly informed of all you do and intend doing, and of all news from Khartoum and of the enemy.' Metemmeh was 180 miles from Korti, and one is struck again by the way in which any idea of speeding up communications by use of heliograph was ignored.

Buller reached Jakdul on February 2, and on the following morning Lord Cochrane came in with the news that Khartoum had fallen and that Gordon was presumed dead. Cochrane went on to Korti, which he reached on the evening of the following day. On receipt of the news Wolseley wrote to his wife:

Oh my dear child I am in despair—News just in that Khartoum was taken by treachery on 26th January. My steamers reached Khartoum on

28th just in time to see it occupied by the enemy. . . . Poor Gordon! for his sake I sincerely hope he is dead. . . . I should think this blow will kill poor old Gladstone. He alone is to blame.

A few days after this he gave General Grenfell two boxes of cigars, saying that he would never smoke again. It was a vow he kept.

*

The news reached London before dawn on the morning of February 5. The Queen was at Osborne, and when she heard it she hurried to Sir Henry Ponsonby's cottage nearby, and appeared in the drawing-room, crying 'Too late'. She telegraphed in clear to Gladstone, Granville and Hartington:

> These news from Khartoum are frightful, and to think that all this might have been prevented and many precious lives saved by earlier action is too frightful.

To Hartington she added a sentence expressing sympathy with Wolseley, and her prayers that Gordon might still be alive. In her Journal she noted that the Government was to blame, and she sent Ponsonby to London to discuss 'the alarming state of affairs'. Gladstone was staying at Holker Hall with Hartington, whose resignation, threatened once more on the subject of the form of enquiry to be made into Egyptian finances, had been yet again averted. He returned to London at once, with his wife and Hartington, and a Cabinet was summoned for the following day. Gladstone must have been greatly occupied, but he found time to write a reply to the Queen in the tone of mellifluent righteousness that so much infuriated her. To her this was a time for weeping and for action, to him it was a time for words, words that recited once more the battle of the routes, words which acknowledged the likelihood that 'abundant wrath and indignation' would be poured out on Ministerial heads, but words which still discovered

> a partial consolation (in) reflecting that neither aggressive policy, nor military disaster, nor any gross error in the application of means to ends, has marked this series of difficult proceedings, which, indeed, have greatly redounded to the honour of your Majesty's forces of all ranks and arms.

R

Had the Government erred at all? He admitted the possibility, for it is human to err, but he felt that the most difficult argument to answer would come from those who said that Britain's business was the protection of Egypt and not the Sudan, 'and that the most prudent course would have been to provide it with adequate frontier defences, and to assume no responsibility for the lands beyond the desert'. Gladstone's biographer, John Morley, thought that these well-rounded phrases adequately closed an unedifying and tragic chapter in national history, but their effect at the time was to anger the Queen further and to make her send another telegram urging 'a bold and decided course' upon the Cabinet. When they met on the morning of February 6 they were bold and decided enough even for her. Wolseley had asked for further instructions, and the Cabinet in effect capitulated to military and public opinion, deciding to give the Commander-in-Chief *carte blanche* to carry on further operations in any way he wished, recapturing Khartoum if he thought it advisable, or advancing on Berber as Gordon had suggested. They had also decided to send out an expedition to Suakin. The Queen approved what was being done, but stressed to Hartington 'in the *very strongest* manner' that Wolseley must now be left 'entirely unchecked'.

Gladstone had been concerned by the possibility that the messages sent in clear by the Queen had been passed on by the telegraph clerks, and this must have happened, for the last editions of the *Daily Telegraph* and the *Daily Chronicle* on February 5 contained the news, so that it was on the streets at just about the time that Gladstone first heard it himself. A public announcement was made by the War Office just before noon. The papers were bought as fast as they could be got on to the streets. 'Men, youths, and even ladies, stood at the street corners and on the pavements',[1] reading and discussing the news. Strangers spoke to each other. The War Office was inundated with requests for further information, and Pall Mall was filled with officers talking to each other and adding rumours of their own to the meagre news put out. 'It is many a long day since the clubs at the West-end have been

[1] *Daily Telegraph*, 6.2.85.

so well filled before noon.'[1] In the life school of the Royal Academy the students were assembled and the news read aloud to them. Egyptian stocks fell immediately.

The sense of shock was increased by the optimistic tone which had been taken for several weeks in almost the whole of the Press. When word came on January 6 that Stewart had reached Jakdul, a leader in the *Daily Telegraph* suggested that 'the worser half of the Desert March is already an achievement of the past', and that what remained was easy work. As soon as the troops arrived on the bank of the Nile Gordon's relief would be a certainty, and on the 31st, when the news of Gubat became known, the paper suggested that Wilson 'by this time has probably shaken hands with General Gordon'. On the same day, when Gordon was already dead, *Punch* published a cartoon of him shaking hands, not with Wilson but with Wolseley. In the following issue this was supplemented by a mournful Britannia saying 'Too late'. It was this over-confident atmosphere that prompted the first re-action, which was in many provincial cities a positive refusal to believe that Khartoum had fallen. Later, the telegrams were pinned up outside newspaper offices, and people crowded round to look at them. By the evening there was no further doubt, and Conservative Associations all over the country were expressing their 'deep regret and bitter humiliation', and condemning the Government's dilatoriness. On the following day photographs of Gordon began to appear in shops and houses, and a few days later this form of mourning for the dead hero had spread to Paris and Berlin.

Could the Government survive? At the beginning of the year Gladstone had thought, as he had so often thought before, of 'letting the outworn hack go to grass', but the actual prospect of defeat stirred him to vigorous action. A vote of censure by North-cote was debated at the end of February, as was a left wing Liberal amendment of Morley's regretting that troops had been sent out at all. This was easily disposed of, but the vote of censure was another matter. Gladstone's speech in answer to it was so full of qualifications that it was often difficult to discover a worm of

[1] Ibid.

meaning wriggling through the rhetoric. Referring to the possibility of reoccupying Khartoum he said:

> What we say is that we are not prepared, at the present moment, to say
> that there is no obligation upon us to use, according to circumstances,
> efforts, if we go there, to leave behind us an orderly government.

The obscurities of Gladstone and the bombast of Harcourt
appeased the Radicals, but it was the struggling honesty of Hartington's winding-up speech that swayed the doubtful. His
admission that 'the Government was not, until a comparatively
late period, convinced of the absolute necessity of sending a military expedition to Khartoum' was balanced by his assertion that
much had already been accomplished, and that they would go
on to achieve the object that Gordon had at heart. The Government scraped through with a majority of fourteen, and Gladstone
said to a colleague: 'That will do.' Did he mean, as Hartington
thought at the time, that the majority was small enough to justify
resignation? It proved that he did not. In the Cabinet he carried
the day for the Government's continuation in office, against the
feeling of several Ministers on both sides of the party, including
Granville, Hartington, Northbrook, Chamberlain and Dilke.
The Queen read with dismay his letter telling her that 'the circumstances, however arduous, would not warrant their (the
Government) tendering at the present moment their resignation
to your Majesty'. In the country, anger turned to gentle regret.
On Friday, March 13, commemoration services for Gordon
were held at St. Paul's, Westminster Abbey, and in hundreds of
churches throughout the country. Everywhere the national
colours were flown at half-mast. Nothing adulterates anger like
tears, and politicians and clergymen set about canonizing Gordon,
leaving the soldiers to avenge him.

So again Hartington had saved the Government in Parliament,
but really they had been saved by the immediate decision to give
Wolseley a free hand. This piece of political realism delighted and
amazed him. To Hartington he wrote that the decision had
astounded him, and to his wife that 'for England's sake, for
Egypt's sake, indeed for the sake of suffering humanity', he was
happy that 'our weak-kneed Cabinet have at last determined

upon an energetic policy for the Sudan'.[1] At the same time he warned Hartington that a summer campaign against the Mahdi would be 'simply madness'. The Mahdi would now be able to concentrate the whole of his army, and the guns he had taken at Khartoum, on the British force, so that 'a repulse would mean annihilation'. He would have to stay where he was for some time, limiting himself to the capture of Metemmeh and Berber while the new force at Suakin destroyed Osman Digna. In the autumn he would be ready to besiege and take Khartoum, which would be 'a very interesting operation, but one of some considerable magnitude'.

This idea of a months-long campaign was accepted in February without question. Certainly the position of the River and Desert Columns gave little reason for thinking that the campaign would be a short one.

[1] Letters, 8.2.85.

CHAPTER NINE

THE RIVER COLUMN: THE BATTLE
OF KIRBEKAN

THE fact that Brackenbury was to organize the movement of the River Column was a guarantee that this would be efficiently done, but efficiency does not necessarily imply speed. The battles of Abu Klea and Gubat had been fought, and Wilson had just set off on his vain journey from Metemmeh, when the River Column started out from its base at Hamdab, some forty miles up the Nile from Korti, sending first of all to the Commander-in-Chief, a telegram reading: 'Just off; all going as well as possible; troops in high spirits, longing for a fight; no sick.' Probably the delay had been unavoidable, for many of the troops were still struggling along between Wady Halfa and Hannek when Stewart made his first march, and Earle himself did not reach Hamdab until early in January.

Brackenbury's abilities were stretched to full capacity. Much of the whalers' gear had been lost or stolen, and no more than eight oars and two poles were available for each boat. Wolseley's decision that this, too, must be a flying column with no line of communications back to Korti meant that they had to carry a hundred days' provisions in the whalers. Even at Hamdab Brackenbury noticed that many of the provisions had been spoiled by poor packing, and he arranged that when they reached Abu Hamed the deficiencies should be filled by a convoy coming over the desert from Korosko. There was a great deal of superfluous hospital gear, including coffee mills, bellows, pewter measures and beer taps, and all this was weeded out. More stringent, or it might be said less eager, than Stewart, he restricted the load on the transport camels to 300 lbs., believing that this was the maximum weight they could bear while remaining in good condition. It proved, however, that no baggage camels at all were available for the River Column. When Earle asked for some on January 17, Buller replied that he had not a camel or a driver to send because they were all in the desert. Two or three days later he obtained some, and told Earle that he must be thankful for small mercies. There was trouble with the Mudir's agent, the Vakeel, who was persistently obstructive in obtaining the supplies and giving the military assistance promised by the Mudir. Buller refused Brackenbury's request for the Vakeel's dismissal, saying that it was undesirable to take the government of the Sudan into their own hands and also that he did not wish to upset the Mudir. In the end the Vakeel with his troops unwillingly accompanied the Column. To crown Brackenbury's troubles, a problem arose concerning the voyageurs. Their engagements had been for six months, which ended early in March, and they were asked to sign re-engagement forms for a similar period. In spite of an offered fifty per cent increase in pay, few of them signed. A personal appeal by Denison had some effect, but against it was the Canadians' fear of the hot African summer that lay ahead, dislike of the treatment some of them had received from the regular soldiers, and in some cases personal commitments in Canada. Less than a hundred men re-engaged. The rest returned to Canada, without any particular consciousness of having played a unique part in a unique expedition. One of their officers said with some exaggeration that they were drunk all the way home. Many of those who stayed were the original incompetents, who were no doubt a good deal more competent by this time. Together with the soldiers, who had themselves learned something about poling and tracking up the Nile, they faced the practically unknown and inadequately mapped difficulties of the Fourth Cataract. Altogether, it seems surprising that they made a start as early as January 24, but decisions were reached quickly because the telegraph line had been extended from Korti to Hamdab. During the days in camp the troops practised formation changes into square ('I shall form square in ample time, for these battalions are sufficiently well drilled to be able with care to move easily in that formation', Earle wrote to Wolseley[1]), and the cavalry made some reconnaissances, one of which brought a sharp rebuke from the Commander-in-Chief, to which Earle replied stiffly that he would not make excuses, but hoped that his further proceedings would command approval.[2] The high spirits of the Headquarters party were soon slightly dampened by the sight of boats in difficulties. During the first day nine boats had to be unloaded, hauled up and repaired, either by their own crews or by the boat-repairing party that Brackenbury had provided to accompany the Column. It was like that terrible passage between the Second and Third Cataracts over again.

There were differences, however. One of them was that many of the men were now adept oarsmen and skilful in steering the boats, another that the River Column was a smaller, more purposeful and more homogeneous group than the army that had moved up the Nile to Korti. There were no fancy Guardsmen on camels to irritate those sweating in the boats, and the nearness of the enemy bred excitement and constant alertness. The pattern of the days did not vary. The cavalry, under Butler's command, ranged ahead of the boats every day, looking for Arabs and reporting back on the best place for the advanced troops to camp. Butler operated on the left bank of the river. Sometimes a similar reconnaissance was made on the right bank, along which the Mudir's three hundred soldiers marched or rode on their donkeys, often burning villages as a reminder by the Vakeel to the inhabitants that they should pay their taxes to the Mudir. Each night a zereba was built round the chosen encampment, and the men slept in their clothes with rifles beside them, often in the form of a square. There were picquets, guards, and double sentries.[3] They had only distant views of the Arabs, although occasionally deserters came into camp with confused

---

[1] Hove, 24.1.85.
[2] Ibid., 22.1.85.
[3] *The Nile Voyageurs*, p. 189.

and confusing tales. Spies returned from Berti, some thirty miles from Hamdab, to say that a considerable Arab force was stationed there, ready to attack the River Column when their boats were separated in the cataracts.

Such separation was unavoidable. The river was intersected everywhere with islands, so that it was difficult to know which of half a dozen channels to follow, and the desert plains were succeeded, a few miles from Hamdab, by threatening rocks. Colvile, who accompanied the Column, described the conditions in a rare passage of eloquence: 'The pent-up stream becomes more rapid, and sand and alluvium give place to tumbled masses of black rock, which encroach in places almost to the water's edge, leaving only at wide intervals scant room for a meagre patch of cultivation. From a military point of view the conditions are as adverse as from an agricultural. Instead of the rolling plains, so favourable to large range fire, and so fatal to an enemy whose strength lies in the impetuous charge of his spearmen, are here found cramped and tortuous passes, down which a company could scarcely march in line. The rocky ground is almost impassable for cavalry.'[1] Through such country the boats struggled, past the unmarked cataracts of Ederini, Kab el-Abd, Umbahoah and Rahini. Denison, working in conjunction with Colonel Alleyne, was immensely useful in finding back channels which by-passed the main rapids. At the Rahini Cataract the Black Watch took four days to cover seven miles, losing two boats and one man drowned during this time. On the last day of their travail Denison took his boat up a side channel, accomplishing in less than four hours a journey that had taken them all day. The boats were full of lice, which infested clothes and hair, and Earle sent a message to Rundle at Korosko asking not only for horse-shoes, nails, paint and other boat-repairing materials, but also for trousers, because the existing ones were in many cases 'not sufficient for decency'. There was often little to drink but water with a residue of sand, the physical labour was intense (enough, Ian Hamilton thought, to make any modern union call a strike), and the nerves of both

[1] Colvile, ii. p. 84.

officers and men were strained. It was with relief that the advance guard came to the little oasis of Berti, to find that the Arabs had retreated and that they could rest while waiting for the other boats to come up. Butler reconnoitred five miles beyond the camp, and found baggage and provisions left beside the river, but no Arabs.

The houses at Berti were of a solidity that the men had not seen since Korti. Various relics of Colonel Stewart's party were found, including French and English books, and fragments of a barometer. These were discovered in the house of Suleiman, who was known to have played a prominent part in the murder, but Suleiman himself was not to be found. The Vakeel had already suggested that Suleiman and his allies should be trapped by a promise of safety if they surrendered, and had been surprised and hurt when the British officers refused to contemplate such an idea. One object of the Column's expedition had been to punish those who murdered Stewart and his party, and in the absence of Suleiman the Cornwalls destroyed his houses, waterwheels and palm trees, these last with some difficulty because the fibrous bark of the trees blunted their axes. Berti was occupied on February 4, and on the following day Earle received a cipher message telling him that Khartoum had fallen. He and Brackenbury were both convinced that an immediate recall was to be expected, and instructions were given to halt the advance. Brackenbury went across the river to check Butler, and to tell him the news. It was kept from the troops, and rumours spread immediately that the Mahdi had surrendered and that they were going home. Three days later Wolseley received the Government's instructions to continue the campaign, and told Earle to push on to Abu Hamed and there await instructions. A general order for a further advance was given. It was known that the Arabs, heartened by the news about Khartoum, awaited them some five miles away at Kirbekan, and in due course they found themselves in that area, confronting an unknown number of the enemy.

Kirbekan was full of rocky hillocks, something less than a hundred feet in height, and the Arabs were ensconced among them behind breastworks that commanded by rifle fire both the road onwards to Abu Hamed and the river. Parallel to these hillocks, but several yards behind them, was a ridge about 300 feet high, and they could be seen moving about along its summit. The left of the Arab position was this formidable ridge which was covered with rocks that looked like white marble, the right rested on the river. Between this and the other shore of the Nile there lay the large island of Dulka. The British officers thought that they were opposed by an outpost of only 300 or 400 men, and that as soon as they advanced a sudden attack would be made on them from the hills behind Kirbekan. In fact, there were between 1,500 and 2,000 men of the Monassir and Robatat tribes holding the position.

Earle, Brackenbury and Butler discussed the best method of attack. Butler proposed to move two regiments on to Dulka Island and take the Arab position in reverse, but Earle rejected this daring idea after making a personal reconnaissance. According to Butler, the General wanted to make a frontal attack. Butler demurred from this, saying that success would be achieved only with crippling losses, and suggested instead going round the ridge right to the back of the Arab position, and taking it in the rear. During one of his own reconnaissances he had noticed sandy wadis going round the ridge, and on the afternoon of February 9 he took out a Hussar patrol and moved unseen to within half a mile of the Arabs. Earle agreed that this should be the form of attack, and on the morning of February 10 it was carried out. Two companies of the Staffords, with two guns, made a frontal approach and held the Arabs in play with gun and rifle fire, while another six companies of the Staffords and six of the Black Watch began the march into the desert and then round the enemy position. They marched in line of half-battalion columns at an interval of two companies, with stretcher bearers following their companies and a few field hospital and small-arms camels between the Staffords and the Black Watch. The Staffords wore red coats and the Black Watch their kilts, although the men apparently had been wearing khaki for their work on the river. With them went Earle, Brackenbury, and

the regimental officers. At the head of the column—it is difficult
not to add, *of course*—was Colonel Butler.

The manœuvre was completely successful. With hardly a shot
fired at them the Staffords and the Black Watch marched round
the eastern end of the ridge, turned left, and halted under cover.
By this time the Arabs had seen them, and there was some fire
which hit two or three men. Earle ordered Colonel Eyre of the
Staffords to take two companies and try to capture the ridge
from its western shoulder, sent two companies of the Black
Watch down to the river to cut off retreat in that direction, and
set the rest of the men to drive the Arabs from the hillocks by
rifle fire. 'In open attack formation our men went for them;
destroyed their grand counter-charge of spearmen by fire and
then stormed the heights *from the rear!* No one escaped.'[1] The
trap was so perfectly sprung that there was no chance of getting
out of it. The spearmen's charge against the rifles of the Black
Watch was received with such shattering fire that the Arabs
broke and fled towards the river, to be met by gun and rifle fire.
Earle ordered a final assault and the Black Watch, bagpipes
playing, charged across open ground and stormed the remaining
Arab positions. The battle was over, and the men were searching
for isolated Arabs among the rocks, when Earle was killed. On a
small plateau between two hillocks there stood a stone hut with
a thatched roof. A Black Watch sergeant said that there were a
lot of men in the hut, and Earle ordered the roof to be pulled
down. It was set on fire, an Arab rushed out of the hut on to a
British bayonet and Earle, disregarding a warning from Brackenbury, approached very near to the hut. He was shot through
the head from its small square window, and died within minutes.
He was buried under a palm tree, near to Colonel Eyre and
Colonel Coveney of the Black Watch. The mortality among
officers was high, as it always was during the Victorian age.
Nine other ranks had been killed, four officers and forty-four
men wounded. Estimates of the Arab dead vary between two
hundred (Brackenbury's cautious calculation) and seven hundred (that of the Vakeel, based upon interrogation of prisoners).

[1] Hamilton, p. 178.

The command of the River Column now fell upon Brackenbury. Hamilton has described him as the complete Army
bureaucrat, a man perfectly at home in an office but with no
taste for active fighting. This may be true, and there is no doubt
that Brackenbury's was a careful temperament, but his replacement of Earle made little practical difference to the Column's
movement. Immediately ahead of them lay the Shukook Pass,
a series of difficult defiles described as one of those positions that
a few men could hold against a thousand. The Column's weakness in cavalry made it impossible to seal off the pass from the
farther end, and although Butler made a reconnaissance (observ-
ing characteristically that the red granite rocks showed drawings
of wide-antlered stags and other animals that were not to be
seen in the country), his opinion afterwards was that if the Arabs
had stayed in the Shukook instead of venturing out to Kirbekan,
'the River Column would have found a difficulty in getting
clay enough in this wild land to cover the dead it must then have
had to bury'. Movement through the Pass was necessarily slow,
and was not completed for nearly two days. It was easy to get
lost and Brackenbury, travelling with the baggage convoy, was
misled by a guide into a labyrinth of rocks over which the
loaded camels hopelessly stumbled. Brackenbury saw that
Earle's estimates of times had been much too optimistic, and he
replied with dampening realism to a telegram from Wood
which assumed that both he and Buller would reach Berber by
February 28. Brackenbury said that not only was this out of the
question, but that any date must be purely conjectural, 'being
dependent upon condition of unknown rapids and unknown
movements of the enemy'. Alleyne, investigating the rapids
ahead, pronounced them swift, shallow and studded with rocks,
and they proved to be even worse than they looked. Unmarked
obstacles like the cataract of Sherrari caused great delay, and
damage to many boats. The Staffords and the Gordons each lost
a whaler, and although repairing materials had been sent up
from Korti, they were not adequate for all that had to be done.
Stoved-in planks were repaired by patches of tin from biscuit
boxes, nailed over the leaks.

Progress was steady but extremely slow, not more than three or four miles a day. By the night of February 23 they reached Huella, and here the whole force reassembled for the first time since it had left Hamdab. They were still thirty miles from Abu Hamed, and nearly 150 from Berber, but they were through the hostile Monassir country, and there were no visible rapids ahead. The men were extremely fit and in high spirits and Brackenbury, indulging for the first time a little optimism, felt confident of their ability to defeat any Mahdiist army that lay between them and Berber. Rockets were fired to tell Rundle's scouts of their position. Brackenbury thought that they would reach Abu Hamed in four days, Butler in three. There they would find fresh supplies, and move on to Berber and to Buller.

They had just begun to move off on the following morning when a native messenger arrived with a cipher despatch from Korti, for delivery of which he had been promised £50. It told Brackenbury that Buller had evacuated Gubat and was now at Abu Klea waiting for camels so that he could fall back on Jakdul. It hinted that the transport of the Desert Column had collapsed. It ordered the retreat of the River Column. The Journal of the Column says tersely: 'The troops in boats dined at 11 a.m. and moved down the river at 12 noon.'[1] Butler took a few Hussars out on a last patrol, and looked at the river that had played so large a part in their defeat:

> It lay a blue belt amid the waste of yellow drift, far stretching to the east, with a rugged outline of purple mountains in remotest distance. A few red and black hills rose in the bare level of the middle distance, and one lofty rock, shaped like a gigantic sphinx, stood looking at us from across the river.[2]

On the way back they carried on further their punitive mission in relation to the deaths of Colonel Stewart and Power. At Hebbeh, between the Shukook Pass and Huella, they had found more traces of the murders—some of Stewart's visiting cards, a shirt-sleeve stained with blood, various papers. Hebbeh had already been half-destroyed, but now the work of destruction

---

[1] P.R.O., W.O. 32/129.
[2] Butler, *Campaign*, p. 367.

was completed, and all the water-wheels were chopped up and burned. With this work done, they continued their descent of the rapids, guided by the voyageurs. Brackenbury thought afterwards that if Wolseley's despatch had not reached him at Huella he would have gone on to occupy Abu Hamed, and the whole British position in the Sudan might have been improved. Yet the change could not have been important, or the improvement lasting. Butler saw more truly when he said, with his usual floridity:

> Ever since the fatal news of the 6th February it was only too clear that all our labour had been in vain, and that the great cheque we had drawn upon future history had come back to us, unhonoured by Destiny.[1]

[1] Butler, *Campaign*, p. 367.

CHAPTER TEN

THE DESERT COLUMN: COLLAPSE OF
THE TRANSPORT

BULLER reached Gubat with six companies of the Royal Irish Regiment on February 11. He had stayed at Jakdul four days while Wolseley waited for instructions from the Government. Neither man had much doubt that the force would be ordered back to Egypt ('I feel already like a beaten cur', Wolseley wrote), and Buller left for Gubat with instructions not on any account to let his force be shut up, but to withdraw it while he could do so easily, while 'avoiding the appearance of running away before this rabble of the Mahdi's'. When Wolseley learned of the Government's decision to continue the campaign he countermanded these orders, telling Buller to take Metemmeh as soon as possible and then co-operate with Earle in attacking Berber. By the time Buller received this message, however, the evacuation of Gubat was in full swing.

'Buller, thank goodness,' Marling wrote in his diary for February 11, and the arrival of the stout red-faced choleric General immediately lifted the spirits of the men. They were happy also to see the Royal Irish, who had marched all the way from Korti in eleven days, a proof that the use of camels for the men was not essential, and a part-justification of their commander's complaint that he was the Colonel of a regiment of soldiers, not sailors, and could march them up to the front. No doubt they were glad to see Kitchener, who had accompanied Buller, and some stores that had come in from Korti were very welcome. But it was the arrival of Buller that really heartened the force. Ian Hamilton has commented on the strange fact that even Buller's failures in the South African War did not shake the faith of the rank and file in his abilities, and during the retreat of the Desert Column officers and men put complete trust in him, a trust based less on what he did than on the kind of man he was. The fact that during a critical moment in the retreat he was discovered laughing heartily over an old copy of *Punch* increased rather than diminished their belief in him. To say this is not to belittle Buller's achievement in bringing order at Gubat into what had been rapidly approaching chaos. Within twenty-four hours of his arrival he had arranged for a convoy to take the sick and wounded back to Jakdul, and had sent a clear and decisive memorandum to Wolseley setting out the situation. He said that there would be no difficulty in taking Metemmeh, but that in view of the condition of the steamers and the state of the transport there was no point in capturing it. Beresford had told him that the two steamers left were of no use for serious offensive purposes, although the *Safieh* could still be used for short raids, to capture cattle and sheep. The camels Buller described with moderation as emaciated. 'Indeed I do not think we have enough camels to get this force out at one go.' He had therefore decided on withdrawal, and he was not moved from this decision by a series of increasingly optimistic letters from Wolseley, who had been greatly cheered by the news that 'the Goverment of jellyfish character had become vertebrate animals', as he put it. The letters, all written in ignorance of the true situation, discussed possible courses to be pursued after the taking of Metemmeh. 'I should have liked to go at Metemmeh very much, but on the whole I concluded that I ought not to attack but to march out, so out I marched,'[1] Buller wrote to his wife.

The seventy-five sick and wounded, including Stewart, left Gubat on the morning of February 13, together with some Egyptian soldiers and camp followers, with an escort taken from several regiments. They were attacked after they had gone eight or nine miles, but were rescued from what might have been an awkward situation by the opportune arrival of the Light Camel Regiment from Jakdul. On the following morning they reached Abu Klea,

[1] Melville, *Buller*, i. p. 237.

rested there for the day, and then went on unhindered to Jakdul.
When they were a few miles from the Wells, Stewart died. An
hour or two before his death he scribbled a last letter to his idol,
Wolseley. It is impossible not to be moved by the high military
romanticism of the letter and by the last line, which refers to some
houses that the Wolseleys had bought on Stewart's advice, written as it was in the context of immediate death.

> My dear General
> Bad luck but glorious—you will agree with me more than any man in
> the world. Oh I have tried hard to do as you would do yourself and oh I
> do so hope you will write to my poor little wife and say—satisfied. Oh
> my dear General thank you a thousand times for your numberless kind-
> nesses. My last wish is that you may finish off gloriously this campaign
> and be soon home again. See my son sometimes if you ever have time.
> Kindest regards to Lady Wolseley. Tell her I am sure the houses will be a
> success in the end.
>
> H. S.[1]

Wolseley had always been worried by the fact that Stewart
was an unbeliever in revealed religion, but he found consolation
in the thought that a merciful God would surely forgive him. His
deep personal distress is evident in the letter that he wrote to Lady
Stewart, telling her that 'I would rather be his widow than the
wife of most of the men I know'. Stewart was buried near the
Wells from which he had set out on his first independent command in battle. Wolseley lost in him the fellow officer for whom
he had most affection. All the others irritated him in various de-
grees, and now that the dogmatic Buller had gone, he found himself driven almost mad by the acting Chief of Staff, Evelyn Wood.
He had received a sharp rebuke from the Queen for a characteristically injudicious remark in a letter, when he said that he hoped
they would be able to wipe out the disgrace of Wood's ignominious peace at Majuba. Smarting under words that he thought
'ungracious to a General in the field fighting her battles', he felt
in no kindly mood towards Wood, and reflected that in spite of
the Chief of Staff's fine soldierly qualities he was 'not to be named
alongside of poor Herbert Stewart or Buller'.

At Gubat, Buller had his hands full. The whole of February 13 was spent in making camel returns and destroying stores in preparation for departure. To their chagrin the men, who had lived on short rations for the past ten days, had to dispose of the greater part of the stores that had come in from Korti because the number of camels left was sufficient only to carry three days' rations in addition to kit. The tins and cases pierced and then thrown into the Nile included more than 20,000 lbs. of beef and as much of flour, 3,000 lbs. of biscuit and about 1,000 lbs. each of tea and bacon. Five boxes of rockets were similarly disposed of, and at the end of the operation the river bank was strewn with broken boxes. The *Safieh* and *Tewfikieh* were sunk, and the six brass guns brought down from Khartoum spiked to render them useless. Soldiers were allowed to take as much food in their private kit as they could carry, and the champagne and port that had come in the guise of medical comforts was all drunk. On the following morning, a beautiful day with a cool breeze and fleecy clouds in the sky, the force of 1,700 men marched off. All of them, Camel Corps and others, were now on foot, with the exception of the Hussars on their ponies. The Royal Irish, who were fresh and eager for action, acted as rearguard, and Buller stayed with them. A large force of Arabs followed the British, but made no move to attack, and after marching ten miles one day and sixteen the next, they reached Abu Klea. Here Buller was made painfully aware of the danger in which he stood. More than 100 camels had collapsed during these two days, and had been left in the desert. The water supply at Abu Klea was not sufficient for the men, let alone for the camels, and there was practically no forage. It would be impossible to move the stores left at Abu Klea, and the hovering clouds of Arabs seemed likely to attack at any moment. Buller ran the risk of being pinned down at Abu Klea, with no transport at all. He decided to send all his spare camels back to Jakdul while they were still able to walk, together with the baggage, stores and Sudanese troops, escorted by part of the Guards and Heavy Camel Regiments, while he remained with the rest of the column at Abu Klea, awaiting a fresh supply of camels and ready to beat off any attack.

They stayed for six days at Abu Klea. It was, as Marling put it, a most unpleasant hole. The thick, muddy water was rationed at three pints a day, dust covered everything, and the Arabs kept up a continual worrying fire, although they never ventured to make an actual charge. The defence was conducted with determination and ingenuity, Major Wardrop of the Guards distinguishing himself on one occasion by persuading the Arabs that he and only three companions were subjecting them to a serious flank attack. The men kept fit and in good spirits, thanks largely to the intrepidity of Buller, who ignored Wolseley's instructions by going out into the desert with the Mounted Infantry. His A.D.C. voiced the general thought when he said that if Buller were wounded they would never get away, and in fact he was struck on the arm by a spent bullet. He wrote to his wife:

> I for the moment could think of nothing but how much I should like to go back to you with all my arms, etc., and was intensely bored with myself at finding that I had suddenly stopped in the conversation I was having with a man.[1]

Their fifth day at Abu Klea was a Sunday, and Buller ordered a church parade, during which the chaplain was two or three times almost hit. Marling shot his dying camel, cooked and ate part of the hump and gave the rest to his men, commenting that it was horribly tough and full of maggots, but a change from bully beef. On this Sunday, at last, a convoy of 782 camels returned. It was now possible to move out, and indeed necessary to do so, for the Medical Officer said that it would be impossible to transport any more wounded if a battle took place. The Arabs had received reinforcements, and were massing for attack.

On the morning of Monday the 23rd Buller was at breakfast when his A.D.C. told him that the Arabs were passing by in thousands, and asked if he wished to change the timing of his plans about moving out. He placidly replied that he did not. The sick and wounded, and the regimental transport, left in the afternoon, the rest after nightfall. All fires were left burning, and the Last Post was played as usual. Before they left, a difficult question arose. With so many thousands of Arabs nearby, and no doubt anxious to water their ponies, would it not be wise to fill up the

[1] Melville, i. p. 236.

wells to delay them? Buller was reluctant to do anything so un-
sporting, but was persuaded by the Intelligence Officers, Kitchener
and Verner, that it was necessary. He consented only to the filling
of the largest wells, but it seems likely that the officers under his
command filled them all. When the incident was reported, it
brought an anxious telegram from Hartington, who was mollified
when he was told that only a few wells had been filled. With the
wells filled they left Abu Klea, in darkness and in silence. The
Arabs did not learn of their departure until the following morning, and then did not follow. Perhaps they were too happy to see
the British go.

The return to Jakdul Wells took three days' hard marching,
and during it tempers often frayed. The mens' boots, which were
of poor quality to begin with, had been rotted by water and eaten
by ants. The sailors marched barefoot, some of the men cut up
old rifle buckets and tied them under the soles of their feet with
string, and others walked with their soles flapping. Their uniforms
were so worn, torn and ragged that they were hardly distinguishable one from another. They were all unshaven. Some felt the
effects of the sun, like Major Gough of the Mounted Infantry,
who was 'quite off his head and got no end damned by Buller' on
one day, and was suspended from his command on the next for
making an unauthorized halt. At last they limped into Jakdul.
Wood, who had been sent out to meet them, sent back a minute
impressing on Wolseley the fact that although the men were
extremely fit, their equipment was ruined and their transport
almost non-existent. The Heavy Camel Regiment had only
twenty-two riding and ten baggage camels left, the Mounted
Infantry ninety-five, and the Guards just over 200. The Remount
Department at Wady Halfa had practically ceased to exist, because all spare camels had been sent up to Korti. Even at Korti
the shortage was such that Wolseley's own camel and those of
the staff had been pressed into use for carrying the sick and
wounded. Now Wood told Wolseley: 'The troops cannot get
to Korti without transport to move all of them, as also for the
stores. I assume every effective will walk.' And most of them did
walk, still bootless or wearing boots which had been hurriedly

sent out from Korti and were so small that many of the men could not get their feet into them. The officers wore anything they could find at Jakdul, from field boots to tennis shoes. Back at Korti they enjoyed the pleasures of 'pyjamas, clean shirts, a new sponge, baccy, a complete change of attire, and a spare pair of boots'.[1] There were other pleasures too, for those friendly with Buller. On the march the General had despised the use of his tent, sleeping out in the open and eating what the men ate, but things were different at Korti. Marling, and his friend Bimbash Stewart the champion looter, dined with Buller, on the night of their return. After a meal accompanied by 'lashings of fizz' Stewart told stories of the return, digging Buller in the ribs while asking for his confirmation. At last Buller said 'Damn you, Bimbash', and pushed him over, chair and all, on to the sand.

It was not until he saw the men come back on March 16 that Wolseley realized how completely the Desert Column had become, in the words of one officer, a force incapable of undertaking active operations because of their lack of equipment. The River Column had returned already, taking little more than a week to come back down the rapids that had been so painfully ascended, although they lost several boats in the process. Bitterly, he assessed the situation. There could be no question of advancing again across the desert, or of moving to capture Berber. If it were taken, what would be achieved to compensate for a further lengthening of the line of communications? He told Hartington that the force would now take up summer quarters along the Nile. In the meantime, General Graham had again been appointed to command the force being assembled at Suakin. A contract had at last been signed with a firm of private contractors, Lucas and Aird, to construct the famous Suakin–Berber railway. Graham was to act against Osman Digna, but to consider himself under Wolseley's orders. Hartington thought that it would not be possible to do much during the hot weather, and that perhaps most of the force might be kept at Suez then. It looked like a long war.

[1] Gleichen, p. 247.

CHAPTER ELEVEN

THE END OF THE CAMPAIGN

BETWEEN the latter part of February and early April the process of reorganizing the battered little army, and of settling into summer quarters, went on. Stations were formed at several points along the Nile, from Dongola up to Korti and Hamdab, and garrisons were allocated to them. Flying columns were organized, ready to resist attack at short notice. Mud and straw huts, which were thought necessary as protection against the summer heat, were put up, a procedure which was expedited by the expulsion of the Mudir of Dongola from his province to Cairo. The extension of the Wady Halfa railway for nearly fifty miles, to eliminate some of the worst rapids between the Second and Third Cataracts, was begun, or at least the materials were ordered. A number of river craft were ordered too, including stern-wheel boats, steel barges, and 300 more whalers. Furse drew up a report on buying camels and obtaining drivers for the autumn campaign. Graham's force at Suakin, which had swelled to 13,000 men including Indian and Australian contingents, and was blessed with the novelty of a balloon detachment (the balloon proved generally unusable because of the high wind) fought one or two minor engagements. Eighteen miles of railway were laid down by Lucas and Aird, but the difficulty of working while marauding Arabs were near proved as great as Wolseley had expected. He told his wife of a plan for forging the seals of the Mahdi and his principal followers, so that false proclamations could be issued under their authority. 'Everything is fair in war', he said, but asked her if she thought the idea villainous. Before there was any chance to use this trick, however, he returned at the Government's request to Cairo, as a convenient place from which to direct the two forces he was now commanding. He reached Cairo on April 11, and two days later the blow fell. A telegram from Hartington told him: 'In the condition of Imperial affairs it is probable that the expedition to Khartoum may have to be abandoned, and the troops brought back as soon as possible to Egypt.' Within a few days the probability had become a fact. Khartoum, Berber, and the whole of Dongola province were to be abandoned to the Mahdi, and the expeditionary force was to return home. Wolseley's immediate reaction was to write a letter of resignation, but his wife, who had come out to Cairo, persuaded him to accept the decision without overt protest.

The 'condition of Imperial affairs' that occasioned this second reversal of Government policy was an incident on the Afghan border. The line of demarcation there was in perpetual dispute, and a joint Russian–British Commission had been convened to settle it. On March 30 the Russians attacked Afghan troops and occupied Pendjeh. Few people in England had heard of Pendjeh, but the Russian action immediately became a cause for Gladstonian alarm. He conveyed to Hartington and others his sense of shock and danger, and suggested that since war with Russia was a possibility, Wolseley should be brought home at once to give advice on the conduct of operations. The Grand Old Man, as he moved into action, drowned the doubts of his colleagues in a flood of words. Morality once again raised its noble head as he asked them whether there was 'any obligation of honour or any inducement of policy (for myself I should add, is there any moral warrant?) that should lead us in the present state of the demands on the empire, to waste a large portion of our army in fighting against nature, and I fear also fighting against liberty (such liberty as the case admits) in the Sudan?' A tremendous memorandum questioning 'the moral basis of the projected military operations' battered them, in terms that few could resist. Wolseley had not helped his own case by saying incautiously that the advance on Khartoum would be the most serious military operation since Waterloo, and by asking for very large reinforcements to conduct the autumn campaign. On the one hand there was this morally dubious expedition, for which many people had lost appetite since the confirmation of Gordon's death, and on the other an urgent need to support that sovereign ally of Britain, the Emir of Afghanistan. In Parliament Gladstone, full of fine moral feeling, solemn about the Afghan problem ('We cannot close this book and say we will look into it no more'), asked for and obtained from the House of Commons a war supply vote of £11 million, of which £4½ million was to meet Sudan expenditure, and the rest to be used for general military preparations. Within days of this war supply vote being passed without Unionist opposition, the Pendjeh problem was suddenly found to be capable of solution by arbitration, and it was generally agreed that actions on both sides might have been a little hasty. There was, however, no question of rescinding the decision to evacuate the Sudan.

How far this master stroke of Gladstone's, by which he had obtained a large sum of money to cover the Sudan operations including the expensive and now useless Suakin–Berber railway, was a piece of political chicanery, and how far he believed in the Russian threat, is something that perhaps he did not know himself. The happy way in which political convenience and moral imperatives chimed together was something upon which he remarked himself, not in those words. But some of his Cabinet were indignant at the way in which they had been persuaded or deceived, and between the middle of April and the middle of May more than half of them threatened resignation. 'A very fair Cabinet today—only three resignations,' he said with good humour after one meeting. The Liberal Government, full of dissensions about Ireland, the Franchise Bill and Gordon, was staggering to its end, and early in June defeat came through an alliance of Unionists and Irish Nationalists, on the trivial issues of increased duties on property and on beer. Lord Salisbury formed a Government with the aid of the Parnellites, but the new Government made no change in the policy of evacuating the Sudan, which had become by this time almost irreversible. The sudden death of the Mahdi on June 20 made no difference, nor indeed did it affect the power of the Mahdiist movement, or the slow development of a Mahdiist state under his successor, the Khalifa Abdullah. Hartington had, after all, managed to get through the Government's five years without resignation, but as his biographer says he must have been profoundly relieved by its defeat, and have gone to Ascot races in that same week of June with an easy heart.

So it was settled. Baring, as well as the soldiers, was anxious to hold on to Dongola province, but this advice was rejected. The voyageurs returned to Canada. Wolseley, talking to Denison at a time when an autumn campaign still seemed likely, said that he would want four or five hundred of them later in the year, but no tinkers or tailors. Now there was to be no autumn campaign, and sadly and bitterly the troops came home. There were pleasures in Cairo for the officers, cold drinks, English breakfasts, table-cloths and sheets. Lieutenant Bower of the Mounted Infantry beat up a policeman in a festive mood, and Bimbash Stewart made love to Nubar Pasha's daughter. When asked by Nubar about his intentions and means, he said that he was an officer in the Gordon Highlanders, with a castle in Ayrshire and a good claymore. Nubar thought this an inadequate provision for his daughter, and rejected Bimbash as a suitor. But these alleviations, and the pleasures of the brothels for the other ranks, did not touch the sense of frustration felt by officers and men. On July 5 Brackenbury, who was in charge of the rearguard, 'evacuated Dongola, bringing with him all whalers, stores and steamers', in the words of the Official History. The withdrawal of the troops at Suakin began in May. On June 27 Wolseley handed over to Stephenson command of the troops in Egypt, and left for England.

*

During his last weeks in Egypt the Commander-in-Chief was much concerned with fixing military responsibility for the failure to reach Gordon in time. On April 16 he wrote a personal letter to Hartington, reiterating the thesis so often denied by the Duke of Cambridge, that selection for promotion should come through merit and not through seniority, and implying that this had been one cause of the Expedition's failure:

> There are now serving under my command some regimental Lieut-Colonels who are entirely unfit for their positions . . . to the Brigadier or General under whose immediate orders they serve, these officers are a source of constant anxiety. Owing to their ignorance of the first principles of tactics or of the military art, it is always necessary for him, in order to avoid disaster, to keep them under his own personal observation, or to send some well-trained Staff Officer to take care of them. . . . I have often on active service seen splendid battalions kept in the rear, or broken up for work along the line of communications, whilst others of inferior quality were sent to the front, because the General commanding did not dare to employ against the enemy corps whose commanding officers were manifestly incompetent.[1]

He named no names, but appealed to Hartington for action to change the 'entirely and radically wrong' system under which 'the lives of gallant soldiers' were handed over to 'men who are deplorably ignorant of the elements of their profession'. The outburst seems to have been ignored, and although Wolseley repeated it in a magazine article under the sobriquet of 'Centurion', the letter and the article had no effect except to annoy the Duke of Cambridge. One particular soldier, however, was picked out by Wolseley as a man who could have saved Gordon had he been more enterprising and energetic. In forwarding on February 15 Wilson's report on the attempt to reach Khartoum by steamer, Wolseley omitted any comment on Wilson's own part, although he praised the men in the boats. 'It was not through any lack of zeal or want of energy on their part that these steamers only reached Khartoum two days after it had fallen,' he said, adding that had the steamers reached the town on the 25th instead of the 28th there was 'little doubt that the place would not have been surrendered'. Privately he said much more than this, telling his wife that he could not bear to have Wilson in his sight, and commenting on the fact that the *Bordein* had emerged unscathed from the gunfire directed at her, and so evidently had not pushed as far as she might have done into Khartoum. When, a little later, Wilson was asked to explain the reason for the delay at Gubat

[1] Maurice and Arthur, *Wolseley.*

he realized that he was cast for the role of scapegoat. His dignified reply placed the cause of delay on fear of attack by an Arab force, and the need to clear off the useless Egyptians from the steamers. The reply is not wholly convincing,[1] and it certainly did not convince Wolseley, who passed it on saying that he did not propose to add any remarks of his own, and that 'the reasons given by Sir Charles Wilson must speak for themselves'. Hartington consulted with the Duke of Cambridge, but the Duke had already been much impressed by Wilson's unselfishness in giving Boscawen active command of the square, and was in any case not inclined to support Wolseley in such a criticism. Hartington told Wolseley that there was no disposition in London to blame Wilson. At the end of June he said an official good-bye to the Commander-in-Chief, commenting that although they had just missed success this should not be attributed to 'any fault either of design or execution on your own part, or on the part of your officers and men'. Wolseley responded with genuine good feeling, expressing his hope that Hartington would be the next Liberal Prime Minister. 'My only regret to the arrangement will be, that we shall not have you at the War Office.' He always remembered Hartington as, next to the reforming Cardwell, the best of the civilian War Secretaries under whom he had worked, and certainly he was the most compliant.

*

During the months after Gordon's death there seemed to be really no need for a scapegoat. Gordon himself was a natural subject for one of the sentimental orgies by which Victorian society transformed disagreeable reality into noble myth. Gordon Clubs for boys, Gordon Boys' Homes established by national subscription, Gordon windows in churches to commemorate the

---

[1] It is, however, more convincing than Mr. Allen's ingenious suggestion, based on a conversation with Stuart-Wortley many years later, that Wilson waited in the hope that Beresford would be able to accompany him—so that Gordon may have died because of the boil on Beresford's bottom! This seems to be contradicted by Beresford's own *Memoirs*, and by Wilson's comment that Beresford offered to go with him, but that he felt he could not deprive the force of its only naval officer.

Christian soldier, in these and a dozen other ways the uncomfortable memory of the real Gordon and his fate were put away. And if Gordon had died the best of all possible deaths for God and country, had not those who tried to save him deserved well of the people also? When, on 12 August 1885, Lord Salisbury as Prime Minister rose to move that the thanks of the House should be given to Wolseley and to all those who accompanied him to Egypt, this was agreed to *nemine dissentiente*—unless, indeed, the Duke of Cambridge, who made a speech referring to Wolseley only in one sentence and even then going on to mention immediately how ably he had been seconded by Buller, might be thought of as a dissenter. When awkward questions came up concerning Wilson they were turned away with soft equivocatory answers, when the cost of the expedition was estimated at nearly £3 million, the matter was not debated. Wolseley's last despatch praised almost everybody and everything, as is customary. The army was a wonderfully efficient military machine and had greatly improved in moral tone, thanks partly to the abolition of flogging. They had been immensely healthy, the sick and wounded had never been better cared for, the Ordnance, Transport and other Departments had worked well, the voyageurs had shown a high military and patriotic spirit. Buller, Wood, Brackenbury, had all done splendidly, Butler and Alleyne deserved great credit for their work on the whalers, Beresford's resource was equalled only by his daring. Even Wilson received carefully phrased commendation: 'In the intelligence Department Colonel Sir C. Wilson kept me fully supplied with information as to the enemy's doings and intentions, and showed himself eminently qualified to conduct the duties of that Department.' These officers did not go unrewarded. Wolseley did not become Duke of Khartoum but he was created Viscount, Buller and Wilson were both made K.C.B., Brackenbury was promoted Major-General. Some of the incompetent Lieutenant-Colonels got nothing at all. Wolseley obstinately refused to sanction any decoration for the Prince of Wales's friend Lieutenant-Colonel Stanley Clarke, who had decided that the war and Egypt were too much for him, and had gone home in February. Wolseley told his wife that she could say, without mentioning Clarke, that 'any officer who went home now except on the most urgent private business would not be allowed to rejoin this Army again, or to serve with any army in the field it may ever be my lot to command'.[1] The Prince also deprecated Clarke's conduct and agreed that promotion for him was not to be thought of, but he suggested that C.B. might be managed for him, or if not, C.M.G. When Wolseley finally refused to make any award at all, the Prince was driven to speculate that there must be 'some Turkish decoration given with the sanction of the Sultan',[2] and that Clarke might be eligible for that. In the long run, friendship had its way. Clarke ended his Army career as an honorary Major-General, but he had to wait until 1897 for his C.M.G.

The cracks were thus plastered over, yet echoes of the expedition's failure reverberated for years, both within and outside the Horse Guards. A special committee on Small Arms heard evidence from indignant officers and men of the jammed rifles and bent bayonets at Abu Klea. When Colonel Talbot, the commander of the Heavy Camel Regiment, was asked by the committee on what occasions the rifles had jammed, he replied: 'On all occasions,'[3] and said that at least half of them stuck or jammed at Abu Klea, so that a man would throw down his rifle and snatch another belonging to a wounded comrade. The bayonets which had proved unsatisfactory were the sword bayonets, which could be detached and used separately as sword or dagger, and not those of triangular shape. These sword bayonets had been put to service in cutting grass and chopping wood, and many of them had become so blunt that when thrust at a body they turned harmlessly away from it. The committee did its best to minimize the failure of these arms, and recommended solid-drawn cartridge cases and a stiffer and more powerful cartridge extractor, but the days of the single-shot rifle were numbered, and within a few years the magazine rifle had been approved and adopted. An enquiry was also held into the Gardners. Tests carried out in 1881 had seemed to

[1] Letters, R.U.S.I., 11.3.85.
[2] Hove.
[3] War Office Records, Report of Committee on Small Arms, 1886.

THE END OF THE CAMPAIGN

show that the Gardner was a more convenient and considerably more dependable weapon than the Nordenfelt or Gatling, but now Wolseley in a memorandum said that he could not recommend any large expenditure on the Gardner in its present form. He expressed his own preference for the Nordenfelt, with its horizontal instead of circular firing action, and ended his memorandum prophetically: 'The machine-gun is still in its infancy. Its power when in its prime will in my opinion astonish the world.'[1] Neither Wolseley, nor anybody else for some time to come, realized that the development of the machine-gun implied the end of cavalry as a fighting arm. There are limits to prophecy.

'I turn my back upon Khartoum with a sinking heart,' Wolseley wrote, and in the end it was his reputation, rather than that of any subordinate officer, which was damaged by the failure to capture Khartoum. 'What a host of enemies I have!' he had written to his wife in January from Korti. 'Do you suppose it is only the usual number that a successful General has, or is there something about me that makes men bear me ill-will? I believe there would be many who would rejoice if this expedition failed, because its failure would be mine.' Dislike of him was indeed prevalent outside his immediate circle, particularly within the Indian Army. Ian Hamilton has confessed that in those days he would have given anything he possessed to see Roberts raised up and Wolseley and the Wolseleyites brought low. This did not happen, and indeed outwardly little was changed in the War Office hierarchy. Wolseley remained Adjutant-General until 1890, and then went to the command in Ireland. During these years he continued the battle for army reforms against the Duke of Cambridge, enlisted the Duke of Connaught in his campaign for the adoption of khaki as a uniform in the field (the Nile Expedition had emphasized its usefulness, and red jackets were never again used by the army in action), and brooded on real or imaginary frustrations. He never made any attempt to fulfil that last duty imposed on him by Carlyle, but in 1888 his public criticism of political leaders was expressed in such barbed, contemptuous terms that he was compelled to make a public withdrawal in the

[1] Wolseley Papers, R.U.S.I.

House of Lords. In 1895 the enforced retirement of the Duke
brought him to the position he had always longed for, that of
Commander-in-Chief of the army. Now at last he was supreme,
now there was no Great German Sausage (as Wolseley privately
called the Duke) standing four-square against all reform. But he
took office at a time when his powers were already failing. He was
still able to write sharp, admirably worded minutes, but his
memory showed alarming lapses, and his power of concentration
had gone. The improvements he effected in training and in the
use of weapons were only a small fraction of what he would have
achieved a few years earlier, and the end of his reign was clouded
by the disasters of the South African War. These were not greatly
ameliorated by the fact that the mobilization for which he was
directly responsible had worked with wonderful smoothness, and
Wolseley suffered the humiliation of being confronted with a *fait
accompli* when Roberts was appointed as supreme commander
in South Africa in place of Buller. His cup of bitterness was full
when, upon his retirement in 1900, the hated Roberts replaced
him.

Of the other principal figures involved in the Expedition Buller
is the best remembered, although the remembrance is not a happy
one; and even before his death in 1907 many of the Victorian
parents who had called their sons Redvers were regretting it.
Wolseley said in 1885 that Buller was the best man in the army.
'His manner is against him, but as a fighting soldier and as an
organizing staff officer he is A.1.' Buller, like Wolseley, sat behind
a War Office desk for many years, and he was a painstaking and
successful administrator, whose principal achievement was the
combination of supply and transport into what later became
known as the R.A.S.C. Too much good living and too little
action softened him mentally and physically during these years,
and when at the beginning of the South African War he went out
in supreme command of the British forces, his generalship was
not only tactically feeble, but was marked also by a hesitancy that
can be discovered in several incidents of his early career. He stayed
in South Africa after his supersession by Roberts, never lost the
respect or affection of his soldiers, and received a tremendous

welcome on his return to England. He wrecked his career finally
after his appointment to the Aldershot command, by an indiscreet
speech at a public luncheon. He was removed from the command, and never employed again.

Neither Wood, Brackenbury nor Wilson held another field
command. Wood spent the rest of his army life in carrying out
Wolseleyan training reforms at Aldershot, and in the War Office.
In 1903, at the end of his career, he was created Field-Marshal.
Brackenbury occupied several important positions at the War
Office and on the council of the viceroy of India, and was brilliantly successful in reorganizing the supply of munitions during
the South African War. The rest of Wilson's life was marked by
the slur which he felt had not been removed by his official excul-
pation from blame. Acquittal by his military superiors was something that he would have valued much more, but this he never
received. He was for several years director-general of an Ordnance
survey of the United Kingdom, and thereafter held a post in
charge of military education.

The fate of the turbulent Butler deserves a separate paragraph.
He was given command of the troops on Egypt's new frontier,
and in December 1885 led a brigade under Stephenson when the
Mahdiists made their last attempt to invade Egypt and were
decisively defeated at Giniss. Within a few months Butler had
exasperated the patient Stephenson so much that he wrote to
Wolseley, who sent an admonishing letter to Butler, and a little
later had him brought home on sick leave. There he learned that
he would receive no gazette for Giniss, and found himself put on
half pay. A couple of years later he was asked to prepare a report
on the Army Ordnance Department, and expressed himself in
such terms about the civil side of the War Office that the
printed copies of his report were recalled and destroyed. The
crowning misapplication of his talents came when in 1898 he
became commander of the British troops in South Africa and
temporary High Commissioner in Sir Alfred Milner's absence on
leave in Britain. Just as he had sympathized with the Arabs against
the Turkish and Egyptian pashas, so now Butler took the side of
the Boers against what he thought of as the Houndsditch Jews

T

of Johannesburg. In his capacity as General in command he
scouted the likelihood of war with the Boers and said that if it
came an enormous army would be needed to defeat them, in his
capacity as acting High Commissioner he cheerfully ran counter
to Government policy by espousing the Boer cause against the
pro-British South African League. As soon as Milner returned
Butler was relieved of his civil duties, and Milner's obvious distrust of him combined with a sharp reproof from the War Office
to induce him to offer a resignation that was promptly accepted.
He returned to a home command until his retirement in 1905.

Among the politicians chiefly involved, Gladstone emerged,
not triumphant exactly, except so far as it may be called a triumph
to have emerged at all as the leader of a Liberal Party which
bounced back into power again in 1886, when a General Election
returned a number of Liberals exactly balanced by the number of
Unionists and Parnellites combined. In the short-lived Government that followed, which was primarily concerned with Irish
Home Rule, Granville was Colonial Secretary and Chamberlain
president of the Local Government Board. It was Granville's
last post in any Government, and for Chamberlain it was a parting
of the ways. He accepted the post with reluctance, and after a
few weeks he resigned, although it was not until 1895 that he
accepted office under a Tory Prime Minister. Dilke, already in
the toils of his divorce case, was not included in the Government.

Hartington's conscience refused to let him join a Government
pledged to the idea of Irish Home Rule, and his appearance upon
the same platforms as Salisbury was a presage of the break-up of
the unhappy Liberal Party. In 1887 he led his followers, who
called themselves Liberal Unionists, into the lobby with Chamberlain and Bright to defeat the Government, and at the subsequent election a deep fissure was apparent, when the Liberals
were split into 191 Gladstone and seventy-eight Hartington
Liberals, against 316 Unionists and eighty-five Parnellites. In this
delicate situation Hartington twice refused Salisbury's offer to
support him as Prime Minister, and instead sat upon the Front
Opposition bench and gave the Unionists the support which
kept them in power. He had three times declined to be Prime

Minister, and it was not until he had succeeded to his dukedom and left the House of Commons that at last, in 1895, he joined a coalition administration of Tories and Liberal Unionists, accepting under Salisbury the post of President of the Council. He occupied this position for several years. His conscience had come to rest at last.

CHAPTER TWELVE

POSTSCRIPT AND POST-MORTEM

THE postscript to the Nile Expedition was written thirteen years after its end. During those years Kitchener had been in Egypt, first as Governor-General of Eastern Sudan, with his headquarters at Suakin, battling with the threat constantly posed by Osman Digna, then as Adjutant-General of the Egyptian Army, and from 1892 onwards as Sirdar. He prepared slowly and carefully for the reconquest of the Sudan, preferring an advance up the Nile to a move across the desert. There was no need for speed, and hence no question of attempting to move up a falling Nile. In 1896 the dervishes were driven out of the province of Dongola, and during the next two years Kitchener pushed forward his plans for advance on the Sudan. These plans were delayed by troubles, any one of which would have been sufficient to destroy the hopes of the Nile Expedition: an outbreak of cholera in the army, severe storms which washed away a twelve-mile stretch of recently built railway, an explosion in a gunboat specially designed to attack the dervish forts along the Nile. But time was not of vital importance to him, and in July 1897, he captured Abu Hamed, and soon had in operation a railway running 103 miles across the desert from Wady Halfa. The railway had been seven months in preparation, and Kitchener was able to feed supplies along it to this farthest point of his advance. A month later he occupied Berber, but his advance from there was delayed until January 1898. In April he defeated the Arabs at the battle of the Atbara, and in September finally destroyed the dervish power outside Omdurman. On 4 September 1898, the British and Egyptian flags flew again over the ruins of the palace at Khartoum. The Mahdiist state was at an end, and the Khalifa Abdullah was hunted down and killed. He had ruled for thirteen years, during which he had established complete personal control over the country, and had given it an effective administration operated through a great range of new taxes. The British did not free the Arabs from anarchy, as was maintained at the time. They replaced the Mahdiist state by Imperial rule.

Kitchener was hampered in this River War, as Winston Churchill called it, by the fact that he took his orders from the Foreign Office through Baring, now Lord Cromer, so that the need for economy was continually urged upon him. If in the end he possessed a superiority in material and weapon power that made defeat unthinkable except through gross incompetence, he owed much of this to Wolseley, who as Commander-in-Chief continually urged forward his plans. There was a time in April when Kitchener seems to have lost his nerve, to the point of asking a startled Cromer whether or not he should attack. When he decided at last to do so and won the battle of the Atbara, Wolseley sent him congratulations and a mild rebuke. 'Were I in your place, I would not ask such a question. You must be a far better judge than Lord Cromer or me or any one else can be. You have your thumb upon the pulse of the Army you command, and can best know what it is capable of.' After Omdurman he noted in his diary that Kitchener was a fine fellow, and added: 'God be praised. We can once more hold up our heads in the Sudan.' He might on this occasion have been forgiven a little envy, but there is no indication that he felt anything but pleasure when Sir Herbert Kitchener became Baron Kitchener of Khartoum, and was acclaimed by the British public as the man who had avenged Gordon.

So far the postscript. Kitchener's River War was so prolonged, and in conception so different from Wolseley's, that it helps very little in answering the questions it is natural to ask in a post-mortem on events from the despatch of Gordon to the time of his death. Who was responsible for sending Gordon? Was it right to send him? Why did the Expedition fail to reach him? Could it have arrived in time? Most of the answers are implicit in the narrative, but they should be set out explicitly too.

They have a political and a military side. The Government were collectively responsible for sending Gordon to Khartoum. No member of it knew much about him personally, or took the trouble to find out that the 'bee in his bonnet' was not small, as Granville believed, but a real queen bee. Yet had the full extent of Gordon's eccentricity been known, it is doubtful whether the Government would have been deterred from sending him. The decision assumed an importance afterwards which was in nobody's mind at the time. It was essentially an act of expediency. Had the mission been confined to the original idea of reporting and returning, probably no more would have been heard of Gordon in relation to the Sudan. For the subsequent confusion about his mission, Granville was chiefly responsible. He should have realized the danger of the situation even before Gordon arrived in Khartoum. It was plain that a man who had been appointed Governor-General of the Sudan had been entrusted with a mission quite different from a simple examination and report. From February onwards Granville (and some other Ministers too, but he was the principal culprit) at times accepted that Gordon had been given supreme power in the Sudan, and at other times spoke as if his original instructions still held good. This contradiction was not at the time realized by anybody. Baring's attitude was wholly logical. He disagreed with the use of Gordon, but saw that once he had been sent he must be given complete support.

It is not possible to assess Gordon's own behaviour by ordinary standards. There is no doubt that he began by trying to evacuate Khartoum, and some of his later suggestions were full of good sense, yet one is left with the feeling that if the Government had disregarded the inevitable Parliamentary storm and acceded to his request for Zobeir, Gordon would have imposed some conditions making Zobeir's appointment impossible. He realized that Khartoum was the crown of his life's work, and resisted any attempt to make him leave and to ensure his personal safety with a passion which suggests that he half-consciously wished to end his life there. When Wolseley said in

November that he hoped he would have no trouble with Gordon, he was anticipating a refusal to leave Khartoum which he might well have received. Gordon's only mistake in a purely military sense was his consistent underestimation of the power and attraction of the Mahdi, and a corresponding overestimation of his own influence. His actual defence of Khartoum was a marvel of improvisation. By staying there he was forcing the Government's hand, and trying to make sure that they followed his policy of leaving an orderly government in the Sudan instead of merely scuttling out of it—or at least, that is what one would say if Gordon had been a rational human being. As it is he can only be said to have acted according to his lights, which may be called those of a monstrous egocentric or a Christian hero. Perhaps the two designations are not incompatible. In considering Gordon's last months in Khartoum, one is sometimes reminded of the definition of a martyr as somebody who moves along the path of least resistance to a desired death.

The indignation of Gladstone and Granville in March and April 1884, sprang from a genuine belief both that Gordon was ignoring his instructions and that he was trying to impose his will on the Government. It followed that he could get away at any time he wished, and that no help should be sent him. To this view Gladstone tenaciously adhered through the months of May, June and July, with an obstinate self-righteousness equal to Gordon's own. He was deaf to the arguments of Baring and the wavering complaints of Hartington, and his refusal during these three months to accept the overwhelming evidence that Gordon was in danger and would have to be rescued, is one of the blackest marks against him as a man and as a statesman. Besides Gladstone's obstinate refusal to recognize reality, the muddle-headedness of Granville and the vacillations of Hartington are comparatively unimportant. The whole episode may be seen on a personal level as a battle of wills between two men equally bathed in an odour of sanctity. Gordon paid for his obstinacy with his life, Gladstone for his by the popular dislike which led the G.O.M. to be named thereafter the M.O.G., or Murderer Of Gordon.

Had Gladstone sanctioned an expedition in May or June instead of in early August, it would of course have reached Khartoum in comfortable time to save Gordon. But at that point the military questions begin. Given the existing conditions, would Khartoum have been reached in time had the Suakin-Berber route been adopted? Could it have been reached by the Nile route? Was the expedition a military failure, as it was certainly a political one?

To the first of these questions it is impossible to give a definite answer. Ian Hamilton's caustic remark that only Wolseley could have persuaded the Government, in the days of railways, to travel up the Nile in boats rather than a short distance across the desert by rail, is pointed enough. Yet when the laying of a railway began, under the protection of Graham's force, it reached a distance of less than twenty miles in several weeks, and after Osman Digna had retreated into the mountains, Graham found it impossible to reach him or to stop occasional attacks on the line. In 1896 Kitchener carefully considered both routes and decided in favour of going up the Nile. Such evidence as exists suggests that in the particular circumstances (with Berber occupied, and marauding parties ranging round Suakin) the choice of the Nile route was the right one.

It is equally hard to be dogmatic about the second question. Some part of the Desert Column could certainly have reached Khartoum before it fell, had there not been a hold-up over the coal, or had there been more camels, or had Wilson not waited at Metemmeh, but whether the appearance of a few British soldiers would have scared off the Mahdi's army permanently is a matter of conjecture. It seems likely that the saving of a couple of days (by Wilson) made little difference, but that the saving of two weeks (ten days were lost through the coal failure) might well have meant the arrival of a considerable force in Khartoum before Gordon had quite reached the end of his resources. The second question is linked with the third, and the third with Wolseley's reputation, which was once so high and has now sunk so undeservedly low, largely because of the Nile Expedition's failure.

Nobody who examines Wolseley's whole career, and in particular the campaign against Arabi which ended in the battle of Tel-el-Kebir, can have any doubt about his talents as a fighting commander. This lightning campaign, with its deliberate false trail laid to newspaper correspondents and others, its surprise night march and its storming attack on an entrenched camp in early morning, is like a modern *blitzkrieg* in miniature. Every move and action is marked by that decisiveness which is the mark of a fine commander. Wolseley was a lucid and incisive military analyst but he was not, like Ian Hamilton, a writer of elegant memoranda who failed when put to the supreme test of individual command. Major-General Fuller, writing in the thirties, called him the ablest British soldier of the past hundred years, and his contemporaries and immediate successors had no doubt of his transdendent merits as an organizer. Sir John Fortescue, the historian of the British Army, called Kitchener a sorry organizer compared with Wolseley, and suggested that the British Expeditionary Force of 1914 should have been called Wolseley's Army. And in the course of a searing criticism of the administrative confusion prevailing in South Africa under Roberts, he remarked that neither Wolseley nor even Buller 'had they started, as did Lord Roberts, to march with 30,000 men from the western railway to Bloemfontein, would have lost an all-important convoy on the fourth day's march, and reached Bloemfontein only with men and animals starving, to stay there paralysed and inactive for nearly two months.'[1] Even Ian Hamilton, no friend of Wolseley's, acknowledged his supremacy as an organizer. How, then, did it come about that the Nile Expedition was not more coherently organized and more energetically led?

It is necessary to understand that the Expedition had from the beginning no more than a moderate chance of reaching Khartoum in time. In all military enterprises some things go wrong. Orders are misinterpreted, transport breaks down, supplies are sent north instead of south, commanders attack at one point instead of another. The two World Wars contain hundreds of

[1] Fortescue, *Following the Drum*, p. 170.

such instances of human error, and they are all excused by
victory, magnified by failure. It may reasonably be maintained
that little went seriously wrong during the Nile Expedition, and
that many aspects of it were dramatically successful. The building and despatch of the whalers was carried out with extraordinary speed, the voyageurs proved their worth time and
again, and the medical services—which included the use of
women nurses at Wady Halfa—were by Victorian standards
very efficient, even though the report exaggerated which said
that 'a sick man, when seated on one of these (cacolets) with an
umbrella over his head and an interesting book in his hand,
could pass the time across the desert, comparatively speaking,
very comfortably as well as pleasantly.'[1] The food was well
chosen, the health of the men was good, the movement of
supplies up the enormously long line of communications was
maintained with few serious breaks. The things that went wrong
did so partly because of slackness in Egypt, like the failure to
report on the condition of the Wady Halfa-Sarras railway,
partly because of inefficiency on the civilian side of the War
Office, which was responsible for the inadequate packing of
supplies, partly because the subordinate commanders were so
quarrelsome. Probably regular soldiers in positions of power are
quarrelsome as a group, but it does seem that many members
of the Wolseley Ring found it exceptionally difficult to co-
operate with anybody. Buller was notorious for his shortness of
temper and his refusal to listen to criticism, Wood hid behind
the barriers of deafness and vanity, and Butler showed time and
again that it was almost impossible for him to work with any
commander but Wolseley. When Furse, the inexperienced
Director of Transport, made representations to Buller about
camels it is likely that he got short shrift, and Wood took any
criticism of his handling of the line of Communications as a
personal insult. A permanent quarrel went on between Webber,
the Director of Telegraphs, and the Egyptian officials. Most of
them would listen only to Wolseley, and it was impossible for
Wolseley to be everywhere at once. As one of the Expedition's

[1] War Office Records.

most intelligent critics has said: 'Too much depended upon individuals, and particularly upon the Commander-in-Chief.'[1]

In a wider sense, the chief lesson of the Expedition is the inability of Victorian military commanders to use their staff. At Tel-el-Kebir Wolseley had been in effect his own Chief of Staff, and at Omdurman Kitchener relegated his Chief of Staff to the rear and rushed from point to point directing the battle in person. Wolseley was a commander in this tradition, and the failures of the Expedition reflected his inability to exercise personal control over the whole line of communications. It is true that particular commanders had their own areas of responsibility, and Buller spoke more than once of his own freedom to act as he thought fit, but Wolseley concerned himself individually with many things that should have been quite outside his direct control. In the many petty Colonial wars of the Victorian era this individual command was practical, and even beneficial. In the Nile Expedition it caused much hesitancy and confusion. A proper staff system was needed, and it did not exist in the British Army until shortly before the First World War. The absence of it was responsible for diverting Wolseley's attention from the vital to the trivial. The disregard of the need for heliographs in the desert, and the failure of the supply of camels, reflect directly upon Buller, but by extension also upon Wolseley. He showed also, in the last weeks before Gordon's death, a strange and uncharacteristic inability to act as a Commander-in-Chief. Just as Hamilton at Gallipoli never exerted the kind of command that might have ensured success, so Wolseley here let command slip away from him, never pressing Buller sufficiently about the camels, never positively demanding that heliographic communication be established, never trying to force the hand of the Mudir of Dongola. It may be that by this time nothing could have saved Gordon, yet the image left of Wolseley on the Nile Expedition is that of a man cut off from the fighting part of his army, and no longer fully in control of events.

Wolseley ever afterwards thought of the Nile Expedition as the time in his life when his luck changed, and believed that

[1] *The Nile Voyageurs*, p. 46.

after it nothing went right for him. Was he in truth, as Fortescue believed, a commander of genius who never met a worthy opponent in the field? The image of failure left by the Expedition could never be corrected, for this was his last campaign. When he died in 1913 and was buried in St. Paul's near to Wellington, his fame had faded, and many people hardly knew the name of the man who for so much of the Victorian era had been 'our only General'.

BIBLIOGRAPHY

MANUSCRIPT SOURCES

War Office Records and Papers (W.O. Records).
Wolseley Papers at Hove (Hove).
Wolseley Letters and Papers, etc. Royal United Services Institution (R.U.S.I.).
Public Record Office Papers (P.R.O.).
Gladstone Papers at British Museum (Gladstone).
Gordon Papers at British Museum (Gordon).
Thomas Cook & Co. Archives (Cook).
Brocklehurst Papers (Brocklehurst).

SELECT BIBLIOGRAPHY—PRINTED MATERIAL

SIR JOHN ADYE, Soldiers and Others I Have Known (1925).
MICHAEL ALEXANDER, The True Blue (1957).
BERNARD M. ALLEN, Gordon and the Sudan (1931).
SIR GEORGE ARTHUR, Life of Lord Kitchener (2 vols., 1924).
REGINALD H. BARNES and CHARLES E. BROWN, Charles George Gordon (1885).
ADMIRAL LORD CHARLES BERESFORD, Memoirs (2 vols., 1914).
W. S. BLUNT, Gordon at Khartoum (1911).
D. C. BOULGER, Life of Charles George Gordon (2 vols., 1896).
MAJOR-GENERAL HENRY BRACKENBURY, The River Column (1885).
SIR WILLIAM BUTLER, The Campaign of the Cataracts (1887).
Autobiography (1911).

SPENCER CHILDERS, Life and Correspondence of the Rt. Hon. H. C. E. Childers (2 vols., 1901).

COLONEL H. E. COLVILE, Official History of the Sudan Campaign (2 vols., 1889).

JOHN MASON COOK, Mr. John M. Cook's Visit to the Sudan (1885)—pamphlet.

EARL OF CROMER, Modern Egypt (2 vols., 1908).

DOUGLAS DAWSON, The Desert March (1866), *Quarterly Review*.

SIR GEORGE DOUGLAS, Life of Major-General Wauchope (1904).

LORD DUNDONALD, Life (1926).

VISCOUNT ESHER, Journals and Letters, Vol. I (1934).

LORD ESMOND FITZMAURICE, Life of Lord Granville (2 vols., 1905).

ARCHIBALD FORBES, Memoirs of War and Peace (1895).

SIR JOHN W. FORTESCUE, Following the Drum (1932).

A. G. GARDINER, Sir William Harcourt (2 vols., 1923).

COUNT GLEICHEN, With the Camel Corps Up The Nile (1888).

MAJOR-GENERAL C. G. GORDON, Journals at Khartoum (1885).

GENERAL CHARLES GEORGE GORDON, Letters to his Sister (1888).

MAJOR-GENERAL SIR GERALD GRAHAM, Last words with Gordon (1887).

FIELD-MARSHAL LORD GRENFELL, Memoirs (1925).

STEPHEN GWYNN and GERTRUDE M. TUCKWELL, Life of Sir Charles Dilke (2 vols., 1917).

LIEUTENANT-COLONEL ANDREW HAGGARD, Under Crescent and Star (1895).

IAN HAMILTON, Listening for the Drums (1944).

BERNARD HOLLAND, Life of the Eighth Duke of Devonshire (2 vols., 1911).

P. M. HOLT, The Mahdiist State in the Sudan (1958).

ROY JENKINS, Sir Charles Dilke (1958).

MRS. AUBREY LE BLOND, Day In, Day Out (1928).

MAJOR-GENERAL SIR HUGH MCCALMONT, Memoirs (1924).

ALEX MACDONALD (under pseudonym 'A War Correspondent'), Too Late for Gordon and Khartoum (1887).
Why Gordon Perished (1896).

PHILIP MAGNUS, Gladstone (1954).
Kitchener (1958).

BERNARD MALLET, Thomas George, Earl of Northbrook (1908).

SUSAN COUNTESS OF MALMESBURY, Life of Sir John Ardagh (1909).

SIR PERCIVAL MARLING, Rifleman and Hussar (1931).

MAJOR-GENERAL SIR F. MAURICE and SIR GEORGE ARTHUR, Life of Lord Wolseley (1924).
Letters of Lord and Lady Wolseley (1922).

COLONEL C. H. MELVILLE, Life of Sir Redvers Buller (2 vols., 1923).

JOHN MORLEY, Life of Gladstone (3 vols., 1903).

LADY DOROTHY NEVILLE, Life and Letters (1919).

FRANK POWER, Letters from Khartoum (1885).

MELTON PRIOR, Campaigns of a War Correspondent (1912).

JOHN PUDNEY, The Thomas Cook Story (1953).

W. FRASER RAE, The Business of Travel (1891).

COLONEL C. P. STACEY (Editor), Records of the Nile Voyageurs (1959).

SUDAN NOTES AND RECORDS, 1930 and 1936.

HISTORY OF 'THE TIMES', Vol. 3.

COLONEL R. H. VEITCH, Life, Letters and Diaries of Sir Gerald Graham (1901).

WILLOUGHBY VERNER, Sketches in the Jordan (1886).

COLONEL WILLOUGHBY VERNER, Military Life of H.R.H. the Duke of Cambridge (2 vols., 1905).

LETTERS OF QUEEN VICTORIA, Edited by George Earle Buckle. 2nd Series, Vol. 3 (1928).

FREDERICK VILLIERS, Pictures of Many Wars (1902).
Peaceful Personalities and Warriors Bold (1907).

SIR CHARLES M. WATSON, Life of Major-General Sir Charles William Wilson (1909).

FREDRIC WHYTE, Life of W. T. Stead (2 vols., 1925).

CHARLES WILLIAMS, How We Lost Gordon (Nineteenth Century, 1885).

SIR CHARLES W. WILSON, From Korti to Khartoum (1885).

MAJOR F. R. WINGATE, Mahdiism and the Egyptian Sudan (1891).

SIR RONALD WINGATE, Wingate of the Sudan (1955).

SIR EVELYN WOOD, From Midshipman to Field-Marshal (1906). Winnowed Memories (1918).

Also consulted:

Newspapers and magazines of the period.

Official publications on Egypt, 1883–1886.

INDEX

U